ABOUT THE SERIES

Culture shock is a state of disorientation that can come over anyone who has been thrust into unknown surroundings, away from one's comfort zone. *CultureShock!* is a series of trusted and reputed guides which has, for decades, been helping expatriates and long-term visitors to cushion the impact of culture shock whenever they move to a new country.

Written by people who have lived in the country and experienced culture shock themselves, the authors share all the information necessary for anyone to cope with these feelings of disorientation more effectively. The guides are written in a style that is easy to read and covers a range of topics that will arm readers with enough advice, hints and tips to make their lives as normal as possible again.

Each book is structured in the same manner. It begins with the first impressions that visitors will have of that city or country. To understand a culture, one must first understand the people—where they came from, who they are, the values and traditions they live by, as well as their customs and etiquette. This is covered in the first half of the book.

Then on with the practical aspects—how to settle in with the greatest of ease. Authors walk readers through topics such as how to find accommodation, get the utilities and telecommunications up and running, enrol the children in school and keep in the pink of health. But that's not all. Once the essentials are out of the way, venture out and try the food, enjoy more of the culture and travel to other areas. Then be immersed in the language of the country before discovering more about the business side of things.

To round off, snippets of basic information are offered before readers are 'tested' on customs and etiquette of the country. Useful words and phrases, a comprehensive resource guide and list of books for further research are also included for easy reference.

D1157896

CONTENTS

Chapter 7
London at Play 202

Chapter 8
Learning the Language 237

Chapter 9
London at Work 243

Chapter 10
London at a Glance 253

INTRODUCTION

Why buy a guidebook? Maybe you want to get a head start on some of the experiences that will be available to you at your destination; maybe you want to get a grip on what interests you there; or maybe you just want to fill the vacuum of your knowledge about a place you've never visited before.

Nearly any up-to-date guidebook will serve these general purposes, and there are many to choose from: a whole industry exists to inform you about the ways that you can spend your time and money when travelling abroad. You will notice, however, that most guidebooks start from the premise that you are a tourist; that your visit is transient; and that your goal is to go home with a 'been there, done that' experience under your belt. If this is the aim of your trip to London then you will probably be happy with the mainstream of popular information.

However, if the goal of your visit is to experience something a little bit richer, more memorable or more meaningful than what suffices for the tourist throng, this book will be one of your most helpful companions in London.

London is the tourist city par excellence. It receives nearly 30 million visitors a year. The tourist layer of London is too thick to be penetrated with the blunt instrument of the ordinary guidebook, no matter how skillfully you wield it. In fact, London guidebooks do not help you to penetrate the London tourist experience at all; they merely help you navigate it.

This book, on the other hand, is designed to immerse you in the real London. It guides you into making your stay as trouble-free as possible, and at the same time helps you discover what makes people tick in this exciting capital. For business people, the book will provide much needed advice on dealing with the locals and making your time in London a success. Whether your visit will last a day, a week, a month or a year, you will find within the tools you need to experience London on your own terms. Read on and enjoy!

Orin Hargraves

I am ever grateful to the directors of the International Meditation Center USA who put me up, and put up with me, while I was writing this book.

I thank the visitors to CompuServe's UK forums who have answered my queries from time to time. I deeply appreciate the Guildhall Library in the City of London, and its many helpful staff. Countless hours of investigation and miles of pounding London's pavements were saved by their presence.

Finally I thank the Londoners, past and present, whose kindness and friendship have ensured that London is always a home for me: Hilary Arnott, Erroll Bowyer, Yadi Nejad, Maria O'Shea, Neil Pavitt, Majid Suleiman, Irfan Torbas and Frances Webber.

MAP OF GREAT BRITAIN

ATLANTIC OCEAN

SCOTLAND

NORTH SEA

NORTH CHANNEL

EDINBURGH

NORTHERN
IRELAND

IRISH SEA

REPUBLIC
OF IRELAND

ENGLAND

ST GEORGE'S CHANNEL

WALES

CARDIFF

LONDON

ENGLISH CHANNEL

FRANCE

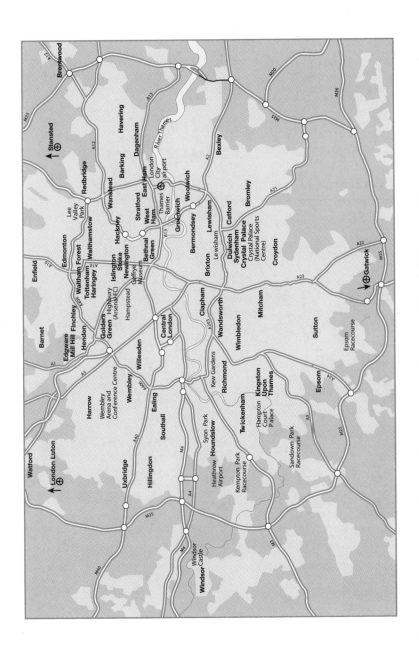

There are many outstanding landmarks and places of interest in London, Saint Paul's Cathedral being one of them.

FIRST IMPRESSIONS

'Behold now this vast city; a city of refuge, the mansion house of liberty, encompassed and surrounded with his protection; the shop of war hath not there more anvils and hammers waking, to fashion out the plates and instruments of armed justice in defence of beleaguered truth, than there be pens and hands there, sitting by their studious lamps, musing, searching, revolving new notions.'
—Milton's *Areopagitica*

PEOPLE COME TO LONDON for the first time in all sorts of ways: in planes, in trains that may have crossed through the channel tunnel, in buses that started at the coast after a boat ride across the English Channel or the North Sea. A not inconsiderable number of people come to London for the first time hidden in the back of a lorry and go on to make London their home. What can any of these first-time arrivals expect?

SPEAK ENGLISH!

It may come as a relief or a shock to you, but it will certainly not escape your notice: London is officially a one-language city, and that language is English. This is not to say that you won't hear other languages in London—indeed, the average ride on a London bus exposes you to two or three languages other than English, whether whispered between old ladies, shouted back and forth between teenagers on the top deck or droned into someone's mobile phone. But these are all private conversations. The public business of London is conducted in English. Signs, whether in the street, in restaurants or offices, or in the Underground, are in English only. Unless you are in one of London's many ethnic neighborhoods, anything you want to buy, learn, sell or impart is likely to meet the most success if English is the medium. You will probably figure this out very early on—in fact, during your encounter with the immigration officer if you were required to deal with

one on your way in. There is no second language in London that has dependable status, and the degree to which you can comport yourself in English will be a barometer of your success. Accent doesn't matter—every accent is heard in London, and Londoners are used to sorting out the wheat from the chaff in what you're saying. What matters is that you put your English to work, whatever state it is in; making the effort to bring it up to the best possible standard is well worth your while.

MIND YOUR MANNERS

While London can be a maddeningly busy place, there is an underlying order to the way that people conduct themselves in public that is based on generations, if not centuries, of respect for privacy and common decency. Because London compresses so many people into a small space, people who live there very often build a wall of sorts around themselves for protection. Don't mistake this for rudeness: it is only a symptom of the English character adapting itself for busy urban life. As a rule, strangers do not routinely make eye contact on the street, and greetings are not exchanged between people who don't know each other. When contact between people on the street is sudden and unexpected—in a collision of pedestrians, for example—even here the veil of privacy is often not breached: a typical Londoner's response is simply to mutter 'sorry' and walk away, often without so much as looking at the other party involved, and no matter who was at fault.

When contact between strangers is intentional, however, a completely different rule prevails, and you will have the greatest success by making an effort to be polite and courteous. Friendly greetings to shopkeepers, market traders or uniformed people whom you are required to deal with are always the best way to start. Say 'please' and 'thank you' for what you request and receive, even if it is the other person's job to tend to you. Don't be intimidated about approaching a stranger if you have a good reason—to ask directions for example. Though people may have a gruff exterior, you can usually melt it very quickly by approaching in a courteous, friendly and sincere manner.

FORM A QUEUE

Whether you come from a culture where order prevails in the provision of services or where chaos is the rule, you will be shocked and awed by the instinct in London to observe the rule of 'first come, first served'. Whether at the post office, the bus stop, a fast-food restaurant or the till at the chemist's, you cannot go wrong by just joining the queue—and you will certainly go wrong if you disregard one that is already there. The rule in London is one at a time, in order.

THINK LEFT

The downfall—literally—of many first-time visitors to London is a failure to take into account the implications of a deeply-held British convention: keep left. Traffic, you will notice, is on the left side of the street. In all of London's busiest areas, 'Look Left' or 'Look Right' is prominently painted on the roadway at intersections to remind you of the direction from which traffic is flowing in the first lane that you will cross.

Pay attention to these warnings! Also note that the rules do not change when you are out of central London, but the reminders will not be there. You just have to remember!

Similarly, the general instinct of Londoners is to regard the left side of any pathway as the one to walk on, the one to move in, or the one to overtake someone in. If your instinct is to regard the right-hand side as the place to do this, you will need to retrain yourself. You will notice that the Underground, to the degree possible, herds people to the left. On Underground escalators, which are usually wide enough to accommodate two abreast, note that people who wish to simply 'ride' up or down stand on the right; those who wish to climb or descend do so on the left. If you are idly standing on the left-hand side of an escalator, do not be surprised if a hurried and somewhat impatient pedestrian is suddenly breathing down (or up) your neck.

KEEP YOUR SHIRT ON (OR NOT)
You may find Londoner's response to the weather very different from your own. Everything will fall into place if

you remember this general pattern: Londoners react to the weather in direct proportion to how unusual it is. At most times of year, cloud cover in London is the rule, and sunshine is the exception. It sometimes pours rain, but the more usual form of precipitation is drizzle. So, if it's overcast, drizzling and slightly chilly, Londoners generally just go about there business: this is not weather that bears responding to. You may wonder that they're not all freezing with so few clothes on, but you'll see: you get used to it after a while.

Extreme weather for London comes in two forms: hot sunshine, and (quite rarely) snow. On a hot summer day, do not stare aghast when grown men rip off their shirts in the park and expose their manly chests to solar radiation. They don't often get a chance to do this, and it is a yearly ritual. If there is snow in London—and this doesn't happen every winter—expect general paralysis in the city's services and the population.

IS THIS ALL THERE IS?

Anyone who goes to London and doesn't have a great time there is very likely to have made a very common mistake: spending the entire visit in Tourist London. If all you ever saw of London was the few blocks around Tottenham Court Road Tube station or Petticoat Lane market on a Sunday morning, you could very easily conclude that London was the world centre for cheesy souvenirs and grotesquely decorated youths.

Whether you come to London for a day or a year, make a plan early to get off the beaten path. You may want to take in the main tourist sites if you've never seen them, but the most delightful parts of London are the ones that don't show up prominently on the tourist map. Get out and explore! The other chapters in this book will help to show you the way. With a TravelCard in hand, all of London is at your disposal for a song. Hyde Park, smack in the middle of London, is a pleasant enough green space but it can't compare with the peace, tranquility and majesty of Richmond Park in west London. The guidebooks may point you to Portobello Road market to experience local colour, but you'll find a lot more of it in Hackney's less-renowned Ridley Road market. Don't hesitate to take the roads less travelled!

LONDON IN A NUTSHELL

CHAPTER 2

'London is a modern Babylon.'
—Benjamin Disraeli

THERE IS PROBABLY NOT A LITERATE PERSON in the world for whom the word 'London' doesn't conjure up some image: a red double-decker bus, the tower of Big Ben, or perhaps the ceremony of the changing of the guard at Buckingham Palace. London's influence internationally is no doubt diminished from the days of the British empire, but its power to make itself known around the world is still as strong today as that of any world city. For three hundred years, it has been among the most populous cities in the world, and for a hundred of those—most of the way through the 19th century—it was without dispute the biggest. Today, it ranks only as number 20, but it continues to maintain its rank as the largest city in Europe, a distinction that only Paris threatens to upset.

London will, however, drop out of the top 20 world cities by 2010, for the first time in its long history.

Nevertheless, London has always been, and will remain, a name to conjure with. It is the seat of British royalty and government, and also of the highest English courts of law. It is Britain's manufacturing and commercial centre, and remains Europe's preeminent financial centre, despite occasional bids from lesser cities. It is the cultural capital of the United Kingdom, and it has a very good claim as the cultural capital of the English-speaking world.

Millions listen attentively to the words "This is London" that precede the BBC's World Service broadcasts, whether or not they are spoken in English, and millions flock to London yearly simply for the opportunity to learn and use the language.

If you want to acquaint yourself with London through reading and other media, there is no end of material to choose from: no city in the world is better documented in English. So the first task is to decide which of three Londons you want to know about.

First there is the London of the imagination, the one that is the most real for many people in the world because they have never been to London and know about the city only second hand. Every book, film and television programme about London will help you to know it in this regard.

The second London is nearly as well known, living as it does in the memory of millions, and entering the memories of millions more every year. This is tourist London, and it is nearly as well documented as the London of the mind. Guidebooks are the best accompaniment to this London, and these are also easy to come by.

London Guidebooks

The average bookshop in London carries a dozen titles, and all of the guides published would fill several library shelves. You can choose from *Pauper's London*, *London on £ 1,000 a Day*, *Green London* or *London by Night*, to name only a few.

Lastly, there is the London that is home for six or nine million people, depending on how you count them. This is the London that persists after the armchair excursion or the two-week tour, and the one that eventually supplants the London of the imagination and tourist London if you come to live here.

This book is about that London, the London that people call home. It doesn't pretend to be a substitute for the experience: the only way to make London home is to live there. This book sets out to expedite the process of settling you happily into London, to steer you clear of things that might put you off the place, and to help you find your niche in what may seem at first a very big and impersonal city. To start that process, we look at London in summary: facts and statistics that make the place what it is today.

WHERE IS LONDON?

There are a couple of things to note about where London is besides the ones that you already know: that it's in England, and that England is on an island off the north-west coast of Europe.

First, note that London is not on the sea, nor is it technically any longer a port. Old movies, paintings and stories may give the impression that you can look out to sea from the banks of the Thames, but in fact you have to go about 58 km (40 miles) downstream to do so. London ceased to be a seagoing port with the building of the Thames Barrier (completed in 1982, to remove the threat of flooding in London), which made the Thames unnavigable for big ships above it. London's port business was moved 40 km (25 miles) downstream to Tilbury in Essex, with some North Sea ports taking some of the business as well. The association of London with Britain's maritime glory is all history now.

The second thing to note about London's location is that it is really quite far north in the world. It is one of only two cities in the world north of the 50° parallel with a population of more than five million (the other is Moscow). This means that it has rather dramatic variations in the length of daylight between winter and summer: summer days are as much as 18 hours long, and winter nights are the same. London's place on the globe would have made it a chilly place, if not for the Gulf Stream, discussed later when we get to the weather.

WHERE IN LONDON?

Though it sprawls over more than 1554 sq km (600 sq miles), the experience of London as home is often a very small and local one, with peculiarities that belong only to a particular area. When you say you live in London, the next question from anyone who knows the city is likely to be, "Where in London?" To answer that question, you need a sense of the parts that make up the vast whole. The shape of and divisions within London have varied considerably over time. Here is a very contemporary perspective that will help you to locate yourself, and others, within the metropolis.

The simplest thumbnail division of London, and one that is as old as the city itself, is provided by the Thames (pronounced 'temz'). It is a physical, as well as a psychological barrier that divides London roughly in half, flowing west to east through the middle of the city. But it is a slightly uneven division, for the larger part of the city and the vast majority of what makes London famous lies north of the river. Journalists are fond of playing up divisions between north and south Londoners, suggesting that those from one place are averse to people and things in the other. But this split, if it exists, is a phenomenon limited to a fairly small, socially immobile group of natives. Londoners today are likely to live or move to where they can most conveniently get to work, or where they find the house or spouse that they like, regardless of which side of the river they are on.

North, South, East or West?

There is a vague but widely felt sense that north London is rather nicer than south London, and an even stronger idea that west London is a cut above east London. But these are very general notions, and within each large area of London there are much smaller areas, with associations that may run counter to the prevailing notion about the area. Thus, while east London may be regarded as rather down-at-the-heels, Saint Katherine's Wharf near the Tower of London is posh by any standard, and north London, whatever its merits, has neighbourhoods generally thought quite dodgy such as Willesden or Tottenham.

The political divisions of London are quite important, because at present, there is no overall authority that governs the city. Many very important services, including education, sanitation and some taxation, are handled at the level of the elected borough council. Today, the city is divided into 32 boroughs and the City of London. As we will see in Chapter Five, London boroughs have reputations, and where you live may say something, rightly or wrongly, about who you are, as well as have a direct impact on your life.

Demographers divide London into three parts: the City, Inner London (made up of 13 boroughs) and Outer London (made up of 19 boroughs). Together, these compose what is called Greater London, which is for statistical purposes a county of England. These distinctions are not necessarily familiar to Londoners themselves, especially transplanted ones, but they will help you to get a fix on the city as a whole. We start in the centre of London and move outwards.

The City

The oldest part of London is officially called the City of London, or for short, the City. The capital C is important, for without it, it may be assumed that you are talking about London as a whole (as is the case in this book). Covering only a square mile (and thus often called The Square Mile; 2.6 sq km), the City today is London's financial centre.

By day, the City is home to more than 350,000 workers, but fewer than 5,000 souls will be found there at night. The City is largely shops, office buildings, banks and company headquarters. There are only a few, generally very expensive, dwellings, notably in the Barbican Centre, and a handful of less grandiose flats managed by the City or by housing trusts. Some of London's most famous historical landmarks are in the City, including the Monument, Saint Paul's Cathedral and the Bank of England.

Westminster

Though officially one of the Inner London boroughs, Westminster insists on calling itself a city rather than a borough, and it is in many ways distinct from the rest of Inner London. It lies immediately west of the City and was originally a separate settlement, but has long since grown to meet its neighbour. Any famous London landmark that is not in the City is probably in Westminster: Westminster Abbey, the Houses of Parliament, Piccadilly Circus, Buckingham Palace, the British Museum and Trafalgar Square, to name only a few, are all here. The tourist's experience of London is largely centred on Westminster, and many come to and go from London having seen little else.

Inner London

The Inner London boroughs more or less form a ring around the City. They are, starting at 12 o'clock and proceeding

Vintage London: grey skies, bricks, cobbles and iron.

clockwise: Islington, Hackney, Tower Hamlets (here we cross the Thames), Southwark, Lambeth, Wandsworth (here we cross the Thames again), Fulham and Hammersmith, Kensington and Chelsea, Westminster and Camden. Inner London contains London's poshest and poorest neighbourhoods. Like Westminster, much of Inner London was once villages that have now grown together to form part of the metropolitan area. Only 150 years ago, you might have crossed vast open spaces to travel from the City to, say, Hammersmith, or Highgate (in Camden), but today hardly so much as a bare spot of ground intervenes.

Outer London

The Outer Boroughs form the outer limit of Greater London. Beyond them lie the Home Counties (see below). Outer London is a mixture of older villages and planned suburbs, and grew up largely in Victorian times. It is as a whole more uniform than Inner London, with relatively fewer big businesses, more open spaces and many more detached houses. The boroughs are, again starting at 12 o'clock and proceeding clockwise: Enfield, Waltham Forest, Redbridge, Havering (we cross the Thames), Bexley, Bromley, Croydon, Sutton, Kingston, Richmond (the Thames runs through it), Hounslow, Hillingdon, Harrow and Barnet.

Intermediate Boroughs

The astute statistician will note that we have named 24, not 32 of London's boroughs. Here we part company from official demography to list boroughs that are intermediate in character and in location between the inner and outer boroughs. Their inmost parts tend to resemble Inner London in character, their outer parts are more like Outer London; and they border neither on the City nor on the Home Counties. The letter following each indicates whether it is officially designated as an Inner (I) or Outer (O) borough. North of the river are Ealing (O), Brent (O), Haringey (I), Newham (I) and Barking and Dagenham (O). South of the river are Lewisham (I), Greenwich (O) and Merton (O).

The Home Counties

The Home Counties are not officially a part of London; they form a ring around it. Part of their population is taken into account by those who count nine million (rather than six million) people in London. The Home Counties are generally prosperous, and are in effect London's commuter belt of wealthy suburbs. North of the river are Buckinghamshire, Hertfordshire and Essex; south of the river are Kent, Surrey and Berkshire. There are good roads and excellent rail connections from all of the Home Counties to London, and a significant part of the working population commutes daily. An area popularly called the Green Belt more or less separates London from the Home Counties. It consists of land bought from the Home Counties in the 1930s to prevent London's unchecked urban sprawl. Most of it is still under conservation today.

Middlesex No More?

The part of Greater London that lies north of the river today was once largely the county of Middlesex. Middlesex ceased to exist officially in 1965, but by then the Royal Mail had already set in stone its division of London into postal districts with their associated post codes. So today, Middlesex still exists as a kind of phantom county in the addresses of some Outer London areas, notably Uxbridge, Wembley, Enfield and Twickenham.

North of Watford

London's pre-eminence among UK cities is mostly responsible for a much-chatted about 'north-south divide' in the UK, wherein the south is seen to be prosperous and to have the full attention of the central government, while the north is poor and neglected. This attitude is summed up in the phrase 'north of Watford,' which people use to indicate all of England lying outside of London—Watford being a town just to the north-west of Greater London.

THE LONG SHADOW OF THE PAST

Since our concern is mostly with London of today, its long and glorious past will get rather short shrift. A city that has been continuously settled for 2000 years has a lot of stories to tell, and a whole industry that exists to tell them. For an overview of this perspective, you can't do better than to go to the Museum of London in London Wall EC2, where the city's history is laid out in rich detail.

For the contemporary Londoner, the city's history is a living thing that comes to your attention in a dozen little ways every day. The remains of Roman London lie mostly buried and crushed under centuries of development, but some of the straight roads the Romans laid out persist to this day among the maze of London's twisting and turning routes: Bishopsgate and Kingsland Road leading north, the line of Holborn-Oxford Street-Bayswater Road leading west and Edgware Road leading north-west were all established in Roman times as major routes between London and other Roman settlements in Britain. A guided walk through the City of London will take you along the route of the London Wall, which for 1,500 years defined the limit of the city as well as provided defence. And hardly a London neighbourhood is without its historical markers, indicating glorious or infamous things that happened there, and blue plaques affixed to houses that tell of famous personages who once lived within.

In short, if history is your interest, you won't find any shortage of material in London. The city's architecture, the development of its precincts and the names of its streets and neighbourhoods all proclaim its long past and invite investigation. Borough museums and libraries contain a wealth of local history, which will enable you to find out how the place where you live got to be the way it is.

GEOGRAPHY AND CLIMATE

We have noted London's high latitude: it lies roughly along the 51st parallel of North latitude. Its longitude is effectively 0, being defined in relation to the Greenwich Meridian, which runs through the London borough of Greenwich. Most of London is only marginally above sea level, and it is largely quite flat; only north London has areas that are appreciably hilly and afford views over other parts of the city. The average elevation is about 15 metres with a couple of hilly places just over 130 m (426 ft). Newspapers are fond of printing sensational maps showing which parts would go under first if sea levels rose, for all of south-east England is slowly sinking.

London's geographic position and the weather that comes its way are inextricably linked. If the earth should ever change its ways dramatically, as some think it threatens to do, London would probably be in for some rude shocks, for it currently enjoys a climate far more pleasant than its place on the globe would suggest is possible. The sine qua non of London's (and Britain's) climate is the Gulf Stream, the north-eastward flowing, warm current of Atlantic water that effectively heats the British Isles and parts of Northern Europe all year round. Without it, London's winters would probably be more like Moscow's, and furry hats would be de rigueur.

The mitigating effects of the Gulf Stream and London's high latitude result in a climate that is generally devoid of extremes. It is never very cold, and never very hot. A typical London day, which can appear at virtually any time of year, is completely overcast (but not raining), with moist but not damp air (relative humidity averages 80 per cent throughout the year), gentle winds from the south-west, and temperatures between 10–16°C (50–60°F). This is not to suggest that London enjoys no variation in the weather at all; summers can in fact be hot and dry, and snowstorms, though appearing on average only every few years, are not unheard of in the winter. The natives, as if to compensate for the lack

of extremes, respond to these variations with alacrity. When temperatures reach the mid-20s°C (mid-70s°F) in summer, businessmen strip off their shirts in the parks on their lunch hours. A winter snowstorm finds everyone dressed up like Eskimos, and the city grinds to a complete halt, for there is little infrastructure to deal with snow on the ground: you just have to wait until it melts.

A widespread misconception about London is that it rains all the time. It certainly rains often enough to dampen many a holiday, weekend or outing; but in fact, London is one of the driest places in the British Isles, averaging about 62 cm (24 inches) of rain per year. This compares with 89 cm (35 inches) for Belfast, 91 cm (36 inches) for Cardiff and 97 cm (38 inches) for Glasgow. Londoners can quite easily get away without their umbrellas more days than not. Rain, when it does come, tends to be spotty, intermittent and light: drizzle rather than downpour is the rule. An average day of steady rain in London brings only half an inch.

With that as the general picture, here's what you can expect throughout the year. We start where the year begins, in January. If snow is to come at all to London (it always comes to Scotland and northern England, but doesn't necessarily hit the south), it will probably come in January and February. These are the coldest months, with frost common by night and the odd day when the temperature doesn't rise above freezing. The average temperatures, however, are 7°C (44°F) by day and 2°C (35°F) by night. There is usually not a lot of sunshine during these months, and rain (occasionally snow) is frequent. Fog is also not uncommon at this time of year, but the fogs for which London was once famous were largely due to fuel particulates from coal burning, and thus no longer appear.

Towards the end of February, there are already signs of spring. In an average year, bluebells and crocuses will be well out of the ground by then, with daffodils not far behind. A day or two with a warm spring breeze will appear, and the days grow appreciably longer.

T S Eliot may have called April the cruellest month, but in London, March joins it. These two months are a battle between winter and spring, and just when you think the latter has come to stay, the former will come along to undo all the progress. There will be some lovely, balmy days when you can go out without bundling up, but also some stormy days, with driving rain and biting winds out of the north-east (south-west winds dominate at other times of the year). Nevertheless, flowers continue to make their appearance, and daffodils by then will be in their glory. April average temperatures are a high of 13°C (56°F) and a low of 4°C (40°F).

By May, you can be cautiously optimistic about having more fine days than foul. London is abloom with tulips, bluebells, the first roses and spring-flowering trees and shrubs. It's not summer yet, but it's the closest thing to it: May runs a close second to June for being the sunniest month of the year. Daytime temperatures will usually be in the teens and 20s°C (50s and 60s°F), but don't be surprised by the occasional day that is a throwback to the dreary winter.

In June, Londoners begin speculating about whether summer will arrive. Summer weather patterns tend to be quite persistent, often sticking around for six weeks or more, so summers in London tend to be much of one thing or another. The stereotype of cool and rainy summers has hardly been borne out in recent years. London has had drought conditions for half of the summers since 1985, and new records for heat or drought are now being set regularly. Remember, however, that in London, a drought is by definition a fortnight without rain, and a heatwave means temperatures around 30°C (mid to high 80s°F) for several days running. It is rarely muggy, except before and after thunderstorms, which if they come at all to London come in the summer. Midsummer average temperatures are a high of 22°C (73°F) and a low of 13°C (55°F). The non-summers that Londoners are fond of complaining about have little sunshine, lots of rain and temperatures forever in the 15–20°C range.

September is very often a pleasant month in London, not only because the worst ravages of the tourist season have passed, but also because the weather usually remains mild, with a fair amount of sunshine. This is a good time of year for taking walks in the parks, which will still have lots of flowers blooming.

October and November will remind you that winter is on the way. Leaves wither and fall, flowers fade and rain becomes more frequent. Violent storms may also come: the famous hurricane that rocked southern England with 100-mile an hour winds in 1987 came in October. Average temperatures at this time of year are a high of 15°C (58°F) and a low of 7°C (44°F).

December is a continuation of this pattern, with even shorter days and cooler temperatures. But when a sunny day comes along, it is quite extraordinary; for by this time of year, the sun is quite low in the sky and casts long shadows even at midday through very milky, luminescent air. On more days than not, you will be comfortable outdoors with a light jacket, once the chill of the morning has passed.

London Air

Air quality in London is spotty at all times of the year, owing to the incredible volume of slow-moving traffic that produces noxious gases and harmful particulates. Whereas it is nearly always safe to breathe the air, there is hardly a day when you would call it wholesome. Air quality is generally worst during still, clear winter or summer days, when ozone and carbon monoxide levels occasionally get dangerously high. When it is necessary for warnings to be issued (this happens quite rarely), they are usually given as part of the weather report.

WHO RUNS LONDON?

Government and politics in London have a very long and tumultuous history, in which new chapters are continually being written. The current situation, in which a single authority runs the city, came about as a result of a referendum in 1998 when Londoners voted in favour of the establishment of a new overall authority for London. In 2000, London elected Ken Livingston as mayor, along with a separately elected assembly of 25 people. This assembly is composed of 14 people representing different areas of London and 11

London-wide members. The new Greater London Authority (GLA) has its own budget and is responsible for transportation policy, economic development, police, environmental policy and fire protection.

For some, this may have echoes of the Greater London Council (GLC), which governed London in a very left-leaning, liberal way from 1974 to 1986. Margaret Thatcher's government disbanded the GLC in 1986. The reason is rather obvious: any representative body for London would be by definition Labour-dominated, and the Conservative governments that prevailed until recently would not tolerate a de facto, powerful legislative opponent. The ironic twist to all of this is that in 2000, Londoners elected as their mayor the very man who was the leader of the GLC when it was disbanded. And as a final coup de grace, although a Labour government was in power when the London mayoral election took place, the Labour party completely disowned Livingstone in favour of a more moderate candidate of their own—whom the voters were not impressed with! The mayor and the government still have fences to mend, but for the first time in many years, London enjoys the relative simplicity of a single governing authority.

As in most respects, the City of London is quite distinct in its affairs from the boroughs. It is governed by a corporation that has existed since medieval times, and in fact remains quite medieval in its complexity and secrecy. It has an elected Lord Mayor who serves for a term of one year, and councillors and aldermen who represent residents and business interests. The City has few residents and so the main business of City government is to safeguard the conditions favourable to commerce and manage the Corporation's extensive land holdings (it owns Hampstead Heath and Epping Forest, as well as 30 per cent of land in the City and various other parcels in and around London).

London is policed by a single force, called the Metropolitan Police, or the Met for short. It reports to the Home Secretary and its headquarters is Scotland Yard (more properly New Scotland Yard, located in Westminster, roughly between Victoria Station and Parliament Square). Scotland Yard also has a consultative role in national police affairs. The City has its own separate police force, called appropriately enough, the City of London Police.

THE LAY OF THE LAND

A big part of really feeling at home in a city is knowing where things are and what they are. This is something that you absorb naturally over a long period of residence, by simply going about the place, studying maps and learning from others. But London is a vast environment to become acquainted with and so it helps to have some idea of the major features on the map and what makes them renowned.

We end this short introductory chapter then with a primer on London landmarks and common places. Included here are the places that most Londoners have some acquaintance with, in terms of their general location, and just as importantly, in terms of people's associations with them. When someone mentions the Elephant and Castle, it's helpful to know that neither a palace nor a pachyderm is involved, but rather a roundabout in South London where several roads and two Underground lines meet.

Before we get started, however, there are a few conventions about the pronunciation of place names, familiarity with which will keep you from sounding like a tourist. Several syllables that commonly end place names are never stressed and are usually pronounced differently than their spelling suggests. These are:

Spelling	Pronunciation	Examples
–cester	–ster	Gloucester (GLOS–ster) Leicester (LES–ster) Worcester (WUS–ster)
–ham	–em	Clapham (CLAP–em) Streatham (STRET–em) Tottenham (TOT–en–em)
–shire	–sher	Berkshire (BARK–sher) Hampshire (HAM–sher)

–wark	–erk	Southwark (SUTH–erk)
–wich	–ich	Dulwich (DUL–ich) Greenwich (GREN–ich) Woolwich (WOOL–ich)
–wick	–ick	Berwick (BEAR–ick) Chiswick (CHIZ–ick) Warwick (WAR–ick)

- Note however that when 'Ham' or 'Wick' appear as separate words, they are accented and given proper pronunciation: 'East HAM,' 'Hackney WICK.'

Not included in the list below are most of London's famous landmarks. These stand out like a sore thumb on every tourist map, and Londoners tend to view them much as everyone does: as tourist attractions. Some of the terms in bold that appear throughout the book are indexed in the back of the book, so if you're looking for a particular place, you may want to start with the index. We begin in the City, move west to Westminster and proceed in a clockwise spiral until all of Greater London is covered.

The City

If you alight from **Bank** tube station, just in front of the **Bank of England**, you will be more or less in the middle of the City and you can walk to any address in 15 minutes or less. Everything having to do with finance is located in the City, including the **Stock Exchange**, the headquarters of nearly all national banks and international banks that have a presence in London, the headquarters of insurance companies and **Lloyd's**, the insurance market.

The City is also home to **Fleet Street**, formerly the home of most of London's newspapers, and also of the Central Criminal Court, popularly known as the **Old Bailey**. Two of London's four **Inns of Court**, where barristers have their chambers, are in the City: the **Middle Temple** and the **Inner Temple**. Four bridges cross the Thames along the City's waterfront. They are, starting upstream, **Blackfriars Bridge**, **Millennium Bridge**, **Southwark Bridge** and **London Bridge**. All end in Southwark on the other side.

Look for the **Barbican Centre**, a huge arts complex that houses two cinemas, two theatres, a performance auditorium, several cafes and restaurants, libraries and various schools. Two of the tallest buildings on the city skyline are the residential towers of the Barbican and the **Natwest Bank**.

Smithfield Market, a wholesale meat market which is a virtual museum of antiquated labour practices where meat is bought and sold in rather appalling conditions, is at the western edge of the City. So is St. Bartholomew Hospital, or popularly **Bart's**, a major teaching hospital that is scheduled to close—amid vehement protest from the public—in the next few years.

Westminster

Because it is the heart of London and so densely packed with well-known places, Westminster is best broken down into digestible chunks before identifying what each of them contains. We begin with three place names that denote more than actual physical spaces on the map: Westminster, Whitehall and Downing Street.

When used by the media, **Westminster** often means the government of the UK, or it can have the more limited meaning of the area surrounding the **Houses of Parliament**, rather than the whole borough. The street leading northwards from **Parliament Square** towards **Trafalgar Square** is called **Whitehall**. In the hands of the media, Whitehall is the British government bureaucracy, for it is along Whitehall that all the major ministries are located, and here that top civil servants (dubbed Whitehall Mandarins) work. A small and unassuming street off Whitehall called **Downing Street** is synonymous with the government of the day: the prime minister lives at **Number 10**, and the chancellor of the exchequer (chief treasury minister) lives at **Number 11**. In the middle of Whitehall is the **Cenotaph**, a monument to Britain's war dead.

The next most well-known part of Westminster is the **West End**, an imprecise term that is more or less synonymous

Besides its theatres and cinemas, the West End and Soho, in particular, are home to numerous popular restaurants and to London's liveliest nightlife. London's Chinatown occupies a couple of streets behind Leicester Square.

with the area where most of the theatres and first-run cinemas are located. It is bounded roughly by **Covent Garden** (known for trendy shopping) in the east, the top of **Charing Cross Road** (bookstores) in the north, **Charing Cross Station** in the south and **Picadilly Circus** in the west. In the heart of this area is **Leicester Square**. Also within this area, adjacent to Leicester Square, is **Soho**.

The next big chunk of Westminster is bounded by **Regent Street** (expensive shopping) on the east, **Oxford Street** (shopping for the masses) on the north, **Park Lane** (hotels for the well-heeled) on the west and **Picadilly** (everything for the well-heeled) on the south. This area can also be identified by its corners, which are equally well-known: **Marble Arch**, **Oxford Circus**, **Picadilly Circus** and **Hyde Park Corner**.

The greater part of this trapezoid is called **Mayfair**, and if you're *really* rich, this is where you shop for everything, from food at **Fortnum and Mason** to clothes in the boutiques along **New Bond Street** to fine art in the galleries on little streets off Picadilly. Two well-known green spaces in Mayfair are **Grosvenor Square**, site of the grandiose American Embassy, and **Berkeley Square**, where the nightingale of song is alleged to have sung. South of Picadilly is the district called **Saint James's**, where old money, old business and government ministries coexist comfortably. There are two former royal residences here, the **Palace of Saint James** and **Marlborough House**, which now serves as a meeting place for the Commonwealth of Nations.

A trapezoid of equal density that doesn't have a convenient name lies roughly north of the Mayfair one. It is bounded by Oxford Street on the south, **Tottenham Court Road** (computers and entertainment electronics) on the east, **Marylebone Road** (harrowing traffic jams) on the north and **Edgware Road** (Arabs and Middle-Eastern shops) on the west. Within this area can be found **Baker Street** (Sherlock

Holmes, remember?) and **Harley Street** (expensive doctors and clinics). Discounting the sheer madness of Oxford Street, this area contains a vast number of interesting specialty stores and businesses. It's very good for shoppers too faint of heart for Oxford Street and not deep-pocketed enough for Mayfair.

Westminster contains some of London's most famous and pleasant parks. The mother of them all is **Hyde Park**, along with adjacent **Kensington Gardens**. In the north-east corner of Hyde Park, directly across from Marble Arch, is **Speaker's Corner**, where every Sunday morning you can listen to fanatics on soapboxes drone on about politics and religion. Few hearts or minds are won, but it is a diverting spectacle. **Green Park** and **Saint James's Park** are smaller, immaculately tended open spaces just south of Picadilly. **Lord's Cricket Ground** in Saint John's Wood is not so much a park as a national shrine, being the headquarters of cricket's governing body. Finally, most of **Regent's Park** lies in Westminster, which is unsurpassed in its brilliant arrangements of all blooming things. The **London Zoo** (forlorn, caged animals) is also located within the park.

The eastern reaches of Westminster contain **The Strand**, home to several theatres and several dozen homeless people and the **Savoy Hotel**. Just a bit further on, and at the border of the city, is **Aldwych**, home to yet more theatres, the BBC's **Bush House**, where World Service broadcasts originate and the Royal Courts of Justice, popularly called the **High Court**.

Other well-known districts of Westminster are a mix of residential and commercial interests. These are the areas around the two train stations, **Paddington** and **Victoria**; **Belgravia**, where stately mansions sell for a million pounds or more; **Pimlico**, where **Tate Britain** (British painting from the 16th century to the present day) is located; and finally **Bayswater**, a haven for London's Middle Eastern population. Seven bridges span the Thames from Westminster to Lambeth on the other side. They are, starting upstream, **Vauxhall Bridge**, **Lambeth Bridge**, **Westminster Bridge**, the three **Hungerford Bridges** (trains and pedestrians only) and **Waterloo Bridge**.

Kensington and Chelsea

Of the Inner London boroughs, this has all the credentials for being the poshest. It calls itself the Royal Borough of Kensington and Chelsea (because Queen Victoria was born here), and if you were in the mood for spotting royals, they would as likely be here as anywhere. A small section of **North Kensington**, north of the A40, is the borough's 'other side of the tracks'. Just south of the A40 is **Notting Hill**, where the Notting Hill Carnival, the largest street carnival in Europe, is held each August. The borough as a whole has some of the most desirable and expensive residences in London. **Sloane Square** is here, home of the 'Sloane Rangers', a media designation for the young, high-income, easy-living upper class set. Leading off of the Square is **King's Road**, where many of London's most innovative clothes designers have their boutiques. A more down-to-earth area is **Earl's Court Road**, popular with Antipodeans and Arabs alike, and with a fair share of gay venues as well. The exhibition centre at **Earl's Court** is the venue of many annual and special events that are visited by people from all over Britain. Many of London's most visited museums are in K&C, including the **Victoria and Albert** (human artifacts of all cultures, as well as fine art), the **Natural History**, the **Science** and the **Geology Museums**, all in one complex. **Knightsbridge** is a posh shopping and residential area in the borough, home to several top department stores, most notably **Harrods**.

Fulham and Hammersmith

On the north side of the Thames in south-west London, these formerly separate boroughs are now home to the middle classes. **Shepherd's Bush**, where there is a sizable Irish community, is in the north of the borough, as is **Wormwood Scrubs Prison**, one of London's largest. Three of London's football clubs have their grounds in F&H: **Fulham FC**; **Chelsea FC**, whose grounds are called **Stamford Bridge**; and **Queen's Park Rangers FC**.

Hammersmith Delights

Hammersmith is home to the Hammersmith Apollo, a large concert hall where loud bands play to hordes of badly dressed young people. Olympia is also in the borough, a large exhibition centre that stages various consumer and trade shows throughout the year. Hammersmith Bridge, which crosses the Thames to Richmond, is an out-of-the-way architectural delight.

Camden

Outside of the major tourist zone, probably no borough offers more in the way of variety and interest than Camden. It contains some of London's leafiest and most comfortable neighbourhoods, many of which grew from small villages, including **Hampstead**, **Highgate**, **Primrose Hill** and **Belsize Park**. There are more than 100 blue plaques, indicating the residences of notable Londoners of the past. Only Westminster and Kensington and Chelsea can boast more.

On the map, Camden is dominated by **Hampstead Heath**, a huge open space of nearly 324 hectares (800 acres) with woods, various sporting facilities, riding trails and nature walks. **Camden Town**, the main business area of the borough, has a four-day-a-week market where virtually anything can be bought. **Camden Lock**, on the **Regent's Canal**, is also a popular spot (if you're young and like to drink beer sitting outside), especially on weekends.

The southern part of the borough borders on the City and on Westminster. Here you will find three of London's mainline train stations serving the north of the country: **Euston**, **Saint Pancras** and **King's Cross** (traffic jams by day, prostitutes by night), all less than a mile apart from each other on **Euston Road**. The **British Library** is adjacent to the Saint Pancras station. **Bloomsbury** in the southernmost part of Camden was home to the literary set of the late 19th and early 20th centuries. Around it are the **British Museum** and the **University of London**. London's two other Inns of Court, **Gray's Inn** and **Lincoln's Inn**, are in the **Holborn** section of Camden.

Islington

In north-east London, Islington has equal parts of chic and gritty neighbourhoods. **Angel**, the main business district, is popular with antique traders by day and young students and professionals, who take advantage of the many reasonably priced restaurants, by night. Just south of the Angel is **Sadler's Wells Theatre**, London's premiere dance venue. In the south of the borough, bordering the City, is **Clerkenwell**, home to London's most visible Italian community and to **Arsenal FC**, one of Britain's best and most ardently supported football clubs. **Pentonville** and **Holloway**, two of London's better known prisons, are in the borough.

Hackney

Being the poorest borough in Britain, Hackney is a convenient whipping boy or object lesson for nearly anyone who has a political or social axe to grind. There is little here that draws tourists, but 180,000 ordinary Londoners live here, enjoying such amenities as the **Hackney Marsh**, which consists of big green spaces on the River Lea, and the walkway along the **Grand Union Canal**. Neighbourhoods

Terraced houses in Islington, typical of inner London.

with character are **Stoke Newington**, which manages to be both hip and affordable to ordinary mortals, and **Dalston**, a comfortable blend of a dozen ethnic groups. Because of its relatively cheap rents for large, formerly industrial spaces, Hackney has a large and thriving community of plastic artists. The south of the borough borders the City and contains a furniture manufacturing area and the **Geffrye**

Museum, which displays domestic interiors from the 17th century to the present day. The **Hackney Empire**, a restored Victorian theatre in Mare Street, is a venue for a wide variety of live entertainment.

Tower Hamlets

Two cities exist side by side in Tower Hamlets: the old **East End** of London that always has been and probably always will be colourful but poor; and **Docklands**, a product of the Thatcher years that was to be (and might still end up being) the bright inner city of the 21st century. Neighbourhoods such as **Whitechapel**, **Bethnal Green**, **Stepney and Bow** have always been home to immigrants and the poor. Today, the borough has a large minority of Bengalis. The western edge of Tower Hamlets borders the City and contains **Spitalfields Market**, until recently a wholesale greengrocers, now a revitalised shopping area. Behind the market is **Brick Lane**, home to some of London's best and cheapest Indian restaurants.

The parts of Tower Hamlets that have been developed as a part of Docklands lie along the Thames: from the **Tower of London** eastwards, and taking in all of the **Isle of Dogs**, the big tongue-shaped peninsula around which the Thames winds in a horseshoe in East London. The Isle of Dogs is home to **Canary Wharf**, an office complex that includes the tallest building in Europe, and also to **Billingsgate Market**, a wholesale fish market that replaced its predecessor in the City.

Further west along the river are **Wapping** (where some newspapers now have their offices and production plants) and **Saint Katherine's Wharf**, an upmarket residential and shopping area. This is the part of town where old warehouses have been converted into spacious (and not very cheap) loft apartments. The **Docklands Light Railway** which runs eastwards from Bank station serves most of the area. One branch of the railway ends at **Island Gardens**, where you'll find a pedestrian tunnel under the Thames that takes you to the heart of Greenwich. A little further downstream, the **Blackwall Tunnel** carries motor traffic under the Thames to Greenwich.

Lewisham

Lying south of the river and south-east of the City, Lewisham is neither prominent nor prosperous by London standards. The **Crystal Palace**, which housed the great exhibition of 1851, is no longer standing. Its grounds are now a park with a museum and various sports facilities, including the **National Sports Centre** where athletes train.

Southwark

Southwark spans the riverfront in south central London. Among its well-known locales are **Elephant and Castle**, a name that designates a pub and also a roundabout circling a monstrous eyesore that looks like it was jettisoned by aliens. The **Tate Modern**, a gigantic museum of contemporary art, occupies an old Southward power plant.

The Millennium Bridge—probably more famous for swaying drastically on its opening day and the cost it took to fix the problem—leads pedestrians across to the City.

Right next to it is the reconstruction of **Shakespeare's Globe Theatre** which has an exhibition on the history of Elizabethan theatre.

The **Rotherhithe Tunnel** (motor traffic) crosses under the Thames in Southwark, joining Tower Hamlets on the other side. **Southwark Cathedral**, the earliest Gothic church in London, is in the borough, as is **Guy's Hospital**. The Labour Party has its headquarters on **Walworth Road**, the name of which is synonymous with the party. All three bridges on the City side of the river end in Southwark, with London Bridge ending at **London Bridge Station**. Another Southwark bridge and London landmark, **Tower Bridge**, meets Tower Hamlets on the other side.

Lambeth

The principal attractions of this south London borough are the **London Eye**, a gigantic Ferris wheel offering views of all London, and the **South Bank Centre**, a large and interesting cultural complex. It houses performance halls, cinemas, theatres and museums, as well as cafés and restaurants. It includes the **Royal Festival Hall**, the **Hayward Gallery**, the

National Theatre and the **National Film Theatre**. Right next door is **County Hall**, formerly home of the Greater London Council and now the **London Aquarium** and upstairs, luxury apartments.

Lambeth is also where you find **Lambeth Palace**, residence and headquarters of the archbishop of Canterbury (head of the Church of England). **The Oval** (grounds of Surrey County Cricket Club) is in Lambeth, as is **Waterloo Station** and **Saint Thomas Hospital**. Two well-known neighbourhoods are **Brixton**, with a large African and Caribbean population, and **Clapham**, where you can presumably find 'the man on the Clapham Omnibus', thought to represent London's ordinary citizen.

Wandsworth

The four cream-coloured chimneys that dominate the south London skyline are at **Battersea Power Station**, no longer in use but repeatedly named as the future site of one major project or another, but at present still gathering dust. Adjacent to the station and also on the riverfront is **Battersea Park**. When central London's Covent Garden ceased to be a wholesale market, its business was moved to **New Covent Garden Market**, which now supplies much of London with fresh flowers, fruits and veggies. Five bridges span the Thames from Wandsworth: starting upstream, **Putney Bridge** and then **Wandsworth Bridge** go to Fulham; **Battersea Bridge**, **Albert Bridge** and **Chelsea Bridge** go to Chelsea.

Outer London Landmarks

Places known to Londoners generally become thinner on the ground as you move away from the centre. Places mentioned here, though perhaps infrequently visited by Inner Londoners, have a big enough claim to fame that everyone at least knows where and what they are.

Starting at 12 o'clock, we proceed clockwise: **Alexandra Palace** and the surrounding park provide a large green space and some cultural activities for north Londoners. Further to the east is the **Epping Forest**, a largely undeveloped, ancient wood where you can lose yourself, or get lost. In the borough of **Newham** in East London, you'll find **London City Airport**, serving cities in the UK and on the continent. **East Ham** and **West Ham**, two working class areas now home to large immigrant communities, are also in Newham, as is **New Spitalfields Market**, a wholesale fruit and vegetable market that replaced its predecessor near the City.

Greenwich is south-east London's premier borough, with several notable establishments along the riverfront, including the **Royal Observatory**, the **Royal Naval College** and the **National Maritime Museum**. Further south-east is the borough of **Croydon**, which should hold a special place more in the hearts of foreign than native Londoners, for it is the home of **Lunar House**—the Home Office site where most matters relating to residency and immigration are handled.

South-west London, probably the single most prosperous quadrant of the city, has a number of landmarks, none more beloved than **Kew Gardens**, visited by people from the world over but always available for Londoners. **Wimbledon** is also in the south-west London borough of **Merton**, where the All England Tennis Club sponsors the annual tennis championship. Other green places in the south-west are **Richmond Park**, **Syon Park** and **Hampton Court Park** and **Palace**, a former royal residence now open to the public.

Far west London is chiefly associated with **Heathrow Airport**, the only major airport serving London that is actually within the city. **Southall**, a neighbourhood in the west London borough of **Ealing**, is famous for being almost as Indian as Calcutta or Bombay: Indian residents and businesses abound. North-west London's principal landmark is **Harrow School**, one of a very short list of private schools where Britain's best and brightest (also richest) boys are educated.

PEOPLE

CHAPTER 3

' "People are funny," she mused.
"In London, they don't seem to care about anything." '
—Beryl Bainbridge, *Sweet William*

AT THE BEGINNING OF THE 21ST CENTURY, there were 7.4 million people living in Greater London. Just who are these people? The last major census was done in 2001. It is a statistician's gold mine of facts about the ways and means of Londoners; it also gives a lot of insight to the ordinary mortal about the social fabric of London and who is part of it.

One of the more interesting facts about people living in London is how few of them, in relative terms, are actually from here. Three out of four Londoners were born in England (not necessarily in London); but one out of four was born elsewhere. This one out of four amounts to nearly two million people. About 400,000 of these were born elsewhere in the European Union, including the Republic of Ireland. But the vast majority of foreign Londoners came from a long way off and jumped through all the necessary hoops (legal or illegal) to settle here.

Few cities in the world have achieved and maintained this degree of cosmopolitanism, but in London, it is a fact of life. So if you're a foreigner in London you're not alone; on the contrary, you're one of a very large crowd. A quick glance at the history of London's immigration reveals why it has been, and

Coming to London

Up until 1066, newcomers to London were as likely as not to be part of an invading army. They came with the idea of not only finding a place to live, but also making it into the sort of place they wanted it to be, by force if necessary. Since then, arrivals in London have been of a gentler sort, but the pace has not slackened.

continues to be, a destination for settlers from all over the world.

The proximity to London of major Continental population centres and Britain's ties with foreign countries kept immigration moving apace for centuries following the final invasion of William the Conqueror, for which 1066 is justly famous. London has always been the first great city that travellers from the Continent encounter once they've crossed the Channel, and when Britain began to develop links to other parts of the world through trade and colonisation, its gates were opened up to arrivals from even further afield. These fall into two broad classes: refugees, and those seeking to improve their fortunes.

REFUGEES AND ASYLUM SEEKERS

Throughout its history, London has been a haven for those escaping political or religious persecution in their own countries. The first of these were Protestants from the Low Countries in the 16th century. In the next century, the Huguenots came from France. Early political asylum seekers also came from the United States, where they were not in sympathy with the revolution. A few years later, small numbers came from France for the same reason.

London Jews

London's earliest Jewish immigrants came for trade in the 17th century, but their numbers were greatly increased by refugees in two periods: the years leading up to 1914, when Jews fled the pogroms in Russia; and in the years leading up to and including World War II, when they fled Nazi Germany and the countries under its occupation.

Today, London continues to be a destination for refugees from battered countries around the world. Britain is a signatory to the 1951 UN Convention on refugees, and as such it agrees to entertain the applications of those who come fleeing persecution. The overwhelming majority of asylum seekers now coming to Britain arrive at one of the international airports serving London, and most of them—as many as 85 per cent—settle initially in London. It is only here that they are likely to find others of their nationality and experience, and it is only in London that local governments have made an effort to develop facilities for the housing and welfare of refugees.

In 2002, asylum seekers arriving in Britain—and well over 90 per cent arrive or apply in London—averaged more than 7,000 per month. Over a third were from Africa. Countries with the largest numbers of applicants were Iraq (17 per cent), Zimbabwe (9 per cent), Afghanistan (9 per cent), Somalia (8 per cent) and China (4 per cent). Only a small percentage of these applicants will eventually be granted full refugee status, but a significant number are granted leave to remain in Britain for a number of years while their cases are being considered.

ECONOMIC MIGRANTS

In all periods of history, the most important motivating force for people coming to London has been the desire to find a better life. The modern term for these folk is economic migrant, and it has something of a sinister ring in the ears of some government ministers. In fact, such migrants have been not only welcomed but actively courted in the past. Formerly, the British government and other British employers sought to import cheap and available labour from abroad, often from countries with strong historical ties, such as the former colonies. The 20 years following the end of World War II was the most intense period for these foreign recruitment drives, the most notable of which were in Ireland and countries in the Caribbean.

Since then, as the job market has contracted and full employment has more often been a dream than a reality, the economic migrant has been characterised as an undesirable opportunist by British governments. But welcomed or not, migrants still arrive: some legally under provisions of various laws concerning former colonials or foreign workers, some in the guise of asylum seekers, and others get their foot in the door on a visa that doesn't entitle them to employment. For the last group, there is the hope they will be able to parlay their status into one that allows work, or the possibility of disappearing into the vast gray market of ethnic London—where they can live and work indefinitely, so long as their presence goes undetected by the authorities.

THE UNMELTING POT

Immigration to London, whatever the reason, has nearly always been a group, rather than an individual phenomenon. Even those arriving alone are often very quick to seek the company of their compatriots, and the result is that many foreign communities exist almost intact within London. Assimilation in the arriving generation can be almost nil, and indeed assimilation of any kind may only occur with the first generation of children who are educated in the state-supported school system. But it may be worth asking just what these arrivals should be assimilating to, since one out of four Londoners is a non-native.

Many foreigners in London end up living mostly in this city within a city, what we might call 'foreigners' London'. It's not that the natives are inaccessible, it's just that they can turn out to be rather thin on the ground in places that foreigners are likely to frequent for the purposes of housing, working and socialising. So before we try to dissect the dominant type, the English-born Londoner, we will take a detailed look at the million-and-a-half strong foreign community in London.

THE VIEW FROM THE HOME OFFICE

Grouping people by country of origin is a cherished view of the Home Office (the ministry in charge of internal affairs) because it enables officials to note trends in immigration. For us, it gives an instructive picture of who makes up cosmopolitan London. Census figures show that there are 1,000 or more natives of 70 different countries living in London. Foreign Londoners speak 200 different languages, and it's a rare ride on a London bus when you don't hear at least one of them. Here is a breakdown of foreign Londoners in the biggest chunks.

The Empire Come Home to Roost

The largest single block of foreigners living in London comes from countries of the Commonwealth of Nations, which was

formerly called the British Commonwealth, and before that, with a few changes, the British Empire. People from the 'Old Commonwealth' (Australia, Canada and New Zealand) and the 'New Commonwealth' (Britain's former colonies in Africa, the Caribbean, the Asian subcontinent and South-east Asia) together account for just over half of foreign London (about 800,000 people). Until 1962, citizens of all these countries were full British subjects and had automatic right to residence in Britain. Since then, increasingly strict legislation has limited in various ways the number and kind who may enter without formality, but many still come under various provisions of the immigration laws.

Though no longer part of the Commonwealth, Ireland deserves a mention here since its people, long-suffering under the British, continue to enjoy the right to live and work in Britain—now in their capacity as European Union nationals. Taken together with their neighbours from Ulster (Northern Ireland), the Irish are the largest single-country ethnic group in London, numbering 250,000, making London the third largest Irish city in the world after New York and Dublin.

Euromobility

As a member of the European Union, Britain can place no obstacle in the way of any EU citizen who wishes to live and work within its borders. Nearly 400,000 EU nationals make London their home, with Germans and Italians in the lead (more than 40,000 of each), followed by France and Spain (around 25,000 each). With each successive year, barriers within the EU become less and less restrictive for EU nationals. Although Britain has not, and perhaps will not, sign on to the single European currency (the Euro) that unites many EU countries, it cooperates on every other front, making it an easy and desirable home for Europeans. The status of English as a world language means that it is a second language (and a mandatory one in many cases) for most Europeans, and after their own country, they find Britain the easiest place to settle in. European visitors are often surprised to find many vendors, especially in tourist areas, accept payment in Euros.

The Draw of London

Two other countries deserve mention because of their relatively large populations living in London: the United States, with about 35,000; and Turkey (which has applied for EU membership but is viewed as a long way from getting it), with 25,000. The largely Arab and Muslim countries of the Middle East have around 51,000 nationals living in London.

THE VIEW FROM THE STREET

A look at some of the obvious groupings of Londoners puts the diverse ethnic composition of the city in a more human perspective. We look here at the groups of people whom we tend to put together on the basis of appearance, which happily coincides more or less with the way they group themselves. This view takes us part of the way out of London's strictly foreign community to encompass also the British nationals who belong to one or another of London's ethnic or religious communities with roots abroad.

Ethnic London: a kosher bakery and a Spanish restaurant in Golder's Green.

Asian Communities

It is surely a Western convenience to pigeonhole a third of the world's population in a single category. The diversity of people in London who are grouped under the term 'Asian' represent perhaps the broadest spectrum of nationalities, ethnic groups and languages. There are appreciable numbers of Vietnamese, Burmese and Thai people living in London but the largest subgroups are:

Chinese

The earliest Chinese in London were seamen in the 18th and 19th centuries. A community of Chinese grew up in the East End, around the neighbourhood now called Limehouse, but this area was heavily bombed in the war and nothing remains of the Chinese there except a few street names.

The most visible Chinese area today is, naturally enough, Chinatown in the heart of Soho, where dozens of restaurants, shops and supermarkets are found. But the Chinese live everywhere in London, and there is hardly a neighbourhood without one of their food shops and a couple of takeaway restaurants. London's Chinese community, foreign and British-born, is thought to number about 55,000.

Subcontinentals

People of the Asian subcontinent, that is Indians, Bangladeshis, Pakistanis and Sri Lankans, have been arriving in large numbers since the days of the British Empire, and continue to arrive today. A significant number of Asians in London came from African countries which, in the throes of early independence, made life uncomfortable for Asians and forced them to find another home.

A few areas of London are associated with large communities, notably Southall in the west London borough of Ealing, and in east London, Newham and Tower Hamlets. A pervasive stereotype of the Asian Londoner is that of the small shopkeeper: the family who owns and operates the small neighbourhood convenience store that can be found, usually no more than a couple of streets away, wherever you live in London. It is true that a large number of these shops are Asian-owned and operated, but Asians of the subcontinent are well integrated into all levels of London life, from manual labourers to corporate executives.

The Black Community

London's black community rivals the Asian in terms of diversity. The major division is between those of West

Middle East meets West at Church Street Market.

Indian and Caribbean ancestry on the one hand, and those who come directly from Africa on the other. Black Londoners number about 500,000, and a few countries are represented in large numbers: Jamaica with more than 75,000; Kenya with more than 55,000; and Ghana, Nigeria and Uganda with an average of 30,000 each. Like Asians and other groups, Blacks live in every area of London. A few areas have large concentrations: Hackney and Haringey in north-east London, Lambeth and Lewisham in south-east London.

Jewish Communities

About 150,000 Jews live in London, representing all the different degrees of religious observance and varieties of ethnicity in the Jewish tradition. They make up over half of the Jews in Britain. The only Hasidic community in London is centred around Stamford Hill in north-east London. Other areas associated with large groups are Golder's Green, Hendon and Finchley in north-west London. A popular stereotype of the London taxi driver includes his being Jewish, but as everywhere, so in London, Jews participate in all levels of social, professional and political life.

Despite its myriad communities, London is less 'ghettoised' than many other world cities. Thanks to the availability of low-cost housing provided by housing trusts, housing associations and local governments, immigrants can and do live in every London borough. Four London boroughs have populations that could be characterised as more than one-third ethnic: these are Hackney, Newham, Tower Hamlets and Brent, which have a whopping 45 per cent ethnic population.

A handful of neighbourhoods have taken on a character of a particular group: Afro-Caribbeans account for more than 10 per cent of the population in four London boroughs; Indians make up more than 10 per cent in five boroughs; and Bangladeshis, uniquely, account for 23 per cent of the population in one borough, Tower Hamlets. But the more common pattern in London is for people from everywhere to live side by side.

LONDON TYPES: A FIELD GUIDE

In addition to the groups noted above, there are a handful of types who, because of their numbers or their visibility, can be spotted easily in London. They are stereotypes, but ones that Londoners have generated about themselves. These include:

Eurokids

Everybody wants to learn to speak English. London abounds with schools where English is taught as a foreign language, and also with low paid, relatively unskilled jobs that Britons don't very much like to do (British university students do not normally hold part-time jobs). These elements combine to provide a milieu for young people from everywhere in the European Union. They come to live and work in Britain for a period, ranging from a few months to a few years. This explains why your waitress in the poshest hotels and tearooms in Picadilly may be Dutch or Greek but hardly ever English, and the guy that brings you your breakfast at the B&B near Victoria Station is from Portugal or Iraq rather than Sheffield or Manchester.

High Fliers

Those who work in the City and make a lot of money on arcane investments and dealings beyond the ken of the ordinary person fit into this category. The print media are the main authors of this stereotype, and it is one they usually sneer at—the underlying idea being that there is something disreputable about making lots of money merely for the sake of it. To be a high flier, you have to wear expensive suits, drive expensive cars and never be separated from your mobile phone. The high flier has largely replaced his predecessors, the yuppie of the 1980s and the City gent of an earlier, gentler era.

The Homeless

At the opposite end of the economic scale from the high fliers are London's homeless. Numbers are down from the late 1980s, but the homeless population is still quite visible,

especially around Waterloo Station and in Westminster around Charing Cross Road and the Strand. Limited hostel space is available at night, but many must sleep rough (i.e. outdoors). Begging is widespread, on the streets and in Underground stations. A reliable estimate is of about 75,000 homeless in London, counting those who live on the street (about 2,000), in hostels, in squats (illegal accommodation) and in B&Bs at government expense.

Punks and their Kin

There is a fringe of young people in London distinguishable by their dedication to treating their bodies as a medium for grotesque ornamentation. No doubt they would protest at being lumped in one category, perhaps recognising within their ranks many gradations and nuances of type. But to the ordinary, conformist dresser, they look a lot alike. The baseline seems to be a willingness to pierce multiple face parts: ears, eyebrows, noses and mouths abound with loops and rings. The hair is required to make some kind of statement, either by being brightly coloured, oddly shaped, matted, or unaccountably filthy—perhaps all four—and clothes are ragged and predominantly black, with leather and metal bits conspicuous everywhere. The punk persona seems to be something that one grows out of—none of them looks older than 30 or so—but while they last, they make a very visible contribution to the passing parade, which is perhaps the whole point.

Pensioners

About 17 per cent of London's population is over the age of 65, and one in five households in Greater London consists of only pensioners. The state-funded pension is universal but meagre, and today's pensioners are largely from an era before the advent of private pensions, so many are forced to live quite modestly. The defining feature of the London pensioner seems to be the two-wheeled shopping cart, in which they place their purchases as they travel from shop to shop. Most Londoners take kindly towards them, though unfortunately they are often the victims of muggings in some areas.

Students

Degree programmes ranging from one to four years in every imaginable discipline exist in London, as well as certificated and fly-by-night programmes in the thriving English language industry. The result is that students crawl over every quarter of London, most of them necessarily living on the cheap and filling up the rather grim low end of rental accommodation. The majority are Britons, but sizable numbers also come from the EU, the Commonwealth and other countries around the world.

Tourists and Visitors

In the latest year for which statistics are available, 30 million visitors arrived in London and spent at least one night here—the majority of them tourists, but business and other visitors are also included in the figure. This means that on average, there are more than 82,000 extra folks on the streets every day: a staggering number, but not surprising after you've taken a stroll down Oxford Street, through Trafalgar Square, or around Picadilly Circus in midsummer.

SOCIALISING WITH THE LOCALS

CHAPTER 4

'London is a roost for every bird.'
—Benjamin Disraeli, *Lothair*

CULTURAL NORMS

With all the foregoing as introduction, it may seem unlikely that anything such as a norm could exist in London. This is partly true: the commonplaces of British life and culture are certainly evident here, but often in a limited or diluted way, since so many of the people on the streets aren't in fact British.

But notwithstanding foreign influence, London life has a number of fairly standard cultural and social features that the foreigner, though not required to observe in every case, is well advised to be aware of. These begin where all probes of British society begin, with the phenomenon of class.

A PLACE FOR EVERYONE, EVERYONE IN THEIR PLACE

Entire shelves of libraries are filled with sober reflections and detailed analyses of the distinctions among the classes. The reader who likes that kind of thing is respectfully referred there.

In a nutshell, class is the index that Britons use to establish how they fit in, and how others fit into their society. In other words, it is a significant component of most British people's identity. Despite protests to the contrary, and the stated intention of the government to create a classless society, the class system is still very much alive. The very existence of a full-blown, titled aristocracy at one end and the possibility of taking elocution lessons to obliterate a working class accent at the other end attest to the influence of class divisions. A plurality of people marry others whom they perceive to be of the same social class; and people who identify themselves as working class rarely marry anyone perceived to be higher up the scale.

Speech and livelihood are the indicators that Londoners most often use to place each other in relation to themselves in the class system. Income is not a reliable indicator, not only because it is not openly talked about, but also because in the so-called working class, there is a wide range of incomes, some of which far exceed the dreams of the middle class.

The Class System

The habit of typing people as belonging to a particular class doesn't straitjacket them, it merely enables both parties in a relationship to bring in a whole truckload of assumptions about the other regarding taste, background, social habits and career prospects, many of which are probably quite accurate.

For the vast majority of Londoners, the only class distinction that regularly comes into play is between working class and middle class. Members of the upper classes and the aristocracy are thinner on the ground than others, and also have a less clearly defined niche in the mainstream of society. In other words, they tend to move more with others of their own kind.

Options about livelihood in regard to class are far more flexible than they used to be and along with education, they represent the main avenue of upward mobility, especially for the working class who can make the jump to the middle class easily in a generation if they are inclined to do so—though the majority probably are not. Those inclined to make a bid for the higher ranks could not choose a better place for it than London, where the presence of 6.5 million others makes it relatively easy to leave behind any limiting factors of one's background. As a result, class stereotyping is probably a little less virulent in London than elsewhere in the UK.

As a foreigner in London, even a native speaker of English, you may find to your consternation that you have trouble understanding anyone's accent, let alone distinguishing one from another. But before long, the various kinds of speech tend to sort themselves into types, and after some time, you may find yourself automatically placing people in the social hierarchy according to how they speak.

Learning from the Television

Television is the best place to learn your initial lessons, as speakers (or imitators) of all accents can regularly be heard. *EastEnders*, the long running, dreary soap opera of East Londoners (broadcast twice weekly on BBC1), is a treasury of working class London speech. Television newsreaders generally have a middle class accent. The accent used by members of the aristocracy and the royal family (or more often, those who make a living sending them up) is thought of as upper class.

Remember that for you as a foreigner, the whole business of class is mostly a spectator sport. This is every bit to your advantage: you will be able to communicate effectively with Londoners of all sorts, without limitations that might result from your being typecast in a particular class. If you are viewed at all in terms of the class system, it will probably be in relation to what you do for a living, and to some extent where you live. But the finer points of class distinctions and all that they mean are best left to the natives to enjoy.

THE WAY THEY DO THE THINGS THEY DO

Certain ways of presenting oneself in public can be called truly British because they cut across all class barriers. These long-cherished standards echoing down through the centuries are still strong enough, even in today's cosmopolitan London, to have their effect. The imperative of public behaviour is that decorum shall be maintained, and awkwardness of any kind shall be avoided. The stiff upper lip of the British is no cliche; it's a genetically programmed part of the anatomy. Whether in a boardroom meeting, at a train station ticket window, or in the audience of an emotion-packed film, the rule is to avoid displays of strong emotion: don't shout and don't cry. Only football fans are excused.

When someone does actually make a scene in public, it is viewed as something quite unfortunate, even disgraceful (unless, of course, the perpetrator is a foreigner, in which case it is charitably assumed that the poor thing can't help it). The effort to prevent the social fabric from coming apart is continuous and mostly automatic for true Londoners. They can spot a situation about to get out of hand at 50 yards and will do and say everything to prevent chaos from taking over. How do they pull it off, you may wonder. The answer is, a highly developed talent for being able to say the right thing under any circumstances, and an unfailing sense of humour. Britons have a true genius for never being at a loss for words, and any number of situations that could run into a sticky dead end if allowed to remain serious are saved by the introduction of silliness.

This highly developed system of maintaining social order rests partly on a very old idea: the sovereignty and separateness of the individual. The truly British effort to keep all human relations on an even keel stems in part from a fairly selfish motive: that is, to protect oneself from involvement in other people's difficulties. In a big city where people live, work and move about in close quarters, it becomes even more desirable to have this form of self-protection.

Minding Your Manners

Consider, for example, the standard etiquette for dealing with an accidental mishap in a crowded place. When two people collide, even if it is by the flagrant carelessness of one of them, the response is automatic: both parties say "Sorry!" perhaps without even looking at each other, and they carry on with their business. In a society where everyone is assumed to be walking about inviolate inside the case of their own skin, no other response is possible.

This is not a touchy-feely culture. It is a lot more cerebral than emotional. There isn't a lot of physical contact among people in public, even between those well known to each other, and handshaking is for first meetings and reunions after an absence—not a form of greeting for people who see each other often. If you put a friendly arm on someone's shoulder, they are as likely to draw back in shock as they are to reciprocate. The English poet W H Auden summed up the idea pretty well in the beginning of his short poem:

> 'Some thirty inches from my nose
> The frontier of my person goes,
> All the untilled air in between
> Is private pagus or demesne.'

A related and laudable feature of this cult of the sovereign individual is the fundamental sense of decency that prevails in most mundane relationships. In fact, it has to be this way: a system of social order based on self sufficiency can only work if everyone goes about it with a sense of fair play, or the whole game would quickly degenerate into dog-eat-dog. But fairness does in fact prevail most of the time. Politeness and courtesy among strangers are common, and almost expected. Rules are there to be obeyed: if everyone plays by the rules, there is no need for anyone to get upset, and everyone can continue going about minding their own business.

Is all this pointing towards a conclusion that the true Londoner is quite happy the way things are, thank you, and doesn't really want to have anything to do with you? Fortunately, it is not so bleak. Native Londoners can and do broaden their horizons through contacts with the foreigners from around the world whom they share their city with. But chances are that, unless you too come from a somewhat 'cold' northern culture, you will find the natives a hard nut to crack. You can get to know them, but it won't happen overnight. Everything that really sustains them seems to come from their own culture, and not from anything you can give them, so working your way into the lives of the locals can be a slow, though not at all unsatisfying process. For this reason, and the earlier mentioned factors about where foreign Londoners live or work, you will most likely find that your social life revolves around other foreign Londoners: either your compatriots, or others among the rich and varied foreign community in London.

WHO DO THEY THINK THEY ARE?

We have come this far without getting a very strong sense of just who a real Londoner is—what makes him or her tick. The reason for this is there is no such thing. London is too big, too diverse and too transient a place for any grand, unifying values to take root and prosper. The axes around which a strong sense of group identity or purpose often revolve—religion, politics or family, for example—are infinitely splintered in London. There is room for everyone, but no more room for one particular dogma or way of life than another.

Consider the religion of Londoners. Though the Church of England is the established Church, it suffers lower attendance in London than anywhere in the country, and Britons already have one of the lowest rates of church attendance in Europe. Membership in the Trinitarian churches (Catholic, Anglican and mainstream Protestant) has been in slow decline in Britain for more than 50 years, though it should be noted that non-Trinitarian groups (Mormons, Jehovah's Witnesses, etc.) are growing moderately, and membership in non-Christian religions (Islam, Sikhism, Buddhism and Hinduism) has doubled in 25 years. But this growth notwithstanding, a quarter of Londoners seldom or never attend services connected with a religion.

In politics, the mainstream is very wide, and what lies outside it is tolerated quietly, as almost any non-threatening, nonviolent idea or behaviour is. Parliament itself embraces members ranging from the frightening right to the loud left, and on the streets of London, you can buy papers with a Marxist or a fascist point of view (though hardly anyone does, and the sellers are forced to take advantage of crowds wherever they find them).

Strong family connections are the rule rather than the exception in London's foreign communities. Indeed, it is on the basis of family connections that many communities have grown to their current size, as family members still abroad join those already settled here. But despite this, three out of ten households in London are one person households; and less than three out of ten have any dependent children. So it would be hard to argue that life revolves around the family for Londoners generally.

Listening to the broadcast media, or reading the papers in London might well give you the impression that people are obsessed by politics, but this is not at all the case. It is only the media that is obsessed by politics. The average Londoner is quite bored by and cynical about the machinations of politicians. Londoners are probably more united by political indifference than by political conviction.

What is left? Nothing that can be summed up and neatly packaged. Londoners seem to make their lives out of what they do from day to day: working, being with their friends and loved ones, doing good or making mischief with their disposable income. There are those with grand and driving passions, but they are not typical. In a culture that is more or less at odds with passion, those who exemplify it usually learn to suppress themselves or to channel their feelings into some single-minded and harmless pursuit and thus emerge in an acceptable place—the varied and thriving eccentric fringes of society.

FINDING YOUR NICHE

With the astounding variety of people and cultures in London, there should be no reason that you can't either find and join, or attract a circle of friends who are just right for you. But as in any big city, Londoners can suffer from isolation and loneliness. The daily assault on the senses that living in a big city entails causes everyone to grow a protective shell. It protects you from a lot of things that you don't want to bother with, but it also cuts you off from many things that might interest you if you gave them your attention.

The greatest challenge to the new Londoner is to break down this insularity barrier in others, before your own barrier becomes so thick that you have to fight through it as well to get anywhere. Standoffishness is the natural condition of native and longtime Londoners, and too often it rubs off on new arrivals before they know it's happening: they start to act like everyone else. Don't assume that just because people seem to be walking around inside their own bubble that they like it that way. It isn't so much a matter of liking it as just being so used to it and not knowing any alternative. So you shouldn't hesitate to take the initiative in getting to know people. In many cases, you will simply have to show an active interest in people to get your message across.

SETTLING IN

'It was a good place for getting lost in, a city no one ever knew, a city explored from the neutral heart outward, until after many years, it defined itself into a jumble of clearings separated by stretches of the unknown, through which the narrowest paths had been cut.'
—V S Naipaul, *An Area of Darkness*

GETTING IN, OUT AND AROUND

The Londoner is spoilt for choice in the matter of transportation, whether travelling to, from or within London. It is the gateway to the rest of the UK and to Europe for many travellers, and the gateway to the rest of the world for many Europeans who find better connections and prices for flights in and out of London than can be found in other European capitals. Movement on the ground is necessarily slower, but there is always more than one way of getting where you want to go, and usually there are several. In this section, we will look first at getting you and your possessions to London in one piece. From there, we examine international transportation and gradually work our way down to the smallest goal, getting from A to B within London.

THE PACKING LIST

A major dilemma for the aspiring Londoner concerns what to bring and what not to bring from home. You may want to bring everything with you, including the kitchen sink, simply in the interest of saving money, since replacing the trappings of everyday life may well cost you more than they did where you came from. But this must be weighed against the cost of importing large or heavy goods into Britain. If you're not sure about bringing some of your larger goods, get some quotations from a freight forwarder or moving company, and then decide if the expense (and in some

cases, hassle) of shipping your goods would be less costly than replacing them. Provided that you have the necessary documentation for settling in Britain, you will not be assessed duties on personal property that you bring in for your own use.

Vital Documents

Besides your passport, a few other documents should accompany you to London if you're coming to live. These are:

- Birth certificate
- Copies of diplomas and professional qualifications
- Driving licence
- Evidence of your credit history (bank statements or better, a letter from your home bank)
- Insurance policies (life, health, property, etc.)
- Marriage certificate
- Work permit (if you have been issued one by the UK Department of Employment)

You may also want to bring your medical records if you have a condition whose history would be of interest to your

London doctor. If you can bring a recent set of dental x-rays, it will save you being re-zapped the first time you visit a London dentist.

Electrical Gadgetry

In general, it is probably not worth your while to bring kitchen appliances to the UK, unless they already run on 240 volts. If they don't, you will have to use unwieldy transformers. You may, however, want to consider bringing electronic goods such as computers and modems. They normally have switches for variable voltage settings, and they are very expensive in the UK: as much as 40 per cent more than North American or Asian prices on some items. Modems manufactured to any standard other than that designated by British Telecom are not 'approved' for use in Britain, but in fact, they work in most cases. Of all computer equipment and peripherals, printers are usually the least adaptable; make sure yours works with 240 volts before you bring it along.

Britain uses the PAL television system, which may or may not be the standard where you come from: your Australian TV and VCR will work fine in London, but your North American one will not. You can buy a new television and video cassette recorder, or rent one in London. There are several firms whose main business is to let household appliances for hire, such as Radio Rentals and Granada; you will probably find them in the high street near your home. The minimum term for hiring most appliances is six months.

If you are coming to set up residency, you can import your car duty free in most cases, but only with a licence to do so. Only vehicles that comply with British safety and construction standards can be imported.

Various electronic media that you bring with you to the UK from abroad may well not work on equipment purchased in the UK. Along with the rest of Europe, Britain is in region 2 for DVDs. Playstation games with coded NTSC will not work on a UK PAL system; however, inexpensive converters that will permit this are widely available in the UK.

AIRPORTS AND AIR TRAVEL

Three major and two lesser airports serve London for flights to and from the rest of the world. Your travel may be such that you are tied to a particular airport, but if you aren't, consider the pros and cons of the various airports before booking your flights. There are transportation links between the three major airports but none of them is particularly fast, easy or cheap, so it is worth avoiding a change of airports if you are in transit through London. All London airports have free luggage trolleys that can usually be found where you need them, and left wherever you stop needing them.

Heathrow (LHR)

Heathrow is the biggest and busiest of London's major airports, and the only one actually located within Greater London; it is about 13 km (8 miles) to the west of central London. It is also the easiest and the fastest to get to from London as there is a high speed rail link that runs very regularly from Paddington Station. It will get you to or from Heathrow in less than half an hour, but you pay for the convenience! High speed rail links to other points in London are currently under construction and will be ready in a few years time. Other transport between London and Heathrow is by taxi, Tube, bus or coach: that is the descending order of price, but not necessarily of speed. In heavy traffic, the Tube will take you faster than any road transportation. Allow yourself an hour between a Zone 1 Tube stop and Heathrow. Without heavy traffic, a taxi will get you there in half an hour, a bus or coach in 45 minutes. In traffic, travel time on the road can exceed an hour. There are ramps and lifts everywhere at the airport that enable you to avoid stairs when carrying luggage.

Gatwick (LGW)

Further away from central London (about 40 km south or 25 miles) but better served by rail links, Gatwick is a near rival to Heathrow in terms of passenger volume. North American, European and holiday charter services are all frequent. Trains taking half an hour run between Victoria station and Gatwick four times an hour. Boarding is at station level at Victoria, and one level down at Gatwick, reachable by escalator or lift. Luggage trolleys are not allowed on the train platform at Gatwick. Porters are available, but most people merely struggle down or up the escalators.

Trains taking up to 45 minutes serving five other London train stations also run four times an hour to and from Gatwick. The stations served, in order travelling from Gatwick, are London Bridge, Blackfriars, City Thameslink, Farringdon and King's Cross Thameslink. All of these stations have connections to London Underground except City Thameslink. They are poorly equipped for people travelling with luggage, and you may face long and wearying flights of stairs with no help in sight. This service is slightly cheaper than the one from Victoria, but the savings are more than offset by the poor provision for laden travellers at most stations served.

You can also get to Gatwick by coach from Victoria Coach Station. Buses leave hourly and take about an hour and a half. A taxi takes nearly as much time, but costs a lot more.

Stansted (STN)

Stansted is London's newest, nicest and least busy airport; there is only one terminal and a couple of dozen airlines in operation. Stansted is further still from central London (58 km or 40 miles, northeast) but also served by a high speed, half-hourly rail link (45 minutes) to Liverpool Street station. Boarding is at station level at Liverpool Street. The terminal at Stansted is reachable by escalator or lift from the train platform, which stops inside the airport. There are coach services from London to Stansted, and also from several towns and cities in Essex and Cambridgeshire, which have coach links to the airport.

There are scheduled and holiday charter services to most European cities and to several UK and Irish destinations. Stansted is the airport of choice for anyone looking for a bargain-fare to a European destination. There is hardly any European destination that is not served from here by some low-fare airline. Other destinations served include a few from North America and the Middle East.

Your arrival in London is very likely to be at one of the foregoing airports. In addition to the means noted, all are reachable by car and have the parking facilities you expect at airports: close-in, fairly expensive parking, or further out, cheaper places to park for longer stays. Traffic to and from the airports is very often heavy, especially at peak travelling times, making the rail and underground links the most desirable way of getting to and from the airports in a timely way.

Other London Airports

Two other airports deserve mention: London City Airport (LCY) is located in East London and has flights to the Continent as well as to other British Isles destinations. It is served only by small aircraft. Public transport to and from it is unwieldy for those with luggage, but possible on the Silverlink Metro train, or via a shuttle bus stopping at Canning Town (the nearest), Canary Wharf and Liverpool Street Tube stations. Finally, there is London Luton Airport (LTN), about 48 km (30 miles) north-west of London. It specialises in low-cost airlines serving mainly continental destinations. Rail-and-coach links with London via the Thameslink train service stop at many London stations and also serve Gatwick airport, thus making Luton-Gatwick the only easy airport-to-airport transfer in London.

THE WORLD VIA LONDON

You need only look in the travel section of any of the Sunday papers to see a bewildering array of cheap flights and package deals to every conceivable destination. London is a mecca not only for the tourist, but also for the traveller bound for other ports. The low end of London's travel industry is the 'bucket shop', a travel agent who sells cheap tickets on slender margins, likes cash, and is often hard to pin down to a particular fare until he sees some of it.

Bargain hunting among the bucket shops is a time consuming and often frustrating business, but if economy is an important criterion, this is where you belong: you may find fares that will astound your friends. If your nerves are not equal to the task and your pocketbook can stand the strain, you're better off finding a reputable and convenient travel agency and simply letting them make arrangements for you when you travel by air. If your destination is the home of any of London's large immigrant communities, consider consulting a travel agent in a neighbourhood where such immigrants are concentrated; you may find deals that the general agents don't know about.

RIDING THE RAILS

Railway lines from all over Britain converge in London. The number of services available and the distinctions among different kinds of tickets and travel is a source of confusion for natives and visitors alike, and one that has grown worse since British Rail (BR) was broken up and divided into different railway companies that compete for travellers. This brief primer of the system looks at London stations and services with a view to giving you some facility with using them economically.

Mainline and Other Stations

A mainline station in London is a terminal with direct lines to destinations outside of London, often far beyond south-east England. In a couple of cases, the area served is completely within south-east England—the part of the country for which London is the hub of rail travel—but most of the stations serve places further afield in the UK, and four of them run trains with connections to the Continent. Fast trains that go beyond the south-east are called Intercity services; they have a different pricing structure and ticketing system than commuter trains. Here are London's most important mainline stations, all of which are centrally located in Inner London, and all of which have connections on at least one line to London Underground. We start at 12 o'clock and proceed clockwise.

Euston

Northern and north-western England are served by Intercity trains from Euston, which is located on Euston Road NW1.

There is a service to Holyhead in north-west Wales with connections to Irish ports. Trains also depart for western Scotland (Glasgow), northern Wales and northern suburbs.

Saint Pancras

Though far more glorious in architecture than King's Cross just across the street, Saint Pancras is today mainly a commuter station for cities and towns north of London. A few cities in the north of England are served by fast trains, as well as Luton Airport in Bedfordshire. It is located on Euston Road, NW1. Soon, Saint Pancras will be the destination for Eurostar trains travelling from the Continent via the Channel Tunnel.

King's Cross

Intercity trains for northern England and eastern Scotland (Edinburgh) depart from King's Cross, which is right next door to Saint Pancras station. Cambridge is also served.

Liverpool Street

Located in the City with entrances on Liverpool Street and Bishopsgate EC2, trains from Liverpool Street serve Essex and East and West Anglia (i.e., eastern England north of the Thames), Cambridge and the northern and eastern suburbs of

People with places to go at Liverpool Street Station.

London. There are also boat trains to Harwich, where services continue to the Netherlands, Germany and to Scandinavia.

London Bridge

Located immediately south of London Bridge on the Thames, this is also primarily a commuter station for Kent and East and West Sussex (i.e., south-eastern England outside of London and south of the Thames). As noted above, there is quarter-hourly service to Gatwick, and regular train service to stations north of the river via Thameslink, the only cross river non-Tube train service.

Waterloo

Trains out of Waterloo, located just south of the Thames on Waterloo Road SE1, serve southern England down to the coast and near-western England. The Eurostar service, with trains direct to Paris and Brussels through the Channel Tunnel, currently uses Waterloo station and will continue to do so until the service moves to Saint Pancras station. There are no boat trains from Waterloo.

Victoria

Just north of the river and south-west in central London, Victoria is the main station for services to Europe. Trains connect to ports in France, Holland and Belgium via Dover, Folkestone and Ramsgate. A variety of vessels are available for Channel crossing, ranging from ferries (slow and cheap) to hovercrafts and hydrofoils (faster and dearer). Destinations in southern and near-western England south of the Thames are also served. Though the station is north of the river, trains proceed directly south out of the station and cross the Thames.

Paddington

Fast trains to Oxford, Stratford-upon-Avon, the west of England and Wales leave from Paddington, as well as trains to near and far western and north-western suburbs. Paddington is also a terminal for the Heathrow Express high speed link to the airport. The station is located in west central London on Praed Street W2.

Other stations in London designated as mainline stations but now serving primarily as commuter stations are Marylebone NW1, serving Birmingham and north-western suburbs; Fenchurch Street EC3, serving Essex; and Cannon Street EC4, Charing Cross WC2 and Blackfriars EC4, serving roughly the same area as London Bridge.

Apart from these large stations, there are dozens of railway stations all over London with one or more different services.

Useful Maps

Two maps merit study for anyone wishing to get a feel for the rail system into, out of and through London: one is called *Network Southeast*, and the other is *London Connections*. Both are reproduced in all London railway stations and are also available in a brochure version from most stations. *Network Southeast* shows the whole rail network that has London as its centre, with a convenient colour-coding system to show which lines connect to which stations. *London Connections* shows all the great and small rail stations in London and their interconnections, not only with each other but also with the London Underground.

In recent years, the National Railway companies have taken to calling the people who ride its trains 'customers' rather than 'passengers.' It is worth considering whether this is recognition of the fact that you always pay, but you don't always get where you want to go! In fact, trains are the butt of as much derisive humour as British food and British weather, and it is quite fashionable among commuting veterans to swap train horror stories.

The truth is that the trains run right most of the time, but when they fail, they can fail spectacularly. The rail service seems to be quite easily done in by events that occur with predictable regularity: strikes (labour-management relations are adversarial), weather (one winter it was 'the wrong kind of snow') and 'signal failure' (a time-honoured favourite), to name a few. Thus when using trains, it is wise to have a contingency plan in mind, should you suddenly

Smart Ways to Ride the Train

Here are a few tips for using the trains into and out of London to your best advantage:

- On Intercity trains, book your ticket as early as your travel plans allow; this will not only assure you of the best price, but also of getting a seat. For longer journeys, an APEX fare system operates whereby cheap tickets are available with restrictions. Seat reservations are available for a nominal fee on most trains and recommended at holiday times and on summer weekends.

- You will find travel at off-peak times not only less crowded, but more economical, since the cheapest tickets are not valid during the busiest times. Peak travel times are the morning and evening rush hours, all day Friday and certain holiday periods.

- You can book your ticket via telephone using a credit card for most destinations. Look in the business telephone directory under 'trains' for the numbers. You can also book tickets via the Internet from website: http://www.nationalrail.co.uk/.

- If you will be using National Railways on a regular basis, consider getting a season ticket for your regular journeys, or get a Network card, which entitles you to discount travel on nearly all National Railway services within south-east England, the part of the rail network that includes London. This discount, however, is applicable only during off-peak times, and here off-peak means after 10:00 am weekdays and anytime on weekends and Bank Holidays. A brochure with details and an application is available from almost all staffed stations.

- Railcards offering 20–33 per cent discounts for off-peak travel are available to young people (up to age 26), families, seniors (age 60 and above) and full-time students. Staffed stations have brochures and application forms.

find your journey uncompletable. Here are a few other tips for using the trains into and out of London to your best advantage:

COACH TRAVEL

In local parlance, a coach is a bus that travels between cities. All of the UK is served by the National Express, with other coach companies operating smaller numbers of routes. All coaches in London depart from a single coach station, Victoria Coach Station. People say Victoria Coach Station, with special emphasis on coach, in order to avoid confusion with Victoria Station. The two are only a five-minute walk from each other, in south-west Westminster.

Victoria Coach Station was modernised in the early 1990s, transforming it from a distressing rat hole to a pleasant, modern facility. One thing about the place that didn't change very much is the central ticketing office; it still has one of the truly legendary queues in London. It's a rare day when you don't wait 5 minutes, and it's more usual to wait 10 or 15. Credit card telephone booking is recommended as this enables you to call for your tickets at a special window for which there is usually not a queue. Call Tel: 08705-808-080 or visit the National Express website to book any National Express coach (http://www.national express.com); you will need a credit card and a printer, since you print the ticket yourself.

Coaches serve more destinations in the UK than trains, and they are cheaper; also slower, but this is to be expected. There is also Continental service from Victoria Coach Station, and this is more efficient than you might think. You abandon one bus at the port, cross the channel on a ferry, hovercraft or hydrofoil, and find another bus waiting for you on the other side, all for much less money than the train will cost you.

A few coaches depart from other points in London, notably Aldgate, where there are several commuter coaches, and King's Cross. Coaches will pick up passengers waiting at a few specially marked bus stops; you must already have a ticket in hand in most cases.

DRIVING IN LONDON: A TEST OF NERVES

The motorist in London should always remember that large parts of London were laid out and settled long before the motor was invented. The motor has made great leaps and bounds forward, but most of London has never caught up. Car ownership in London is ever increasing, but roads and parking spaces are not growing proportionately and won't. So driving in London is a trial at the best of times, a nightmare at the worst.

Adding insult to injury, the cost of petrol is exorbitantly high by some standards: now more than 70 p per litre, which translates to nearly US$ 5 per gallon. If you think you really want to have your own car in London, read on for how to make the best of a bad situation, but remember that the best advice is to leave the driving to others. Nearly 40 per cent of Londoners don't have access to a car. If all these people living there go about without a car, there must be a good reason for it.

A guide to public transportation follows after this passage through darkness.

The Basics

London's centuries-old streets, laid out in the day of the horse-drawn cart, serve for the most part today as arteries for automotive traffic. In a few cases, wide thoroughfares have been built in and around London, but streets that can carry two lanes, and sometimes only one lane of traffic in each direction, are designated as the main travel routes through many parts of London. The average residential street in London is not wide enough for two cars to pass when there are cars parked along both curbs. The upshot is that traffic moves very slowly from the morning rush hour right through the late evening in some places, and it is not unusual to come upon traffic congestion anywhere, at any time, within the capital. The average speed is about 16 kmph (10 mph).

Numerous measures are in effect to cope with this unsatisfactory state of affairs. There are one-way systems operating in many congested areas, where the traffic flows through in one direction and around in the other. A few streets are designated as 'Red Routes', indicated by a double red line at the edge of the road, where curbside stopping is not allowed at all. Most major thoroughfares have the leftmost lane (remember, you drive on the left side here) designated for buses, taxis and bicycles only.

Congestion Charging

Congestion Charging is now in effect in the central part of London. This system effectively changes all roads in central London into toll roads between the hours of 7:00 am–6:30 pm, Monday to Friday (excluding public holidays). It is important to note that you cannot drive a car in central London during these hours without having first paid this charge. The fines and penalties for failing to pay the charge are dire. You can read all about the congestion charge, where it operates and how to pay the charge at:

http://www.cclondon.com.

Driving etiquette is an important part of driving in London, and without it, there would no doubt be multiple disasters daily. London drivers are of necessity patient and considerate. This means that drivers very frequently yield to those trying to enter busy traffic, and horns are used very sparingly. Indeed, it is a mark that the situation has really gone beyond the pale when a driver is forced to blast his horn on a busy street (mind, this rule doesn't apply to foreign drivers, who may come from cultures where sounding the horn is the consolation for not being able to step on the gas). Though the practice is officially frowned on, it is fairly standard for a driver to flash his headlights to indicate to you that he has seen you and that he is waiting to let you go in front of him.

Parking

As if merely driving your car were not enough of an ordeal, the time will come quite regularly when you have to stop driving it and leave it somewhere. The traumas of parking can be conveniently broken down into three areas: at home, at work and at play.

Parking your car near your home should be the easiest of the lot: there is on-street parking in all of London's residential neighbourhoods, and crowded areas usually give priority to residents. You must obtain a permit from your borough authority, which, displayed on your windscreen, shows your right to use your neighbourhood's priority parking spaces. This doesn't mean you'll always find a space, but you may derive some satisfaction from the knowledge that you're entitled to one. There is very little private residential parking available, in the form of houses built with parking spaces or garages attached, but these are viewed as quite desirable where they exist. London drivers are very likely to take ease of parking into consideration in their choice of neighbourhoods, and you'll want to do this as well if you know you'll be a car user in London.

Within central London, free parking at your place of work is usually a sign that you have arrived at the top of your profession, because there really isn't very much of it, and so it is doled out sparingly. Metered parking is available in nearly all London business districts, and car parks (private covered or open parking areas that charge by the hour or fraction thereof) can be found in most areas as well: the more central they are, the more expensive. Metered parking tends to fill up early, so finding cheap parking on a regular basis is not very likely in the busiest areas. More expensive parking in private facilities is usually

Meters do not generally permit more than two hours of parking, meaning that if you intend to use a metered space all day, you will have to regularly 'feed the meter,' and run the risk of a parking ticket, since you are not supposed to do this.

available, though the car park in the West End, just off Shaftesbury Avenue, can very often be full day or night. In this area, you are better off parking in the garage under Hyde Park and making your way to the West End from there via Tube or bus. Other centrally located car parks are at Drury Lane WC2 and the Barbican Centre EC2.

Parking in the evening and on weekends for shopping, dining out, entertainment and the like is generally not difficult outside of the very centre of London, but parking in the West

End (the theatre district) is never easy, day or night. If this is your destination, you may find it easier to drive in only as far as you can find a place to leave your car and then use public transportation or taxis.

Security

Three perils beset the unattended car in London: traffic wardens, clamping crews and thieves. The driver who would escape the ravages of all three must be constantly vigilant.

Traffic wardens are independent of the police and exist only to enforce London's parking laws. Some London boroughs have their own squadrons of traffic wardens, who supplement those who operate London-wide. The profession of traffic warden, if you could call it that, is the subject of many jokes, and thought to be what one does when one can't find any other sort of work. Their main responsibility is to issue tickets to illegally parked cars. A central authority keeps track of tickets issued by reference to number plates. If you don't pay a ticket issued to you, there really is no escape; it will catch up with you eventually, usually via increasingly alarming reminders in the post. If you have many outstanding tickets, your car is a sitting target for the clamping crews, the second great peril.

Going nowhere: a clamped car in the City.

Clamping Trouble

Immobilising cars by the use of a wheel clamp became an industry in London in the 1980s and still thrives today. Borough authorities usually contract out the work to private companies, who clamp with gleeful abandon for the obvious reason: the more they clamp, the more they get paid. A car may be clamped for being delinquent in paying parking tickets, but more usually cars are clamped for single, heinous (in the eyes of the authorities) parking violations: parking on a double yellow line, parking with one wheel on the curb where it is not permitted, or parking anywhere in Westminster in violation of particular restrictions.

If you return to your car to find it clamped, follow the instructions affixed to the windscreen to the letter. The whole process of paying the fine involved and getting unclamped can take up to 4 hours, and will deplete your pocket to the tune of at least £ 100. The moral is, don't tempt fate, park legally at all times. Even the costliest private parking space won't cost you as much in time and money as getting unclamped will.

Car theft is also a thriving industry in London. The more desirable your car (or parts thereof), the more likely that it will be viewed covetously by thieves who await the opportunity to whisk it, or its stereo system or other desirable part, away. If you drive a late model car or a prestige make such as BMW or Mercedes, investment in all available security devices is money well spent. Car alarms are now standard features on new cars; you'll know this simply by the number of times you hear them go off in London neighbourhoods. An internal immobiliser, that keeps either the steering wheel or the gear lever from moving, is also a common device. Removable car stereos are also common, as are those that cannot be operated without the use of a code and thus are thought to be undesirable on the black market. Whenever you park your car, day or night, spare a thought for how secure it will be in your absence, and remove any very obvious temptation, such as valuables in plain sight.

Driving Out of London

Driving within London is fraught with complications. It's possible, though not certain, that you'll escape most of these when you drive out of London. Traffic is in general not nearly as congested, parking is easier and crime is less pervasive. A system of motorways (divided highways of at least two lanes in each direction with controlled access) covers the country well to provide fairly quick access to all corners of the Kingdom. Motorways generally don't reach into London proper, so you'll have to wait until you're well out of London before you can really fly.

The motorways that lie partly within London are short lengths of the M1 (going north-west), the M40 (west), the M4 (also west) and the M11 (north-east). Since these serve as main conduits for traffic into and out of London, they can be as congested as any inner city thoroughfares. There are two orbital roads that allegedly facilitate the flow of traffic around the city; these are the North and South Circular Roads, which form a ring through Outer London, and the M25, a motorway making a circle of sorts just outside Outer London. Both of these are subject to frequent and deeply lamented traffic standstills.

As you would expect, the worst times for traffic on these gateways into and out of London are during rush hours. Monday morning inbound and Friday afternoon outbound are the worst; there is also an inbound rush hour of sorts starting in the late afternoon on Sunday, when all of those who drove to the country for the weekend start to return.

THE LEGAL ASPECTS OF DRIVING, WALKING AND CYCLING IN LONDON

It will not have escaped your notice that traffic proceeds on the left in London. In principle, the left hand right-of-way extends to all locomotion, and the natives' tendency is to steer or veer left when a collision of any kind seems imminent. This of course is not a law as regards pedestrians, but it will work more often than going towards the right will.

A few other motoring and locomotion regulations do carry the force of law, and you are well advised to be aware of them.

Roundabouts

In London as in all of Britain, the roundabout is the preferred way of routing traffic where roads meet: vehicles enter a circle and exit from it at the appropriate road. Unless a roundabout has a traffic signal, you are not required to stop; but you must yield to cars that have already entered the roundabout. This means in effect that you yield to traffic on the right, as it will be circling clockwise. If someone says to you, "turn right at the roundabout," they mean enter the roundabout and take the road that is at a 90° angle to the right from where you entered. In other words, turn into the road that would be the right-hand turn if the roundabout weren't there at all and the roads met as an ordinary intersection.

Pedestrian Crossings

There are two kinds: penguin and zebra. A penguin crossing has traffic lights, controlled by those who would cross. The pedestrian has the right of way while the light facing the motorist is red or flashing yellow. A zebra crossing is marked by black and white stripes in the street and two amber coloured lights at either side of the street. These lights, quaintly, have a name all their own (Belisha beacon), and

A zebra crossing, where brisk pedestrians enjoy the right of way.

when they are flashing, they indicate an active zebra crossing in which a pedestrian who has entered the crosswalk has the right of way. Of course, no pedestrian who values his life enters a zebra crossing without first looking in both directions and making a judgment about whether approaching traffic is going to stop. This is the method you should use as a pedestrian. As a driver, it is a good idea to slow down and be prepared to stop on approach to any active zebra crossing that has a pedestrian nearby.

Lights and Helmets

Pedal cyclists who ride at night must have working lights on their cycle front and back. Drivers of all motorised cycles, whether roaring Harleys or mopeds, are required to wear helmets at all times.

Parking

There is no compulsion to park facing one direction or another on a two-way street. Cars on either side of the street can face in either direction. On a one-way street, all cars must, of course, be parked facing in the direction that traffic moves.

Here are the general meanings of lines in the street as they relate to parking:

- Double red lines: Seen only on streets marked as Red Routes. Means absolutely no stopping for any reason whatsoever.
- Double yellow lines: Means no stopping, but if you are merely discharging or picking up a passenger without leaving the wheel of your car, you will not be frowned upon.
- Single yellow line: Means that parking restrictions apply—just what they are can be learned from a nearby rectangular sign.

See *The Highway Code* for more specific details. (See also 'Parking' in the Resource Guide for more information.)

Parking is in general permitted where there is no line on the roadway beside the curb; but keep an eye out for 'resident only' parking in various London neighbourhoods. You will see cars sometimes parked with two wheels up on the curb, especially on narrow or busy streets. This has the effect of widening the roadway, and probably making your parked car marginally safer. But don't park this way unless a sign on the street specifically permits it; you could easily be clamped for doing so where it is not specifically permitted.

Required Motoring Documentation

If you will be living in Britain for a year or more, it is a good idea to get a UK driving licence. It is required for the purchase of insurance, and will generally streamline anything that you have to do with cars and motoring.

Some countries (including all those of the EU) have a reciprocal agreement with Britain, whereby a valid licence in one country can simply be exchanged for a British one. If you're from a country not enjoying this privilege (and there are many), you will have to take a driving test, which includes both theory and practical parts. Schedule your driving test early on; there may be a waiting period as long as five months, and your foreign driving licence is not good for more than a year. You can find the testing station nearest you by looking under 'Transport, Department of' in the business telephone directory. You need to fill out an application form (available from post offices) for the driving test, and send it in to the station where you want to take your test. You can also book your driving test online using a credit card. Visit http://dsa.gov.uk/tests/ for more information. The driving test fee is not refundable if you fail the test.

If you are an experienced driver, you should have no difficulty passing the driving test, but nevertheless it is strongly recommended that you get a couple of driving lessons before going for it. This is true even if you have been driving for years. Examiners watch driving technique very carefully and expect certain ways of doing things that may be completely unfamiliar to you: the way you hold the wheel when you turn a corner, for example, or how you execute a 'three-point' reversing turn. Failure to drive in the prescribed way will result in failing the test, and in fact most drivers do fail the test at least once. It is such an important rite of passage that special greeting cards are sold to congratulate those who have passed.

Once you get your licence, it is valid until you are 65, provided that you continue to live in Britain and that you do not get your licence revoked. You may be disqualified from driving if your points total 12 or more in a period of three years.

The Highway Code

To master all the passive knowledge required for the test, and to learn about Britain's traffic laws in general, pick up a booklet called *The Highway Code*, available from HMSO Bookstores (see 'Government Publications and Information' in the Resource Guide), and from many driving schools.

If you own a car in London, you are required to carry insurance. Insurers advertise widely in the press and on billboards; you may also want to consult friends and colleagues about their car insurance. In addition, you need a Registration Document and a tax disk, officially called a vehicle excise licence. Forms to apply for these, as well as for a driving licence, can be obtained from and turned into most post offices.

PUBLIC TRANSPORT

Though it is fashionable to complain about public transport in London, the truth is no other city of its size can boast of a better system. There is enough redundancy built into the network to allow for more than one way to get from any A to any B within the metropolitan area. It's not always fast, but its usually dependable, and a majority of Londoners use it.

Learning to use public transportation efficiently in London will go a long way towards making you feel at home here. You need never feel that any corner of London is out of the way once you've got used to using the various services. It's a bit like learning a new language, in that your first attempts may seem faltering and ungainly, but the more you use it, the better you'll get at it, and the less you will baulk at situations that require you to use it. As a language learner may know only one blunt way of saying something, so the novice transport user may think there is only one inconvenient way of getting between two points, when in fact further digging and more experience will show you new ways to reach your destination quite efficiently. What follows is a short primer with a few tips, but there is no substitute for experience: the best way to learn the system is to use it.

Zones, Fares and Tickets

London Transport (LT), the authority that oversees all public transport in London, divides the capital into six concentric zones. Fares for travel on all vehicles always have reference to the zone system, so first of all, it is useful to have an understanding of how it works. Get a copy of LT's map Travelcard Zones (free from most stations) to familiarise yourself with the zone boundaries.

Zone 1 is the innermost zone and includes all of Westminster, the City and small parts of the Inner London boroughs. Travel within, and into and out of Zone 1 is the most expensive on all forms of public transport. The remaining Zones 2 to 6 form concentric rings around Zone 1. Parts of Zones 5 and 6 lie outside Greater London altogether but are well within the capital's commuter belt. Travel within and between the outer zones is generally cheaper the further

London transport icons: bus, rails and the Tube.

out you get. To put it another way, the further from the centre of London you are, the greater distance your money will take you.

Tickets for single bus, train or Tube journeys are available, but are the least used of all tickets. Most public transport users use Oyster cards, Travelcards and passes of various sorts because they offer tremendous savings on the regular fares, and also are much more convenient to use than cash. These tickets are available in a bewildering variety of combinations than cannot be easily schematised, but the general setup is like this:

- Oyster cards (validity based on time or the amount of 'charge' on the card) are available for use on all forms of public transport in London. They are the newest addition to the ticket system. They can be purchased online and at LT stations, and are available in the form of Annual, Monthly, 7-Day and Pre Pay cards. Visit the Oyster card website (http://www.oystercard. com) for full information.

- Travelcards (for use on all forms of transport) good for one day or a week; an Oyster card must be used for longer validity periods. The longer the validity of the ticket, the more you save on the individual fare.

- A system of passes for use on LT buses only is also available. For unknown reasons, there are only four bus zones that correspond to the area covered by the six Travelcard zones. An array of bus passes similar in spirit to the scheme described above for Travelcards is also available. These are in all cases cheaper than Travelcards, so if you can limit your travel in London to the buses (they go everywhere, but more slowly), you will save a bundle.

All Oyster cards, Travelcards and passes (except the one-day ones) are valid only with an LT-issued photo ID. These can be obtained free of charge and on the spot by presenting a passport-sized photo at any Tube or staffed train station. Try to do this at a time other than rush hour to prevent a restless queue from forming behind you, as it takes a couple of minutes for the agent to make one up for you.

Travelcards can be purchased at Tube stations, train stations and Pass Agents, who are retail merchants licensed to sell a large variety of Travelcards and passes. Oyster cards are available from Tube stations and at the Oyster card website noted above. Generally, bus passes cannot be purchased at train and Tube stations, but are available from Pass Agents.

> If you make any particular journey four or more times a week, it is worth getting a pass that covers the zones you travel in. If you are out for a day in London, by all means get a one-day Travelcard; it pays for itself after about three rides of any kind.

The Tube

London Underground is the official name of London's mostly underground rail system that is popularly called the Tube. The colourful map of the London Underground has become a cultural icon, reproduced not only in Tube stations and pamphlets, but also in pocket calendars and on T-shirts, postcards and tea towels. If you use the Tube a lot, the map will slowly imprint itself in your brain and you won't need to refer to it for simple journeys, but you will find that it is never far away when you need it.

Underground lines are identified by name and are colour-coded on maps. They are not referred to by their termini as they are in some major cities, except in the case of branching lines. Though the colour-coding system is familiar to regular users, Londoners talk about Tube lines not by colour but only by name, e.g., the Victoria Line or the Jubilee Line. In the case of a branching line, the terminal identifies the particular branch, e.g. the Wimbledon branch of the District Line, the Edgware branch of the Northern Line.

On the Underground map, stations served by more than one line are indicated by a white circle. When you are in such a station, points of transfer are indicated by line name, platform number (which is in fact more or less useless information for the traveller) and direction of travel; thus, you will need to know not only what line you are transferring to, but also in which direction your journey will continue (i.e. northbound, southbound, eastbound, westbound). Example (do this with the Tube map in hand, or it will only make your head reel): You are at Knightsbridge (Picadilly Line) and wish to travel to Turnpike Lane (Victoria Line). At Knightsbridge, be sure you board the train on the eastbound platform. You can take this train as far as Green Park or King's Cross. When you change, at either Green Park or King's Cross, look for signs that say Victoria Line, and northbound, since you will be continuing your journey in a northerly

A quiet platform on the Circle Line.

Four suicide bombers struck in central London on 7 July 2005, killing 52 people and injuring 700. Three bombs went off on underground trains just outside Liverpool Street and Edgware Road stations, and on another travelling between King's Cross and Russell Square. The final explosion was around an hour later on a double-decker bus in Tavistock Square, not far from King's Cross.

Two weeks later on 21 July 2005, four attempted bombings took place around midday at Shepherd's Bush, Warren Street and Oval stations, and on a bus in Bethnal Green. No one was hurt and the five suspects have been arrested and will face trial in September 2006.

direction. This system of platform identification isn't particularly stranger-friendly, and if you don't happen to orient yourself by the compass, it's downright hostile. If you're lost, you can always ask someone who looks like they know where they're going. Also, study carefully the diagram of the line you're on, posted at or near each individual platform. It will show only the stations served by trains arriving at that platform. If you don't see the station you're headed for, either as your destination or your transfer point, you're on the wrong platform.

Travel on the Tube is at present more exit rather than entrance controlled. This means that at some stations, especially outlying ones, you can easily board a train without a ticket but you can rarely leave a station without tapping your Oyster card against the card reader at the gates, putting your ticket through an electronic turnstile or presenting it for inspection, and you'll pay a £ 10 fine for travelling without a valid ticket if you're caught. The moral is simple: always have a Oyster card, valid ticket or Travelcard before you board your train.

The Tube runs from the early morning hours until about midnight. Rush hour trains, though frequent, can be chock-full, but travel at other times of day usually affords seats for all passengers. Very little of London Underground is accessible for the handicapped.

Unfortunately, it must be said that the more you use the Tube, the less you will like it—for after a time, the fairly regular failures of service stick out in your mind rather more than the times when service is adequate. The best way to counteract this sort of creeping aversion to the Tube is to abort its failed missions immediately. If a line is reported to be having delays, don't even give it a chance. Use another line, or find another way to get to your destination.

LT Buses

Although they are operated by a number of different private companies, buses within London use a uniform ticketing system and all of them honour Oyster cards, Travelcards and bus passes. The majority of London buses are red double-deckers, but increasingly, buses of different shapes, sizes and colours operate on the myriad, twisting bus routes around London.

Working knowledge of the bus system is probably a little harder to get under your belt than of the Tube or train system, but it is well worth the effort. Because the network of London bus routes is so extensive, it is difficult to simplify on maps. The current approach, which is to break down the city in sizable chunks and show all the bus routes that pass through a particular part of the city, is useful, but requires study. While you're standing at the bus stop, check out the map reproduced there showing the various routes. You can get copies of these maps from LT information centres, and on rare occasions—once yearly or so—one will appear in your letterbox for the area of London where you live. Bus travel in London will take you to more places than rails, and there is probably no finer way to view the city than from the top front seat of a double-decker. So don't let the seeming complexity of the bus system put you off using it. Here are the ABCs of bus travel, which should give you a head start on using the system.

- All London buses are identified on the front and back by a route number. The front of the bus also has a sign above the windscreen showing its major destinations on its current direction of travel: these may be the names of Tube stations, neighbourhoods or local landmarks. Below this catalogue of destinations is the final destination of the bus on its current direction of travel. It is important to note this, because not every bus goes to the final destination on its route; some reverse direction or end service before reaching the end.

Boarding the bus at Edgware Road: pensioners take advantage of concessions.

- London bus stops are identified by a rectangular placard mounted on a concrete pillar. A Head Stop is serviced by all bus routes identified by the number on the placard. A Request Stop is also serviced by the bus routes listed, but only when you flag the bus. Merely standing at the stop, looking like you want to go somewhere, does not suffice. Wave your arm when you see your bus coming. On busy streets, there may be as many as four adjacent bus stops. A given bus stops at only one of them, so make sure that you're standing at the stop for your bus; it will be identified by number on the placard. If you can take either of two buses that stop at adjacent stops, you can either test your prognostication abilities by standing at the stop of the one you think likely to come first, or stand strategically between the stops, ready to dash for the first acceptable bus that you see.

- If you are using a pass or Travelcard, you need merely show it to the driver when you board the bus. Oyster cards are even simpler to use: you touch them against the card reader on the bus. In central London, you can also purchase a bus ticket good for one ride anywhere from the vending machine at the bus stop; simply show this ticket to the driver. When you are outside of central

London, you can buy a ticket from the driver. You do not need exact change, but drivers generally don't like to make change for banknotes. Bus fare are determined by length of travel and zone boundaries. As with Tube travel, bus travel gets cheaper as you move outwards from Zone 1. If you do not know the fare, state your destination and the driver will determine the fare. Note that you cannot buy a ticket from the driver if you get on at a stop where there is a vending machine.

- When the bus you are riding is approaching your stop, push one of the buttons located throughout the bus to request a stop. If there are exit doors in the middle of the bus, exit through these; it is usually frowned on to exit through the entrance, as this slows down passengers who may be boarding.

The Routemaster

A fond word is in order for the old-fashioned London bus, the Routemaster, which still operates on a dozen or so routes in London. Routemasters are a monument of efficient and effective design, of form fitting function. They are the oldest of the double-deckers in service, with a single, open entrance at the back. These buses have a conductor, who takes care of all ticketing matters. When boarding Routemasters, you should proceed directly to a seat; the conductor will come around to collect your fare, or inspect your Oyster card, pass or Travelcard during your journey. Since drivers are not required to collect fares, Routemasters make much better time than other buses, and their gradual demise, brought about by the twin demons of government strategists and Brussels bureaucrats, is much mourned by London bus riders.

A dilemma that often arises for the bus-riding Londoner is whether to wait for the one bus that will take you all the way to your destination, or to board the first bus to get you on your way, and then change buses somewhere down the line where it intersects another route that will get you where you want to go. This is a little like choosing a queue in the supermarket: you always seem to choose the one that is moving slowest, despite initial promising appearances. If you do take the first bus that comes along, you will sometimes have the experience of seeing the bus you wanted whiz by

you, nearly empty, about three stops further on. If you decide to hold out and wait for your ideal bus, you will sometimes see three or four buses of every other route pass you by and you will come to despair increasingly, wondering if perhaps all of your buses have been swallowed in a black hole somewhere. So there is no fixed strategy for success, but generally, it makes sense on weekends to take the first thing that comes along, since service can be infrequent. During the week, and especially at peak times, it may pay to wait for the one bus you want and have the comfort of riding it all the way to your destination.

The regular bus routes close down by about midnight. At this point, the Night Bus system takes over. All Night Buses either start and end in, or pass through Trafalgar Square. They cover the most important areas of the day bus routes, and in many cases, the routes overlap entirely. Night buses run through the night until the day buses start up again. Fares are marginally higher, and certain passes and Travelcards are not honoured on Night Buses.

See 'Public Transportation' in the Resource Guide for various helpful telephone numbers.

Using National Railways Within London

To some degree, the National Railways within London supplement the Tube, especially in cases where they serve destinations that are not on the Tube. A good case in point is the North London line, a service that travels east and west across North London, stopping at various places where there is no Underground service, or in some cases providing a more direct and faster connection between points than the Tube or buses provide. Single and return fares on trains within London seem rather steep, but remember that whenever you are within the six Travelcard zones of London Transport, you can use any form of public transportation—bus, train, Tube or Docklands Light Railway—with the appropriate Travelcard or Oyster card, and this makes train travel within the capital quite economical.

The Docklands Light Railway (DLR)

Opened in the early 1990s, the DLR is unique in London's transportation system in that it is a railway independent of both the Tube and National Railways. It runs between Bank Tube station and several locations in East London and the Docklands, an area that in the heady 1980s was envisioned as London's showpiece of the future. That hasn't happened yet, but the Railway is a very pleasant and scenic ride, and the best transportation to the Isle of Dogs, Canary Wharf and other East London locales.

Taxis

Two kinds of taxis operate in London: those popularly called 'black taxis', though not all of them are black, and minicabs (not all of them are small!). A minicab is a privately owned motor car with a two-way radio or cellular telephone connecting it to a minicab company. Thus any car can be a minicab for a day, and many are. The main difference between the two kinds of taxis is cost: minicabs are cheaper. Here's a rundown of what you get and what you pay for in London's cab world.

Black taxis are something of a London icon, and driving one is considered a profession more than a job. It involves extensive preparation, commonly called 'the knowledge', wherein would-be drivers trawl the streets of London on motorbikes for months on end to learn all the major and minor routes connecting the various parts of the city with each other in order to pass the cab driver's qualifying test. Black taxi drivers can be assumed to be conversant in English and to know the city very well. Their cabs are metered, and rides can be expensive: £ 5 for a 5-minute ride is about where prices begin. Black taxis can nearly always be found at one's beck and call within central London, and can also be ordered by telephone; the further out you are from the centre, the longer you'll have to wait for one. Very few black taxis now accept credit card payment.

Minicab companies pop up like mushrooms in London and often die as quickly. It is not unusual to receive through your letterbox a couple of cards a week advertising their services. Minicabs are not supposed to be hailed on the street, so they rely completely on telephone orders and walk-ins for their fares. They tend to be neighbourhood-based, and it is unlikely that you can live anywhere in London without being within a few minutes' call from one of them.

Fares in minicabs are fixed between named destinations. When you order your minicab, you should always find out the fare to your destination, then confirm it with the driver when he or she arrives. Fares are in all cases cheaper than those of black taxis, and minicabs are generally reliable, often more reliable than black taxis in Outer London and in non-posh Inner London neighbourhoods. There is no guarantee that your minicab driver will know the best route to your destination, or that he or she will speak English fluently, but more often than not both of these will hold true.

Both black taxi and minicab drivers appreciate tips in the 10 per cent range. This is not

Minicab Drivers

Anyone with a driving licence can be a minicab driver, and it is a moonlighting job for as many people as do it for a living: all you need is a car, a driving licence and a mobile phone. Driving a minicab is a favoured job of many of London's immigrants: some minicab companies operate entirely within ethnic communities, where drivers speak the language of the passengers.

obligatory, but it will get you a much friendlier goodbye than not giving one will.

Personal Locomotion: Cycling and Walking

We save for last the most dependable form of transportation in London: your own two feet, applied to the pedals or the pavement. As European cities go, London is not the best for either cycling or walking, but there are active lobbies for improving the lot of those who pursue both activities, so there are perhaps grounds for optimism about the future of London's walkways and cycle paths and routes.

Cyclists share a lane with buses and taxis on busy London streets. This is not a very satisfactory arrangement for anyone concerned, as the motor vehicles often get stuck behind bicycles, and cyclists get wedged in clouds of exhaust fumes between the motor vehicles. Most London boroughs operate a system of bike routes that bypass the major thoroughfares, and these are much more satisfactory, usually taking fairly direct routes through residential areas that are unsuitable for heavy traffic. Such routes are marked by blue signs with a picture of a bicycle on them, and arrows pointing to various destinations.

Two accoutrements are recommended for the London cyclist: a helmet and a filter mask. You're really crazy to ride without the first, and you'll enjoy your riding more by using the second. The filters remove particulates and many of the grosser pollutants in London's street air by means of replaceable charcoal filters, assuring that your lungs will be supplied with oxygen freed of most of the poisonous gases that clog London's motor-packed streets. Helmets and masks with replacement filters can be bought at any London cycle shop.

Cyclists are expected to obey all the traffic laws that apply to motor vehicles: don't think that because you are on two wheels rather than four, you can get away with anything!

Finally, to walking. London offers some of the world's best and worst urban walking. It's easy to tell the difference: the worst walking is along the busy, congested high streets, jam-packed with shoppers, sightseers, cars, buses, cyclists, lorries, motorbikes and foul air. Only a starry-eyed tourist can enjoy this, and even then not for very long. The circumspect Londoner avoids these scenes and finds quieter, more circuitous routes by which to navigate the city on foot. This is never very hard to do, since the worst traffic is everywhere quite centralised. You need only go a few streets away to find a quieter place, and tiny, centuries-old lanes not wide enough to accommodate motor traffic are still found throughout London, especially in older central areas.

The nicest places to walk in London—and to cycle, for that matter—are in the city's many parks and along its waterways. Here, it is possible to forget that you are in the heart of one of the world's largest cities, for the green spaces in London are quite generous and many are beautifully cultivated and landscaped to give views that rival anything in the countryside. The parks will be looked at in greater detail in Chapter Seven from a recreational point of view. In terms of simple movement across the city, the following 'green routes' are recommended for covering maximum distance, with minimum concrete:

- Kensington Gardens, Hyde Park, Green Park and Saint James Park: an east-west distance of about 3.2 km (2 miles) through the heart of London, all landscaped.
- Hampstead Heath: more than 2.6 sq km (a sq mile) of park and forest in North London, with walking and cycling trails in every direction across it.
- Grand Union and Regent's Canals: 54.7 km (934 miles) of a nearly continuous towpath alongside these canals, once used for hauling coal. Open to both cyclists and pedestrians, starting at Limehouse in East London, running roughly east to west across near-North London, and then turning north-west to end at Rickmansworth.
- Riverside walks: on both the north and south banks of the Thames running through Westminster and the City, there are pedestrian pathways which, though not particularly green, offer nice views of the city, removed from traffic. Further west starting at about Putney, greener paths line the Thames, alternately on the north and south banks, more or less all the way out of London into the countryside.

Navigating the City

Now with all means of transportation at your disposal, it remains only to learn how you actually find an address in London, and how you figure out the best way of getting there. The simple answer is, by using a street guide. Even natives rely on one; people give verbal or written directions to an address only as a supplement to what can be found in a street guide. Most of London was laid out long before the idea of urban planning developed. Thus, there is no overall house numbering scheme, and major arteries connecting different parts of the city are mostly ad hoc in nature, cobbled together from existing semi-direct routes.

The most common guide in use is *London A to Z*; its success is such that *A to Z* is the generic term for a London street guide, and it is in that sense that it is used here. Everyone has an *A to Z*: hardly a passenger car is without one, taxi drivers use them, and it is a rare London home that doesn't have a dog-eared edition lying around somewhere. The detailed maps show all streets, as well as other familiar navigating landmarks: Tube and rail stations, hospitals, post offices and the like. House numbers are shown intermittently on major streets, which is a useful device for locating an address

TRIGL.

since every conceivable scheme is in use to number houses in London. Some streets are odd on one side, even on the other, some are sequential up one side and down the other, and numbers are sometimes completely out of synch with those directly across the street.

If a criticism can be made of the street guides, it is that the scale is sometimes deceptive. Major routes, called 'A' and 'B' roads, are shown much larger than other streets, giving the impression that you can fly down them, bypassing the smaller streets alongside. In fact, many A and B roads are no wider than ordinary streets: they merely carry the designation of a major route, and thus get all the traffic. There are often faster and less congested routes that use side streets, but these don't exactly jump out at you when looking at the *A to Z*. A guide that overcomes this problem for central London is the *London Back Street Map* (published by the Clever Map Co. Ltd), which has a colour-coded scheme for shortcuts of all of Inner and most of Outer London.

The last word about getting around London is that you should never expect to be moving very fast. The average speed of a car in London is 16 km (10 miles) per hour. It is a big, crowded city; unless you're zipping around in the middle of the night, backed-up traffic can appear anywhere, at any time.

A ROOF OVER YOUR HEAD

London accommodates everyone from paupers to princes; the range of accommodation available should leave no one unable to find a place that is just right. Whatever you do find, however, will probably leave you feeling that you couldn't possibly have spent a penny more than you did: London accommodation is expensive by nearly any standard and it is fairly common, especially in rental accommodation, to feel that you do not get good value for your money.

In this section, we will look first at the kinds of dwellings London has to offer, and investigate a few ways that you might want to go about deciding where you want to live. Then the actual property search begins. Finally, we will detail the pros and cons of renting and buying London accommodation.

Freehold and Leasehold

Before our tour of London properties begins, we look at an important distinction in property rights and ownership that pervades dealings with property of any kind in London. This is the distinction between leasehold and freehold property. Freehold is the easy one: you own the building and the land it sits on, and a title with the land registry records this fact. Leasehold, which affects a large percentage of London business and residential property, is in fact also owned outright by someone—the freeholder—but generally, it is not the freeholder who occupies and has rights to the property. It is the leaseholder who does this, and if you live in a leasehold flat or house, the leaseholder is you.

Leases on residential properties are usually long affairs, from 99 to 125 years when they begin (sometimes shorter in central, high priced districts). As a leaseholder, you pay a nominal ground rent to the freeholder yearly. For that, you enjoy exclusive use of and rights to the property (except for odd things such as mineral rights) just as if you owned it, for the term of the lease. When you buy a leasehold property, typically you buy it from the previous leaseholder, not from the freeholder.

If you are living in a property when a long lease expires, you have the right to negotiate a new lease. But in practice, leaseholders rarely see a lease expire in their lifetimes, or during their tenancy in a particular property. Leases are usually drawn up so as not to be troublesome, but merely to provide a trickle of unearned income for the shadowy freeholder, whoever he or she may be.

Who Owns Property in London?

Exactly who owns what parcel of land in London is often shrouded in mystery. There is no public land record and actual owners are often hidden behind various layers of trusts, companies and agents. In the case of owner-occupied, freehold properties, everything is quite straightforward. But vast tracts of developed land all over London belong to various estates and trusts, some connected with lofty, titled personages and royals, who collect rents from leaseholders but have little or no active hand in what happens on the property. This situation doesn't necessarily have an adverse effect on you as an aspiring London resident; it simply means that unless you are in a freehold property that you buy, the actual owner of the place you live in may not be someone you ever deal with or even meet.

Aside from privately owned dwellings and leasehold dwellings, where the occupier is the lessee, there are a couple of other common kinds of housing in London that bear mentioning. First, there is council housing. To a degree that may astound the foreigner, local government in London (and Britain generally) is in the housing business in a big way. The reasons for there being so much government-owned housing are mostly historical, and some would argue they are no longer very relevant, but the fact is that every London borough owns and controls a great deal of rental accommodation that is available at nominal cost to residents of that borough who meet various qualifications. These usually include residence in the borough of at least three years (except in circumstances of exceptional hardship), evidence of need (if you don't have dependent children, you can probably forget it) and proof of right to residency in the borough and in Britain. Council housing is usually in the form of large groups of big buildings of purpose-built flats, called council estates. Generally, it is not considered very desirable housing.

Housing Associations and Housing Trusts

Often working in conjunction with borough councils but independent of them are housing associations and housing trusts. These organisations, all of which run on a non-profit and often on a charity basis, own properties of all descriptions in London. The properties are let to those in need, as opposed to those who only want. The rent is usually quite reasonable, below market rates but higher than council rents, and many of the properties are well maintained and in excellent locations. But unless you are in London as an asylum seeker, refugee or lone parent with dependent children, chances are that you will not qualify for subsidised housing from any of these organisations.

Houses Great and Small

For an overview of the sorts of housing available in London, we start at the very bottom: the bed and breakfast. Though you may think of it as a quaint and comfortable rest stop for the passing tourist, bed and breakfasts provide rather seamy accommodation for a large number of London residents (and huge incomes for B&B owners). The vast majority of those who actually live in bed and breakfasts are people whom borough councils are required to house, but do not have any better accommodation for. Such accommodation is in principal temporary, but in practice, many people—especially single refugees—live in bed and breakfasts for years without being moved into more suitable lodgings. This sort of accommodation is certainly not recommended for the new or aspiring London resident, but you should know that it exists, and that many bed and breakfasts, especially outside the central area, offer weekly and monthly rates at a substantial savings over the day rate.

The next step up in the London accommodation ladder is the bedsitter, also called the bedsit (for short) or the bedsittingroom (for pomposity). A bedsitter is a room in a house of other such rooms, where tenants share one or more common kitchens and/or bathrooms which may adjoin or be rather distant from their sitting room. The leitmotif of most bedsitters is squalor, but it is not impossible to find nice bedsitters with nice people who keep a clean house and show each other consideration. Bedsitters are primarily accommodation for the young, the poor, students and overwhelmingly for single people. Your first look at one will probably tell you whether you could stand to live in it or not. They are all for rent, and virtually none for sale.

From the bedsitter, we move up to the flat, and it is here that we find the majority of Londoners snugly ensconced. Flats come in all shapes and sizes. They are what Americans call apartments (if rented) or condominiums (if owner-occupied). The biggest share of flats are probably one and two bedroom affairs, but there are studio and efficiency flats available (some may call these bedsits)—especially in crowded central areas—and flats with up to four bedrooms are not unheard of. Most flats in tall buildings, called tower blocks, are council flats and are not very desirable. More typically, a flat is in a converted house (in which case it is called a conversion), or in a purpose-built block of two to four stories (which may be called a block of flats). A block of flats may be called a mansion block if it is somewhat luxurious, architecturally appealing and quite large. Buildings fitting this description are mostly in nicer parts of Westminster, Kensington and Chelsea.

You can expect a flat to have a kitchen (sometimes minuscule), a bathroom with a tub or shower that will also have a toilet (or in older flats, a separate water closet), a reception room (which means a room suitable for use as a living room) and the stated number of bedrooms. A flat advertised as a maisonette is supposed to occupy more than one floor of a building and to have its own separate entrance from the street; but since maisonette is a favourite marketing term of estate agents, it may have only one, rather than both of these features. A flat advertised as ex-council was formerly owned by a borough council, bought from the government by its tenant and is now offered on the open market.

A flat may or may not have use of a garden (open space at the front or back of the house is called a garden, no matter how long it may have been since anything was seen growing there). In the case of flats that are in converted houses, use of the garden may be shared among tenants, or the garden may be physically divided to give separate access to some or all of the various flat occupants. Something advertised as a garden flat has direct access to a garden, but is usually at or below ground level, and it is not unheard of for rather gloomy basements to be advertised as garden flats. Occupiers of flats

London housing has been greatly modernised in the last 25 years or so, but most of the buildings date from a more primitive time when features such as modern plumbing and central heating did not exist. Most properties on the market today have been upgraded to modern standards, and they often point this out in advertising: GCH means gas central heating, GFCH means gas fired central heating. A flat or other property that is advertised as needing modernisation probably lacks central heating, modern plumbing or both.

may be either owners or tenants. The majority of flats are in leasehold property, but it is increasingly common for flat owners to acquire the freehold on their property.

From the flat, we graduate to the house. They come in three basic types in London: the terraced house, which shares walls with similar houses on each side; the semi-detached house (semi for short), attached to a mirror image house on one side but open on the other; and the detached house, free standing without attachment to another dwelling. The order given here is ascending in terms of desirability and generally of price. An end-of-terrace house is intermediate between a terraced house and a semi, being the last house in a terrace and therefore open on one side. Houses of all these types can be found everywhere in London, but terraced houses are much more the rule in Inner London, whereas two-story detached or semi-detached houses predominate in Outer London.

London houses have all the rooms you would expect to find, as discussed above under flats. Nearly all houses in London have gardens (as described above), except in the very oldest, central districts. Front gardens tend to be small, with larger, often long and narrow, gardens in the back. Houses in London are more often freehold than leasehold, but some

A Georgian terrace in Kentish Town, Camden.

A typical semi-detached house in Wanstead, East London.

very expensive central London properties belong to wealthy landowners and are bought and sold as leaseholds.

Search Strategies

In a property market as big and varied as London's, the search for a place to live is complicated by having too much rather than too little to choose from. It is a frequent complaint of flat or home seekers that there is so much available, but nothing really nice. This is not at all true. What is true is that there is nothing really nice available for the price you want to pay. To get something that you think of as really nice, you either have to pay more, accept something much smaller than you had envisioned, accept something not very near a Tube stop, accept something fairly non-central or accept something nicely done up in a not-so-fashionable neighbourhood. So if you are going for 'really nice' on a limited budget, you may first want to consider which of the foregoing you could most easily live with.

You will simplify your search for accommodation considerably if you settle on where in London you want to live first of all. Without doing this, you will flounder amid dozens of property descriptions in all corners of the capital that, their location aside, present few differences on which to make a decision. By limiting your search to a particular area or two, you can concentrate on a smaller number of properties, deal with no more than two or three agents (discussed below) and limit the wearying task of tripping all over London to view places on offer for sale or rent.

A number of factors may influence where in London you want to plant your feet. It is likely that you will have your work (or studies) lined up ahead of time and therefore know where you'll be spending most of your time during the week. For most people, this is the most important consideration: how easy will it be and how long will it take to get to where you have to go each day. The popular notion is that accommodation near a Tube stop is the most desirable for mobility, and prices reflect this: neighbourhoods without a convenient stop on the Underground are uniformly cheaper than those with. But remember that Inner London in particular is very well served by bus transportation, and you may be able to get where you want to go just as quickly overground.

Other factors that you may want to keep in mind before settling on a neighbourhood are the same ones that you would use anywhere. Here is a checklist that you can put in the order that suits your priorities:

Transportation
Check for convenient Tube, bus and rail connections. The more of any of these, the better, since any given mode of travel can be unavailable at different times.

Parking and Driving
If you have a car, look for a place that has good lighting and ample parking on the street, so that you don't spend 10 minutes each evening at the end of a long day looking for a space. Off-street parking in Inner London is rare, but a definite plus for drivers. The more central you are in London, the bigger headache owning a car is. But in Outer London, a car can be more of a convenience than a liability.

Shopping and Services
Look for as many of the following as are important to you in the area of your dwelling: supermarket, street market,

convenience food store, off-licence (see next chapter), dry cleaner, barber and/or hairdresser, hardware, DIY centre (for decorating, etc.), electrical appliance superstore, high street, bank and/or building society, post office, doctor's surgery and dentist.

Amenities

If you spend a fair amount of leisure time close to home, you may want to check for the proximity of cafes, pubs and restaurants, entertainment venues such as clubs and cinemas, private or council sports facilities, adult education classes and a public library.

Noise

Motor traffic and trains are the biggest noise makers in London; residents close to them suffer for it. If this will be a problem for you, don't choose a house on or near a busy street or railway line.

Security

Burglary is endemic all over London. If your dwelling will be empty during the day, look for a neighbourhood or a street that is well lighted and where a number of residents stay at or work from home. There are neighbourhood watch schemes in operation all over London, and these have some deterrent effect on household crime.

Education

If you have school-age children, you will want to know what 'catchment area' your dwelling falls in (i.e. which school your children would be expected to attend, barring any special arrangements you make). Individual schools vary widely in reputation and quality of education and can also vary greatly from borough to borough.

Local Government and the Council Tax

The foregoing list aside, you may wish to consider a couple of other factors in choosing where to live in London: first, the quality and political shade of local government, and second, how much council tax you will have to pay. As we have seen already, London has no overall government authority, and individual borough councils are largely responsible for the day-to-day running of services within their borders.

Financing of local government services is partially provided by the council tax. Since it replaced what were called the rates in the early 1990s, it has gone through a number of changes, all of them unpopular. Many people call it the poll tax, since it is often mistakenly thought to be payable by all those on the electoral register. In fact, it is a tax based on property values but payable by each individual living in a property. Within limits set by central government, each borough council determines how much will be assessed on its residents, based to some degree on the sort of dwelling they live in. The rate of tax is calculated per person. If yours is a two-person household, each of you pays the tax. It is assessed on adults, defined as anyone aged 18 and older. Younger people are not liable for any part of the tax. A table of the tax rates is available from the local council offices. Estate agents should also be able to tell you the council tax on any property they are showing.

Taxes for You?

Don't rule out settling in a borough simply because it has a high council tax. Decide first which borough services are going to be most important to you. Boroughs with the highest council tax may well provide better services in an area that matters to you, such as libraries, child care facilities, or street sanitation. In general, the boroughs with the highest charge provide the most extensive range of services for poorer residents.

The political party that has control of your borough council has a very strong and noticeable effect on the conduct of local government and services. You may wish to consider this if you have tender political sensitivities: chances are you will not be happy in a left-leaning borough if you are a dyed-in-the-wool conservative because you will see public money being spent on services that you think are an abomination. Conversely, if you're a bleeding heart liberal, you could well bleed to death in some of the parsimonious, true-blue Tory boroughs that implement some of the most extraordinary measures in order to relieve themselves of responsibility for social services. Any borough resident will probably be happy to characterise the borough council for you. Collect several opinions to get a balanced picture.

Searching by Postcode

Once you've settled on a general area, the easiest way to go about zeroing in on a place to live is to use the London postcode system. It is common shorthand for Londoners and especially for London estate agents to break down the city into postcode areas: virtually every property identified for sale or rent in advertising names the postcode it is located in, and by acquainting yourself with this system, your search will be much easier to carry out. If you limit yourself to looking in only one or two postcodes, your search will be easier still.

An entire London postcode consists of two parts (for example, E8 3BP), which are separated by a space. The first part (E8 in the example) is the general area, and the second part (3BP) is usually specific to a single section of a street. It is the first part of the postcode that estate agents and others use in advertising. All London postcodes begin with one of the following: E (for East), EC (East Central), N (North), NW (North-west), SE (South-east), SW (South-west), W (West) and WC (West Central). The number following these letters identifies an area. It would be convenient and helpful if the lower numbers were closer in to the centre of London and the higher numbers further out, but in fact no such rule prevails.

The following table equates London postcodes with neighbourhoods. For Inner London, which is less homogenous and more densely packed than Outer London, every postcode is listed along with its associated neighbourhood. For Outer London, the postcodes of entire boroughs are lumped together, partly in the interest of saving space, but also because if you are looking for accommodation in Outer London, chances are that exact location in relation to the centre is not terribly important. There is also much of Outer London that the Royal Mail (the post office) does not classify as belonging to London at all. Outermost areas of the capital have postcodes associated with the Home Counties or with the now defunct Middlesex county, reflecting the time before the concept of Greater London was established, when the postcodes were codified. Some postcodes are listed in relation to more than one borough: the Royal Mail does not generally respect political boundaries in its breakdown of London.

Code	Main Area(s)	Borough(s)
E Postcodes in Inner London: all east of the City, north of the Thames		
E1	Bethnal Green, Whitechapel	Tower Hamlets
E2	Bethnal Green, Shoreditch	Tower Hamlets, Hackney
E3	Bow	Tower Hamlets
E5	Clapton, Homerton	Hackney
E6	East Ham	Newham
E7	Forest Gate	Newham
E8	Dalston	Hackney
E9	Homerton	Hackney
E12	Manor Park	Newham
E13	Plaistow	Newham
E14	Poplar (Isle of Dogs)	Tower Hamlets
E15	Stratford, West Ham	Newham
E16	Victoria Docks, N Woolwich	Newham
E Postcodes in Outer London: all east of the City, north of the Thames		
E4 E10 E11 E17		Waltham Forest
E11 E18		Redbridge

Code	Main Area(s)	Borough(s)
EC Postcodes: all in and around the City of London		
EC1	Aldersgate, Finsbury, Holbom	City, Islington, Camden
EC2	Bishopsgate, Cheapside	City
EC3	Aldgate	City
EC4	Saint Paul's	City
N Postcodes in Inner London: all north of the Thames and the City		
N1	Angel	Islington
N5	Highbury	Islington
N7	Holloway	Islington
N16	Stoke Newington	Hackney
N19	Upper Holloway	Islington
N Postcodes in Outer London: all north of the Thames and the City		
N2		
N3		
N11		Barnet
N12		
N20		
N4		
N6		
N8		
N10		Haringey
N15		
N17		
N22		
N9		
N11		
N13		Enfield
N14		
N18		
N21		

Code	Main Area(s)	Borough(s)

NW Postcodes in Inner London: all north of the Thames and north-west of the City

Code	Main Area(s)	Borough(s)
NW1	Regent's Park, St. Pancras	Westminster, Camden
NW3	Hampstead	Camden
NW5	Kentish Town	Camden
NW8	Saint John's Wood	Westminster

NW Postcodes in Outer London: all north of the Thames and north-west of the City

Code	Main Area(s)	Borough(s)
NW2		
NW4		
NW7		Barnet
NW9		
NW11		
NW9		Brent
NW10		

SE Postcodes in Inner London: all south of the Thames, south and south-east of the City

Code	Main Area(s)	Borough(s)
SE1	The Borough, Waterloo	Lambeth, Southwark
SE3	Blackheath	Lewisham
SE4	Brockley	Lewisham
SE5	Camberwell	Southwark
SE6	Catford	Lewisham
SE8	Deptford	Lewisham
SE11	Kennington	Lambeth
SE12	Lee	Lewisham
SE13	Lewisham Central	Lewisham
SE14	New Cross	Lewisham
SE15	Peckham	Southwark
SE16	Bermondsey, Rotherhithe	Southwark
SE17	Walworth	Southwark

Code	Main Area(s)	Borough(s)
SW21 SW22	Dulwich	Southwark
SE23	Forest Hill	Lewisham
SE24	Herne Hill	Lambeth, Southwark
SE26	Sydenham	Lewisham
SE27	West Norwood	Lewisham
SE Postcodes in Outer London: all south of the Thames, south-east of the City		
SE2 SE3 SE7 SE9 SE10 SE18		Greenwich
SE9 SE19 SE20		Bromley
SE19 SE25		Croydon
SW Postcodes in Inner London: south-west of the city and south of the Thames, except *, which are north of the Thames		
SW1*	Westminster, Victoria	Westminster
SW2	Brixton Hill	Lambeth
SW3*	Chelsea	Kensington and Chelsea
SW4	Clapham	Lambeth
SW5*	Brompton, Earl's Court	Kensington and Chelsea
SW6*	Fulham	Fulham and Hammersmith
SW7*	Knightsbridge, S Kensington	Kensington and Chelsea
SW8	South Lambeth	Lambeth, Wandsworth

Code	Main Area(s)	Borough(s)
SW9	Brixton	Lambeth
SW10*	West Brompton	Kensington and Chelsea
SW11	Battersea	Wandsworth
SW12	Balham	Wandsworth
SW15	Putney	Wandsworth
SW16	Streatham	Lambeth
SW17	Tooting	Wandsworth
SW18	West Wandsworth	Wandsworth

SW Postcodes in Outer London: southwest of the City, south of the Thames

SW19 SW20	Wimbledon	Merton

W Postcodes in Inner London: all west of the City, north of the Thames

Wl	West End	Westminster
W2	Bayswater, Paddington	Westminster, K&C
W6	Hammersmith	Fulham and Hammersmith
W8	Holland Park	Kensington and Chelsea
W9	Maida Vale, Paddington	Westminster
W10	North Kensington	Kensington and Chelsea
Wl1	Notting Hill	Kensington and Chelsea
W12/14	Shepherd's Bush, Hammersmith	Fulham and Hammersmith

W Postcodes in Outer London: all west of the City, north of the Thames

W3 W5 W7 W13		Ealing
W4		Ealing, Hounslow

Code	Main Area(s)	Borough(s)
WC Postcodes: both immediately west of the City, north of the Thames		
WC1	Bloomsbury, High Holborn	Camden
WC2	Strand, Holborn	Westminster, Camden

AGENTS

Estate agents are legion in London. There are chains that operate London-wide as well as local agencies that have only an office or two. They come and go out of business regularly, and their numbers are often a reflection of the state of the housing market. When business is booming, agencies seem to pop up on every corner; when business falls, they close up shop. There are two sorts of agencies: those primarily geared for selling properties (estate agents), and those whose main business is rentals (letting agents). Most estate agents have a lucrative sideline in rentals (lettings, as they are often called) especially since the early 1990s when the London rental market—long in the doldrums—began to revive.

A property may be listed for sale or rent by several agents, but agents only have the right to deal with properties specifically listed with them. This means that you may, and probably will, deal with more than one agency in your search, because an agent cannot show you or make inquiries about a property that is not listed with him. Agents advertise their wares in their windows, with descriptions, and often pictures, of properties for sale or rent, identified by neighbourhood and postcode. When you register with an agent, they will regularly send you, or ring you about, new properties that have been listed with them.

It is the general perception of agents that they take the carpet-bomb approach to selling: they inundate you with descriptions of every conceivable property, taking little heed of what you told them you want or don't want. There is very little computerisation or systematisation in listings, and the amount of chaos that prevails in agencies is sometimes quite alarming. If it is any consolation, their service is completely free to you as a renter or buyer: it is the landlord or seller who pays for the agent's services.

ADVERTISING

It is possible to bypass the whole agency experience by looking for properties through private advertising. This will not alert you to as many properties as you would otherwise find out about, but many find it worthwhile to pursue this route to finding accommodation, either alongside of or instead of using agents.

All of the London dailies, in particular the *London Evening Standard*, carry real estate advertising. All are stronger in lettings than in properties for sale, but there are some of each in every issue. However, you are likely to find that weekly neighbourhood newspapers are more useful for getting a general feel of what's available, once you've settled on an area. Every part of London is served by a weekly newspaper of some kind, and estate agents advertise heavily in them, often taking up a third or more of the paper.

Helpful Publications

Another, nearly indispensable guide for the property seeker is *Loot*, an all-advertising paper published five times a week in an edition devoted exclusively to London. It has the best range of privately advertised properties for sale and rent. Some weekly publications, such as *Time Out* and *The Spectator*, have a classified section where small ads, mostly for rentals, can be found.

Finally, you may want to check the small ads posted in local shops of the area you are interested in. As a courtesy, many shops allow local residents to place small, handwritten advertisements in their windows, and many an unadventurous or parsimonious landlord or seller may advertise a house or flat here and nowhere else.

TO BUY OR NOT TO BUY

The London property market goes through fairly regular upheavals. The pros and cons of buying and renting at any given time are subject to change, and the decision you come to in the end will probably have more to do with your circumstances than the state of the market. There are very good reasons both to buy and to rent; whichever you decide to do will probably not be too far wrong.

The Recent Market

The recent history of London's property market has been influenced by three main factors: the health of the overall economy; changing government policies and new legislation affecting home ownership and tenancy; and fluctuating interest rates, which are more or less controlled by the government reacting to what it perceives as economic necessity. While economic factors have generally had a negative influence on the housing market, the general thrust of Conservative governments—in power in Britain from the end of the 1970s to the mid 1990s—was to favour home ownership but also to improve the lot of landlords, who formerly had a number of disincentives to letting or properly maintaining rental properties. The overall result is that today, there is a very liquid and generally improved market in London for accommodation, whether rented or bought.

Property prices in London have been on a somewhat harrowing course in recent times. Throughout the 1970s and 1980s, there was a steady, gradual increase in prices. Beginning in the mid-1980s, prices began to rise sharply, with properties sometimes increasing in value as much as 10 per cent in a period of months. There are varying theories about what makes property prices rise and fall in London, but two things are sure: first, when they fall, they never fall to anything that would be considered reasonable in most other cities of the world; and second, you should never bet on the wisdom of real estate as a short-term investment in London—plummeting prices can start at any time, unpredictably. Throughout the early 1990s, predictions were regularly made about the revival and stabilisation of the property market, and these more often than not did not come to pass. But since the year 2000, prices have generally been on the rise in London and in the UK generally.

Lately, London's housing market has become more fragmented, with an overall pattern of rising or falling prices replaced by one in which certain areas of the city—those deemed fashionable in the opinion of the day—show very sharp increases, while other areas remain stable or slide. The areas least served by public transport are the slowest to appreciate, while those newly served by public transport can shoot up fast. There is really no substitute for making a thorough investigation of the local market if you are going to take the step of buying London property.

Why Buy?

There are a number of reasons why it may be advantageous to you, as a foreigner, to buy property in London. Perhaps the important question to ask is, how long do you intend to stay? If you mean to live in London for two years or more and you have the means, then there are several good reasons to buy, including the following:

- You receive tax relief on a percentage of your mortgage interest which will significantly reduce your UK income tax; no comparable benefit is available for renters.
- If you have adequate and dependable income, it is relatively easy to get a mortgage with only a small down payment.
- The range of available accommodation is wider and better than in the rented sector.

However, lest this begin to seem like an estate agent's brochure, you should also keep in mind that:

- Owning property decreases your easy mobility, in that you will have to either sell or let before you can leave London (unless you want to leave your property empty, which is not advisable).
- You will be at the mercy of fluctuating interest rates: nearly all UK mortgages have a floating rate, with a period of fixed interest usually no greater than two years.
- You will have some expenses that you wouldn't have as a tenant, mainly insurance.
- There is no guarantee that your investment will appreciate.

TO RENT OR NOT TO RENT?

The sheer ease of moving into ready accommodation is perhaps the main incentive for renting property in London. Most lets, especially at the high end, are furnished and you can settle into a house and lifestyle much more quickly if all the props are already there for you. Renting also makes it easy for you to get out, of your house or of London, with relative ease.

Living in Style in London

Single people and couples will find that there is a greater availability of small accommodation to let than for sale: bedsits and efficiency or studio flats are almost entirely in the rental market. If money is no object to you, renting will be advantageous because of London's pre-eminence among world cities. It is certainly in the top five, if not the top three of fashionable world cities in which to cavort, and so a vast market exists for deep-pocketed transients who want more than a hotel room for their stays in London. Deluxe rental accommodation furnished down to the last silver teaspoon is available in all of London's poshest neighbourhoods—at a price that will astound you if you don't already travel with the set who frequents such places.

The single and compelling argument against renting in London is that it is simply not very good value for money. Unless you come from Tokyo or some other northern European capital, you will be amazed at the prices landlords are able to command. There is virtually nothing available for less than £ 80 per week, and that gets you a seamy bedsit, with a filthy communal kitchen and squalid shared bathroom in the most derelict and crime-ridden parts of London. A decent one bedroom flat in a nice neighbourhood will cost between £ 200 and £ 300 per week. And from here it only goes up: a three bedroom house in a so-so neighbourhood will cost upwards of £ 400 a week, and if you want it in a nice neighbourhood, you're looking at £ 600 a week, and so forth. These prices do not include utilities, nor the council tax, which you will have to pay in addition to the rent.

Renting: Step by Step

If this is the route you want to go, start by looking in either or both of two places: the listings of a letting agent or agents in the area you have decided upon; or *Loot*, which has extensive listings for all of London, broken down by style of accommodation, price and postcode. You should be prepared to invest a fair amount of time in looking at properties; look at a number in the same area to get a feel for the general range of quality. No doubt you will have your own list of desirable items to look for in a residence. Specifically with regard to renting, you should ascertain:

- Who pays the utilities—gas, electricity, telephone and water? It will probably be you, though in some cases the landlord will pay the water bill. If you are to pay them, be sure to get the accounts in your name (see below).
- What is the protocol when something breaks down? Don't leave any room for vagueness here. You should find out specifically what your recourse is if, say, the boiler breaks down in the dead of winter. In principle, the landlord is responsible for maintaining everything in working order that is let as part of the property, including appliances.
- Who pays the council tax? Again, it will probably be you, but it is worth asking.
- If there is a TV in the house or flat, does the landlord pay for the TV licence? If not, you will have to get one in your name.
- If there is a garden, do you have access to it or free use of it? Do you have any responsibility for maintaining it?
- What will be the exact nature of the agreement between you and the landlord? (See the following section)

Rental Agreements and Contracts

Despite the availability of a standard, straightforward rental contract, a great deal of property in London is let without one, and without many problems: landlords want to keep tenants, and tenants want a place to live. A formal agreement is not required to rent property in London, but it is highly recommended because it protects you and makes the nature of your relationship with the landlord completely clear.

Legislation in the late 1980s brought into being a new form of rental agreement that is advantageous for both landlord and tenant, by making the terms of the agreement perfectly clear on both sides. It is called an assured shorthold tenancy. If you rent accommodation under any agreement other than this, including a mere verbal understanding with the landlord, you should know that your tenancy is not secure or protected by the law in any way. In other words, you could be turfed out without much difficulty if it suited the landlord for any particular reason.

An assured shorthold tenancy runs for a fixed period of at least six months, and not more than two years. During the period of the tenancy, provided that you pay the agreed rent and do not create any unreasonable difficulties, the accommodation is yours exclusively. You are not allowed to sublet, but you cannot be evicted and your rent cannot be raised. At the end of the tenancy, you may be required to leave, but more typically, there are provisions for you to stay on. When the initial term of a tenancy runs out, the tenancy automatically reverts to an arrangement whereby you and the landlord each have to give the other notice of intent to vacate one or two months in advance. Your tenancy remains in effect then on a continuing basis, but it is the landlord's option to increase the rent after the contractual period of tenancy has expired.

It is the landlord's responsibility to draw up the lease, if he or she is going to use one; you merely have to sign it. You should certainly read it carefully before you do. It should state all matters relating to your financial responsibility clearly: the amount of rent, how and how often it is to be paid, the amount of deposit and conditions for its return, terms relating to any other bills that you are responsible for, and any other specific responsibilities you have for the property should be spelled out. Be sure that the lease also states specifically the date you assume tenancy, and the date the tenancy ends.

It is not advisable to rent accommodation in London under any written agreement other than the assured shorthold tenancy discussed here. Similarly, it is not advisable to rent accommodation with nothing other than a verbal agreement with your landlord, though it must be said that thousands do without any negative result.

BUYING: STEP BY STEP

Many decide to take the plunge into the London housing market after frustration with rental accommodation: simply not being able to find what they want, or finding it but not being willing to pay what is asked. Buying a property in London is not something to be undertaken lightly, but all in all, the benefits probably outweigh the risks, mostly because the thrust of government legislation over the past 15 years has been to favour homeowners.

Mortgages and Solicitors

If buying a property in London is even a glimmer in your eye, you should go to a bank or building society and start talking about a mortgage. Getting an actual mortgage offer is a long and leisurely (on the part of the lenders) process, so it is in your interest to start the wheels turning as soon as possible. Banks and building societies (they are discussed later in the chapter) will be much more kindly disposed towards you if you already have money on deposit with them, so you may want to start by approaching the one where you have your current or savings account. Also keep an eye out for advertised mortgages in the papers.

To buy or sell a property in London, you also need a solicitor, or in other words, a lawyer. Estate agents, even if you use one, are not qualified to scrutinise contracts and in any case would not have your best interests in mind: remember, they represent the seller. The typical setup is for both seller and buyer to engage solicitors, and much of the business of transferring property, or conveyancing as it is called, is handled (sometimes with amazing slowness) by the two firms of solicitors. For this service, you can expect to pay upwards of £ 300, but hopefully no more than £ 500 for the whole deal, assuming that there are no odd complications.

Virtually every high street solicitor handles conveyancing. This doesn't mean that you should engage the first one you come across. If at all possible, get a recommendation from someone you know or work with. It shouldn't be difficult to find someone who knows of a solicitor who performs this work competently, and there is no need for the solicitor to be physically near you or the property: nearly everything can be done by post, fax and telephone.

Picking the Property

As with rental accommodation, there are two avenues to pursue for the prospective home buyer: private advertising and estate agents. Private advertising is certainly the calmer path to pursue, for there you deal initially only with sellers you speak with on the telephone. You can often decide on that basis whether you want to look at a property or not.

As with rental properties, *Loot* has extensive listings of residential property for sale, broken down by style of accommodation, price and postcode. You can save yourself a lot of footwork by having a detailed set of questions ready to ask the seller on the telephone about the property in question. The seller will be much better informed about a property than an estate agent would, and can give definitive answers to questions that agents could only be (purposefully) vague about, so take advantage of the opportunity to find out as much as you can about a property verbally. Then, if you still want to see it, make an appointment. Among the things you may want to ask, in addition to the general features already discussed, are:

- Is the property freehold or leasehold? In either case, make sure you understand all the details (e.g. how many years remain in the lease, is the freehold shared, how much is the ground rent, etc.).
- How old is the property? The older they are, the more that goes wrong with them. But many properties, flats in particular, are in completely renovated older houses.
- Is there or has there ever been any problem with rising damp and dry rot? Are there guarantees against these? They are the dual bugbears of all London property.
- Is the property a former council house or flat? Is it on a council estate? (Yes answers to either question should give you cold feet, unless you're on a tight budget).
- How long has the current owner been in possession? If it's not very long (two years or less), ask a lot of questions about why they are selling.

Estate agents, being in the business of making money from the sale of houses, will do everything they can to see that you buy one, and what they do is sometimes more than you need

Mock-Tudor heaven: orderly living in Haringey.

or want. But they perform a valuable service in connecting buyers with sellers, and their costs are borne completely by the seller so it costs you nothing to register with as many of them as you like. One of the truly wearying things about looking for a place to buy in London is being dragged around by agents to numerous places that, if you'd known what they looked like before you got there, you would never have set foot in. They want to show you as many properties as they can, and they do inevitably show you properties that you know you have no interest in as soon as you step in the front door, if not before. While you cannot arrange to view a property listed with an agent without the help of the agent, you can visit properties, if for no more than a drive-by, to see if there is anything from the outside that would keep you from looking any further. You may also be able to eliminate some properties from consideration by close questioning along the lines above. Remember, every property description from an agent is going to look good on paper—they wouldn't be doing their job if it didn't.

Making the Pitch

Once you see a place that you feel prepared to make an offer on, your approach varies according to whether you are dealing with an agent or not. If an agent is involved, you deal only with the agent, not with the owner, even if you've made his or her acquaintance. The agent will forward the offer you make and get back to you about whether it has been accepted. If you are dealing directly with the buyer, make your offer and wait for the answer. No one offers the asking price initially; you might try an offer in the range of 10–15 per cent below the asking price to see what happens. If your initial offer isn't accepted, you can up it a little bit, or play hard to get. It depends on how much you want the place, and perhaps also on how desperate the seller is to get rid of it. Negotiations of this kind are not usually fraught—if both sides are willing, an agreement is usually reached after not more than two or three exchanges.

Even when your offer is accepted, you have still done nothing that is legally binding. You have, however, done something that is morally binding, and you will be the target of indignation (the Briton's favourite emotion) if you pull out of a deal now. So don't make an offer you are not serious about. There are two practices that may come into play here, both of them justly disparaged because they contravene the sense of fair play, but if people didn't do them, there wouldn't have to be a name for them! One is *gazumping*, wherein a seller reneges on his acceptance of an offer and says he will only sell if the offer is raised. The other is *gazundering*, wherein the buyer reneges on his offer and says he will only buy at a lower price. Obviously these practices can only gain currency in an exaggerated sellers' or buyers' market and they have never been prevalent, but also never unheard of.

If your offer is accepted, it is at this point that you get your solicitor hot on the trail of completing the deal. If you're working with an agent, the agent will get the two firms of solicitors (yours and the seller's) talking to each other. Without an agent, you can exchange names of solicitors with the seller. You must also notify your prospective lender that your offer has been accepted on a particular property. They will complete a survey and decide how much (if any) money they will offer to lend you towards the purchase of the property. This is called the mortgage offer, and is a critical step in the buying process, because it cannot go forward without one.

The solicitors then proceed to do their legal dance, making various enquiries and stipulations to ensure the best deal for their client. At some point, in consultation with you and the seller, they set a date for the exchange of contracts. This is not the point of no return, but it is the next thing to it. On the date of exchange, you have to make your agreed deposit (down payment) on the property, which is not refundable, and all lenders and interested parties are informed of the imminent sale.

From the exchange of contracts, typically two weeks pass (though only a few days is required) until completion: the day you move in, and also the day when the money you have borrowed is transferred into the seller's account. This is all handled by solicitors and banks, but you must be sure you understand all the details and do your part as regards signing documents, picking up keys and so forth.

YOUR MAIL AND YOUR ADDRESS

Once you are settled in your abode, make a point of finding out your full postcode, if you don't already know it. You can learn it from someone who lives or has lived at the same address, or from a next door neighbour. The general part of your postcode, which is the first two, three, or four letters and numbers, such as N1, WC2A, or SE16, can be found on street signs, but the more specific part is particular to a single street and is not posted publicly. If you cannot find this information from a neighbour, you can ask the Royal Mail at tel: 0345-111-222, website: http://www.royalmail.com.

Your personal mail will be delivered to you, probably through a hole in your front door called a letterbox. There are in principal two deliveries per day, both usually coming before midday, but the main delivery is the first one and you may not get anything on the second unless you regularly receive large volumes of mail. The Royal Mail

If you need to receive mail in London before you actually get there and have no friends or colleagues whose address you can use, enlist an Accommodation Address Agent (this is their classification in the *Yellow Pages*) to set up an address. If you haven't got anyone in London to sort this out for you, you should be able to get hold of a *London Yellow Pages* in a good public library.

delivers letters to the stated address and seems to take scant regard of names; thus you may receive at your address letters for people who lived there years ago and whom you have never heard of. By the same token, a letter that bears your name as the addressee but an incorrect address has little chance of finding its way to you.

Your letterbox also serves as an opportunity for the world to bring printed information to your attention. There is no law against literature and leaflets being distributed via letterboxes, and you will regularly find all sorts of advertising coming to you this way, such as takeaway menus, notices of minicab companies and various promotional offers.

UTILITIES: ELECTRICITY, GAS, PHONE AND WATER

Most utilities in London are provided by privatised monopolies—companies formerly under government control that have been sold off at different times under Conservatives governments. A feeling prevails that this situation is the worst of all possible worlds: companies providing essential services who are accountable mainly to their shareholders, and who seem in general to be more interested in maintaining and increasing profits rather than in improving services. All of the utility companies are under the scrutiny of watchdog organisations that allegedly argue the consumer's case, but the watchdogs themselves are largely run by establishment figures drawn from the same lofty socioeconomic strata as the company directors, and it is questionable whether the watchdogs can play any useful role for the consumer when they enjoy such a cosy relationship with the utility companies.

Be that as it may, you may have no choice but to get your services from these providers, and so economical use is the only way for you to save money. Following is a rundown on the four services listed above. If you are in rental accommodation, you should get the account in your name for any utility that you are required to pay for. This will certainly be true of the telephone, but may vary for other services. The general rule is that if your dwelling has its own supply of gas, electricity or water that you do not share with other tenants or residents of the building, then you should have the account in your name. In all cases, you should also be sure that there is no outstanding account for the address of your residence which is owed by a former tenant. If such an account is payable, you must make it clear to the provider in question that you wish to begin a new service, that you have no connection with the former tenant or owner, and that you are not responsible for paying any amount that may be due.

Utilities

Any of the utility companies may require you to pay a deposit in order to establish service. This is particularly true of the telephone. If you are moving into an area or an address known for bill delinquency, or if you speak English with an accent other than that of a native speaker, chances are greater that you will be asked to pay a deposit.

Gas and Electricity

As a result of the government's encouragement of free enterprise and competition, there is an increasingly wide (and confusing) variety of power companies in London that can offer you gas and electricity. While it is possible to get your gas from one company and your electricity from another (in some parts of the capital, you may *have* to do this), companies such as London Electricity and British Gas encourage you to buy both power sources from them by offering you savings incentives; so we treat the two together here. If you are moving into a property that has been occupied before, the easiest thing to do at the outset is simply to take over whatever service arrangement is in place in order to keep the energy flowing; then, when you have more time, you can investigate whether it would be beneficial for you to switch gas or electricity suppliers.

The electricity supplied to London is 240-volt, 50Hz. In all likelihood, the place you move into will already have the electricity hooked up and a meter installed, even if it is a new flat or house: builders usually take care of this. You should contact the existing electricity supplier before moving in to set up your account with them and to verify the date on which service billed to you is to begin. When you move into your property, read the meter yourself and make sure that the first bill you receive shows the reading that was current when you moved in.

Piped natural gas is provided to all homes and businesses in London. The procedure here is essentially the same as for electricity: notify the existing gas company of your intended residency, set up your account and read the meter yourself when you move in.

Consult the seller, landlord or estate agent about what company or companies currently supplies power to your residence. Look in the phone book under 'Gas' and 'Electricity' to contact the various companies offering these services.

Telephones

British Telecom is the main provider of local telephone service in London, but more newly established companies such as Mercury and Orange are beginning to get a share of the market. You have an even greater choice of long distance carriers, though they require either the use of special equipment or the dialling of special codes to access them.

The Trouble with BT

Of all monopoly providers in London, BT is the hands-down favourite for criticism, which in most cases is not far off the mark. Hardly anyone is without a story of their unhappy experience of this large and often unresponsive behemoth. To BT's credit, it has striven to improve its performance record with massive investment in new technology, but if you are coming from any modern, developed country, you may find BT's residential service slow and quaint—and probably expensive to boot.

As soon as you have settled on your residence, determine whether phone service exists there already. If it does, arrange to have the service transferred to your name. This is not very costly (though you may be required to pay a deposit) and is by far the easiest way to get telephone service established. If there is no telephone service where you intend to live, set up an appointment as early as possible to have a line installed; it can sometimes take weeks. You are required to have only the line. You are not required to use BT telephones, which you lease from them at not very attractive rates. You may wish to buy a telephone and/or answering machine from an electronics shop, making sure that it is compatible for use with BT equipment (most phones sold in the UK will meet this requirement). There is a hefty charge for having new service installed, more than £ 100 in addition to the deposit you may be required to pay.

By default, your name and telephone number will be listed in the next published London directory, and will be available to enquirers through directory enquiries. If you wish to be unlisted, you should request for your number to be ex-directory. (See 'Telephone Directories' in the Resource Guide for details on the system of London directories.) There are a number of other services offered by BT, including call forwarding, call waiting and caller ID. These only work on so-called 'modernised' exchanges, and the prevalence of these is rather spotty throughout the capital. If you want any of these services, you can request them when you order your line installation or changeover.

London's dialling code is 020. Telephone numbers consists of eight digits; those beginning with 7 correspond roughly to Inner London, those with 8 to Outer London. Calls within code 020 are charged at the local rate; calls to numbers beginning with other prefixes are charged at a higher rater. You need dial only the eight-digit phone number when calling within London; for calling outside from London, start with the full prefix. You should tell callers from abroad that they omit the '0' before 020 when calling you. The country code for Britain is 44, which foreign callers to you will also need.

> If you expect to be phoning to your home country or elsewhere abroad while in London, take advantage of one of the many telephone companies that provide cut-rate long distance service. They require you to dial a special access code but their rates are vastly cheaper, sometimes as much as 50 per cent less than BT or its main rival Mercury. These companies, such as SwiftCall and First Telecom, advertise in the London dailies.

Water

RWE Thames Water (Website: http://thames-water.com) supplies potable but not very tasty drinking water to all of London, except a tiny corner in the north-west of the capital, supplied by Three Valleys Water (Website: http://www.3valleys.co.uk). As in the case of electricity and gas, chances are good that water will be flowing already when you move in. In most cases water is not metered, but it's possible that a former tenant or owner installed a water meter, in which case you would take it over. Water bills come once yearly and can be paid all at once, or in two instalments at six-monthly intervals. A single person in a one-bed flat can expect to pay about £ 120 per year for water; it goes up from there.

HOME INSURANCE

Before you finally settle down in front of the telly with that cup of tea in your new house or flat, consider what insurance coverage you should have. Remember that burglary is a thriving industry in London, and no neighbourhood is exempt.

If you are a house or flat owner, you will know about required insurance from your lender, as it must be in place when you assume ownership of the property. Typically, lenders themselves offer insurance policies that can be paid for in monthly instalments along with your mortgage. These, however, are rarely the best deals you can get; you will be better off going to an insurance broker, or inquiring yourself of various insurance companies that advertise. The best-known companies often have the reputation of providing the best service, but rarely of offering the best rates.

Household insurance is of two kinds: buildings insurance and contents insurance. Owners need both kinds; renters only need contents insurance, and then only for the things you own; the landlord, in principal, insures everything else. The two types of insurance are drawn up in separate policies and may be obtained from the same or from different companies.

Formulas determine the cost of your buildings insurance, based on a number of factors such as the age of your dwelling, the type of construction and whether the area it is in is subject to subsidence. Generally speaking, you must insure to the cost of rebuilding. The cost of contents insurance depends on the value of goods you want to insure. Most companies have special clauses and charges for high-risk items such as computers, audio and video equipment and bicycles. All of greater London is designated by actuaries for the highest insurance rates in Britain, because of the risk of theft. A few companies may give marginally cheaper rates in selected post codes, but you can generally expect to pay as much as twice what your country cousins pay to insure—it's just part of the price of living in London.

FINDING YOUR HOME ON THE INTERNET

In the years since the first edition of this book was published, the Internet has developed into the almost indispensable information tool that it is today. It can help you find a home even before you get there. Most estate agents have their own websites with sophisticated search facilities; you can use the information earlier in this book to zero in on a location (always the most important first step) and then proceed to the Internet.

Finding Your Home Online

Use a search engine to find estate agents in London, or search on any of these better known agents who serve most areas of London: Allen Douglas Spiro, Bairstow Eves, Bennett-Walden, Castles, Joyce Copping, Shaw & Co. or Winkworth & Co. A search on 'London property' will return you enough hits to keep your fingers walking for some time. You can also access the extensive property listings in *Loot* by clicking on 'Property' at website: http://www.loot.com.

WHAT TO DO WITH ALL THAT MONEY

We've been spending money since the start of this chapter without any notion of how to manage it and where to keep any that may be left. This section will look at the ways to manage your money in London, and to suggest a few other things you can do with it if you have any left after the food and rent.

Sterling

Britain has used a decimal currency system for more than 20 years now, and the last coins in circulation from the old 'LSD' system (which stood for pounds, shillings and pence, curiously) have now vanished. Money today goes by very prosaic names: coins are named for their value (e.g. 5 p, 10 p, 20 p and so forth, up to the newly released £ 2 coin) except for the two smallest: 1 p, which is called a penny, and 2 p, which is called tuppence. Notes come in denominations of £ 5, £ 10, £ 20 and £ 50 and are all named for their value: a £ 20 note, for example. The two smallest have nicknames: a 'fiver' and a 'tenner'. Occasionally, you will hear older terms for money, especially 'bob' for shilling, as in, "It costs 10 bob." Think of this as 10 x 5 p, or 50 p. The slang and informal term for pounds is 'quid', plural 'quid'—"Lend me 50 quid, will ya, mate?" A 'guinea' is a former coin, worth the current equivalent of £ 1.05, and is sometimes used in horse racing and other esoteric contexts.

Banks and Banking

The banking system in Britain is highly developed and well integrated into everyone's household economy. Salaries are usually paid directly into accounts, and it is very easy to arrange for bills to be paid automatically out of your bank account, including your mortgage, all utility bills and any other regular weekly, monthly or quarterly payment. All of this is done from and to one's current account, which is also a chequeing account. It comes with a supply of cheques, deposit slips and usually a debit card that does three things for you:

- You can use it to pay for goods in many shops by debiting your account directly.
- It serves as a cheque guarantee card for cheques of up to either £ 50 or £ 100.
- It is used to withdraw cash from automatic teller machines (ATMs), or cashpoints, as they are usually called.

You should insist on getting this card when you open a current account if it isn't offered as part of the deal; without it, your account is not very practical.

When you open your account, be prepared to show the bank manager evidence of your good credit in your own country. This will be especially useful if you speak accented English or if you come from non-European stock. If you can open an account with a hefty sum, all the better. A letter from your UK employer will also serve as a useful reference, and if you have already established residency in London, bring along evidence of this as well when setting up your account.

The two methods for making automatic payments from your account differ slightly. A standing order is an authority that you give your bank to pay a fixed amount to a named party at regular intervals (e.g. weekly or on the same day every month). A direct debit is an authority that you give to one of your creditors to withdraw varying amounts from your account at regular intervals. Standing orders are useful for regular payments that do not vary in amount from one payment to the next, such as loan repayments or your mortgage. Direct debits are useful for bills that vary in amount, such as your gas or electric bill. All the utility companies strongly prefer that you pay your bills this way, and they will offer you every encouragement to do so.

Banking in the High Street

Most Londoners bank with one of the high street banks, so called because their branches tend to be in high streets (discussed later in the chapter). There are four leviathans: Barclays, HSBC, Lloyd's TSB and NatWest. Banks that were formerly building societies, such as the Halifax, are also popular, along with branchless or 'online' banks, such as First Direct. If you travel widely or often, this is the most convenient kind of bank.

There is little to choose among the high street banks. All of them compete keenly for business, but not so keenly that at any given time you will find one of them offering a much better deal in the way of more interest or lesser service charges. In choosing which to open your account in, the most important consideration is probably the particular branch where you will do any banking that is not done automatically or by machine. And in looking at the particular branch of a bank, the main criterion should be: how long is the abominable queue that you typically have to wait in before you can be served? If you come from anywhere except the developing world, you are likely to find it completely unconscionable that institutions whose fortunes are extracted from the public have so little regard for serving them. But we are told that the English like to queue, so perhaps it is to be viewed as a service of the bank that they provide the opportunity for you to cool your heels for five to 10 minutes while waiting to put money into your account.

The banks' reputations for service vary only slightly; the results of polls appear occasionally in the press showing what the man on the street thinks of his bank, and it usually isn't very much. This may explain why so many Londoners have used the online or branchless banks (such as First Direct), which usually rate far higher in the polls. With these, you can conduct most of your banking via a secure connection on the Internet from anywhere in the world. Anything that requires direct human intervention is handled by telephone communication.

The average working or studying Londoner can do most of his or her banking electronically and doesn't actually need to

visit a branch. Salaries are usually paid directly into accounts, and cash, when needed, can be obtained from cash points. If this is all you need to do in the way of banking, then you may want to choose your bank on the basis of the convenience of cash points in relation to where you work, study or live. In more central parts of London, you're never more than a short walk away from cashpoints of several different banks, but as you get further out, the selection is more limited. The banks cooperate in letting account holders of other banks use their machines. You can use your UK-bank issued card at a cash point operated by any other UK bank without being charged a fee; most machines can also show you the balance in your account, even if the machine is not operated by your bank. Customers of branchless banks can also use cash points without charge, providing that your bank is owned by one of the regular high street banks.

Nearly all cash points dispense money to holders of VISA or MasterCard credit cards in the form of cash advances, which incur fees. Most UK automatic tellers are members of either the Cirrus or the Plus network.

The Right Bank For You

With nearly all the high street banks offering telephone and Internet services of some kind, and with free access to the cash points of nearly all banks, it may seem that one bank is as good as the other. As a foreigner in London, however, it pays to shop around to find the bank that meets all your needs. It is far easier to start banking in the UK than to change banks later, when you have multiple automatic transactions set up. Contact two or more banks and get specifics about how each bank can meet your needs. Here are some points of particular interest to foreign Londoners: Does the bank have a special relationship with your country or with banks in your country? How easy are international wire transfers (see below)? Can you access and manipulate your accounts online and from anywhere?

Building Societies

The choice between banks and building societies in the UK is slowly becoming erased, as building societies convert themselves to banks and increasingly offer all the same services as banks. Historically, building societies have operated as mutual, non-profit institutions that served mainly to hold savings accounts and to offer mortgages, which they still do, but most of them now also offer current accounts that rival in service anything that the high street banks have.

If there is any shortcoming to their service, it is that they have a smaller selection of cash points from which funds can be withdrawn. But this doesn't stop a number of Londoners from doing all their banking at a building society.

Building Societies or Banks?

Abbey National was the first major building society to convert itself to a bank, and now the Halifax Building Society, merging with the former Leeds Building Society, has followed suit. Talk swarms in the media about other conversions.

Moving Money In and Out of London

The 19th century politician Joseph Chamberlain called London the clearing-house of the world. It probably still is that today, as vast sums of money and other negotiables change hands every hour between parties around the world here. What this means for the private citizen is that moving money into and out of London is in general very easy and can be done in any number of different ways. Fees charged by banks for these services are generally a percentage of the total involved, with various minima and maxima relating to different methods—so which method will prove most economical depends on your bank and on the sum involved.

Bringing Money In

For smaller amounts, roughly up to £ 1000, you can use an ATM card from a foreign bank (provided that it works in one of the major networks such as Cirrus or Plus) to withdraw sterling from cash points in London; most of the banks have a limit of between £ 300 and £ 500 per day. The exchange rate is usually quite competitive, as good as you would get for traveller's cheques or cash at any bank. For larger sums, an international wire transfer from a foreign bank to your London bank is the best all-purpose method.

Sending Money Out

For small sums, you may find it easiest to buy traveller's cheques in Sterling or in some other currency. Cheques in the main European currencies as well as US dollars and Yen are available from London banks. For larger sums, there are generally two options: depending on the currency involved, you may be able to purchase a money order or banker's draft in the foreign currency of your choice at only a nominal commission. The post office has arrangements for sending money orders to many foreign nations, especially Commonwealth countries. Banks sell banker's drafts in various currencies. If these methods aren't feasible, arrange an international wire transfer through your London bank payable to a bank abroad.

If you bank with a large, well-known bank in your own country, it may well have an office in London. Normally, these offices exist to facilitate business accounts; but in some cases, they perform services for ordinary account holders, and this is particularly true of banks from the developing world. For large or complicated international transactions, it may be wise to consult the bank in your own country to see if they have representation in London that could help you.

YOU AND THE TAXMAN

If you reside in the UK and have an income, you are liable to UK income tax. This is true even if your income comes from abroad, or if it is nominally unearned, proceeding from investments or interest. The Inland Revenue is the government department responsible for the collection of income tax. If you are regularly employed in Britain, they will already know about you, via your employer, and there is little you will have to do about your taxes, aside from stand helplessly by while you see the sums disappearing from your pay packet. If you are self-employed, you are responsible for monitoring your own income, and making (usually quarterly) payments to the Inland Revenue, towards a return that you file once a year giving a full account of your income and outgoings.

Double Taxes

Most countries have tax treaties with the UK that prevent you from being taxed both in the UK and in your own country. The most usual arrangement is for you to pay UK income tax while resident in the UK, and take a tax credit or exemption in your own country. Authorities in your own country will be the best source of information about this.

The general philosophy that prevails about income tax in the UK is that the Inland Revenue knows what they are doing, and if you just leave them alone, they will take only what is owed them and treat you fairly. A surprising number of people actually believe this. It may well be true, but you are welcome in any year to file a tax return, and as a foreigner in London, it is recommended that you do. Unless you are permanently settled in Britain and have no income, property or other financial ties abroad, your tax situation is probably not as routine and simple as the average working Briton's, and it is worth your while to find out just where all the money is going, and whether the Inland Revenue is really entitled to all that it takes.

VAT (Value Added Tax)

Most retail and consumer goods and services (food and clothing are the main exceptions) in Britain are subject to a whopping 17.5 per cent tax called VAT, which is collected by the Customs and Excise Department of the government. This goes to support the behemoth known as the European Union, which distributes the largesse in a way so inept and inequitable that hardly a day passes without the press exposing some new scam involving immense sums. However, there's no point contesting it, because if you live in Britain, you have to pay it. It is already figured into the asking price of many goods, but for more expensive items, the advertised price may be exclusive of VAT, and if you fail to notice this you will be in for a shock when you reach the till.

If you are a business owner or self-employed, it may be to your advantage to register for VAT. By doing so, you will receive an official VAT number. You have to keep close account of the VAT that you spend and collect, but if you spend a lot more than you receive, you are entitled to the difference in the form of a refund. To find out about this program and whether you can or should be participating in it, visit HM Customs & Excise at website: http://www.hmce.gov.uk.

More for You, Less for Them

Britain's Conservative governments of recent years have encouraged the development of a capitalist mentality for the average wage earner, and have created a number of schemes whereby you can invest your money tax-free, or otherwise get tax relief. In most cases, as a foreign resident of London, you enjoy the same tax incentives that a Briton does, so it is worth your while knowing about them.

Among the more popular deals available are:

- TESSA: This stands for Tax Exempt Special Savings Account, and is available to all UK taxpayers. Money must be kept in savings for a period of five years and can be added to annually. Details are available from building societies and banks.
- PEP: A PEP is a Personal Equity Plan, a scheme invented by the government in order to create a nation of shareholders. You can invest up to £ 6000 per year in securities (shares, bonds, mutual funds, etc.), and in some cases up to £ 9000 per year. Any profits you

make on such trading are not taxed. PEPs are available in high risk, low risk and secure flavours, and are offered by a number of different investment and insurance companies. The daily newspapers are littered with advertisements for them.

- Tax Relief on Mortgage Interest: Interest that you pay on the first £ 30,000 of your UK mortgage (provided that it is for your principal residence) is subject to tax relief. In other words, it is deducted from your income before taxes are assessed. This usually happens automatically in a scheme called MIRAS, which is administered jointly by the Inland Revenue and mortgage lenders. The amount you save is typically deducted from your monthly mortgage payment. Participation in this scheme is usually arranged when you get your mortgage.

- National Savings: The government operates several schemes to encourage savings through an institution called National Savings. Look for advertisements in the Saturday press or pick up leaflets in a main post office, where you can also pay money in and initiate investments of various kinds. One of the more popular of these schemes is Premium Bonds. The bonds you hold earn no interest, but the numbers of the bonds are pooled for frequent drawings, in which the winners are awarded (usually) small or (sometimes) large cash prizes, which are tax free.

Oddly enough, the government doesn't tax lottery and Pools winnings. Maybe you'll get lucky.

HOW TO SPEND

It remains only to set you down firmly in the streets of London with whatever cash you have left in hand and steer you in the direction of places where you can spend it. You should be warned in advance that you will be able to spend it very quickly, and with little effort. London is an expensive city by any standard. Manufactured goods, particularly imported ones, will seem exorbitantly high-priced to you unless you already live in the EU or perhaps in Japan. Londoners on a budget make the best of the situation by shopping in markets (discussed on page 141) when possible, and taking advantage of special offers. Besides the markets, there are a number of other places and districts of London that are more or less designed to part you, amicably if at all possible, from your cash.

Shopping in London is mostly a six-day-a-week affair, but the longstanding tradition of shops closing on Sunday is slowly eroding, and in any case there have always been markets that operate on Sundays. Shops are open from 9:30 am or so to 6:00 pm, but large shops are typically open late one night a week (usually Thursday), while small neighbourhood shops are typically closed one afternoon per week (often Wednesday).

The High Street

The high street in London is as much a state of mind as a place. Its anticipated demise is often remarked on and lamented in newspapers. But it is far from dead now, and the geography of London is probably such that it will always thrive. There are few places to build vast suburban-type shopping centres and malls, and the density of housing in residential areas makes it imperative that a high street containing all essential

A high street in East London: one-stop shopping for the neighbourhood.

businesses and services for the householder be located not very far from where he or she lives.

High streets all over London are remarkably similar in appearance and you will very soon get a feel for the look of them: an endless repetition of small shops with glass fronts and a sign (called a fascia) in some glaring colour across the top of the windows and door. Most high street shops are small and independently owned, so there is quite an eclectic variety. You will also find branches of various institutions (banks, supermarkets, chemists, building societies and travel agents) as well as dry cleaners, florists, hairdressers, newsagents, off-licences and the like. The high street aims to supply all of your regular household needs: food, medicine, hardware, clothing, appliances and so forth.

Prices in high street shops are usually competitive within London, and you won't necessarily find a better deal by going far out of your way.

The Post Office and the Royal Mail

For many people, the central feature of the high street is the post office. In addition to selling stamps and handling mail, post offices offer a dizzying range of consumer and financial services. There are two types of post office: main post offices, which offer a full range of services, and sub-post offices, which are franchised to shopkeepers and are generally found in high streets inside a shop that has some other business—convenience foods, stationery and the like. Both kinds of post offices keep roughly the same hours, which are business hours (Monday to Friday and Saturday morning), though sub-post offices normally have a half-holiday one afternoon per week, typically on Wednesday or Thursday, and they may also close for one hour at lunch.

Several kinds of bills can be paid in a post office: in fact, any bill that comes to you with a payment form attached to it called a Giro. All utility bills can be paid in this way, though the post office may make a small charge for the service. Additionally, post offices:

- Distribute and accept passport applications
- Sell TV licences

- Accept deposits for National Savings
- Distribute forms for driving licences, vehicle licences and vehicle registration applications
- Operate the Alliance & Leicester Giro banking service
- Trade in foreign currencies (at some main post offices)

Finally, benefits of all sorts payable by the Department of Work and Pensions are distributed through post offices. This is largely the reason for the astonishingly long queues, particularly on Monday mornings, when those who depend on government cash injections line up to get them.

Within the UK, two main kinds of postal service are offered: first class and second class. First class is quite reliable and delivers letters almost anywhere in the country on the day after posting. Second class is cheaper and takes two or three days to most destinations.

Markets

Outdoor markets are as much a part of London life as high streets and can be found everywhere, in many cases right on or adjoining a high street. Street markets specialising in food will be talked about in the following chapter. There are markets that sell consumer goods besides, or in addition to,

A market trader hawks his wares.

food everywhere in London. Those in your neighbourhoods will probably come to your attention shortly after you establish yourself. A few others have achieved fame or notoriety beyond their boundaries, and are noted in the box below.

Famous Markets in London

- **Bermondsey Square SE1** (Friday morning)
  Also called New Caledonian market, this is a good antiques and junk market. Come early to get the bargains—it is on the verge of being discovered by the tourist horde.
- **Brick Lane E1** (Sunday morning)
  London's premiere market for secondhand goods, but there is also a thriving section that sells new merchandise. It is centred on Brick Lane but extends into several side streets. You can pick up books, clothing, household items and furniture, all used and on the cheap, but you can also buy a new bicycle, birdcage, or do your grocery shopping for the week.
- **Camden Market NW1** (Saturday and Sunday)
  This is really a handful of markets grown into one. There is a clothing and general market centred on Camden High Street, a collectibles market on the canal and a crafts market around Camden Lock. All are quite popular with young people and have an air of the bygone hippie era about them.
- **Columbia Road E1** (Sunday morning)
  The best London market specialising in plants and flowers. You won't find better prices on bedding plants, trees and shrubs for your garden, bulbs and the like. Cut flowers are also available at knockdown prices, but they won't be as fresh as those from florists; in many cases, they are what the florists had left over at the end of the week.
- **Covent Garden WC2** (seven days)
  This is now primarily a tourist attraction with all the

Shopping Centres and Districts

London has yet to develop many of the enclosed, multi-vendor shopping centres that are found in some other parts of the world. There are a few in outer London, including Bentalls Centre in Kingston-upon-Thames, Brent Cross

attendant irritations of the genre. For the Londoner, the main interest is probably the stalls operated by craftspeople who sell their unique creations which make excellent and unusual gifts for the folks back home.

- **Exmouth Market EC1** (Tuesday and Friday) and **Farringdon Road EC1** (Monday and Friday)
  These are near each other and both offer used books. Go on Friday to take in both at once.
- **Greenwich Market SE10**
  (Saturday and Sunday morning)
  This market offers antiques, aspiring antiques and used books, among some other more tourist-oriented merchandise.
- **Petticoat Lane E1** (Sunday morning)
  Just off Bishopsgate near Liverpool Street Station, this has become a main tourist attraction in recent years. Souvenirs of London are probably cheaper here than elsewhere in the city. There is also a good selection of London-made leather jackets and all sorts of other clothing. Be prepared for the crowds.
- **Portobello Road W11** (Saturday)
  This market has also been nearly completely overrun by tourists, but offers interesting antiques, old prints and books and London memorabilia for those who can stand the crush.
- **Spitalfields Market E1** (seven days)
  On the site of the former wholesale produce market of the same name, this market is relatively new and is still seeking definition. There are food stalls, craft stalls, used goods and various other wares on offer.

Shopping Centre in north-west London NW4, Putney Exchange Shopping Centre in Putney SW15 and Wood Green Shopping Centre in north London N22. Whiteley's in Queensway W2 is the only central London mall; it is relatively new and mostly upmarket.

North-west London has a relatively small but unique shopping mall, in that it houses shops that sell only eastern Asian goods. Oriental City, at 399 Edgware Road NW9, has a vast supermarket with mostly Japanese and Chinese foods, but also sections devoted to Indian, Korean and Thai imports. There is also a large bookstore, a food court, sit-down restaurants and shops selling other imported consumer goods. For the kids, there is one of the best Sega games arcades in Europe.

Other areas of London that are especially associated with shopping are:

- **Oxford Street**
  This is where the world shops, and if you don't believe it, just go on a Saturday afternoon. Many of London's well-known department and chainstores are here, including BHS, Debenham's, Selfridges, John Lewis, Littlewoods and Marks & Spencer, in addition to hundreds of smaller stores selling clothing, food, books and music.

- **Kensington High Street**
  A wide variety of shops and shoppers are here; several big department stores, lots of fashion boutiques and an indoor market catering mostly to the young.

- **King's Road and Chelsea**
  Designer clothes, especially for those with a figure to wear them. If you have a fashion statement to make, make it here on a Saturday morning for maximum effect.

- **Knightsbridge**
  The place to go if you want to spend slightly more money than you would in Oxford Street. Harrods is the flagship; there are many other boutiques and department stores.

- **Picadilly, Mayfair, Saint James**
  If even Knightsbridge can't satisfy that deep urge, these central London districts are guaranteed to turn your

pockets inside out. Designer clothing, jewellery, fine art and antiques are all on offer. Within this area are Regent Street, New Bond Street and Old Bond Street, all associated with the discerning (and wealthy) shopper. Well known shops are Liberty and Dickins & Jones. But there is also Carnaby Street, mecca for the beautiful people of an earlier era and still popular with young people today who dress every bit as strangely as those of 30 years ago.

Finally, here is a thumbnail guide to providers of various kinds of goods with an emphasis on the shopping list of the new arrival in London. The sorts of goods listed below are available widely; this listing merely points you to the areas and/or shops where you can find them in greatest abundance, thus simplifying the task of comparison shopping:

- Antiques: Upper Street and small streets leading off it, just north of the Angel tube stop, have several dealers. A building called Camden Passage in this area is a mall of small antique dealers. See also the Chelsea Antiques Market in King's Road SW3 and Grays Antique Market in Davies Street W1.
- Appliances: The main chain stores are Comet, Dixon's, Curry's and Tempo, all found in the high street.
- Audio and Video Equipment: Tottenham Court Road for top-of-the-line, specialist equipment; chain appliance stores for ordinary TVs, VCRs and home entertainment equipment.
- Beds: There are no sizable chains or special shopping areas. See the Yellow Pages under bedding, futons and mattresses.
- Books (new): Charing Cross Road and smaller streets leading off it; but don't miss Dillon's in Gower Street WC1 or Hatchard's in Piccadilly.
- Books (used): Charing Cross Road and Bloomsbury, in front of the British Museum. Small, independent new and used bookstores can be found everywhere in London. See also under Markets, above, under 'Books' in the Resource Guide, and check out the vendors under Waterloo Bridge on the south bank of the Thames.

Selfridges on Oxford Street is popular with Londoners and tourists alike.

- Computers: Tottenham Court Road for independent, multi-vendor shops. In outer London, PC World, a computer superstore, has outlets in various shopping centres.
- Clothing: London, being something of a clothes-making and fashion capital, have outlets too numerous to mention. For everyday wear, Oxford Street department stores and boutiques probably offer the best selection all in one place. There are small, independent clothing stores in all high streets, and a few chains with a general range of dependable, everyday clothes such as Burton and Top Man (men), Top Shop, Laura Ashley and Jaeger (women), and Benetton, Gap and Next (men and women). All of Britain is alleged to buy its socks and underwear from Marks & Spencer, who also sell a general line of popular clothing.
- DIY and Home Improvements: For the big stuff—shelving, plumbing fixtures, cabinetry and the like—try one of the chains such as B&Q, Do It All, Homebase, Magnet or Wickes. All of these have outlets mostly in Outer London, but there are a few in Inner London. They sell paint and wallpaper as well. Leyland Paints has several high street branches selling their own brand of paint. Two other high street shops selling paint, wallpaper and related decorating needs are Fads and Homestyle; they're owned by the same company.
- Fabrics (High end): Liberty in Regent Street.
- Fabric (Low end): Ridley Road market E8 or Mile End market E3. There is a good middle market selection at John Lewis in Oxford Street. For fabrics cut and designed for various African and Asian garments, try the Broadway in Southall, Ealing and Commercial Road E1.
- Furniture: Tottenham Court Road (Habitat, Heals, Maples and World of Leather are the main stores) for fashionable stuff; Hackney Road E2, for cheaper imitations of the same. For cheap, self-assembly furniture, the chain store MFI is the best place to go. Ikea, the Swedish furniture chain very much in vogue

now, has two London locations: off the North Circular Road near Wembley and in Croydon. Closer to home, London neighbourhoods contain many independent furniture stores.

- Gardening goods: Neighbourhoods have small, independent garden centres with local knowledge and friendly advice. Big chains such as B&Q and Homebase usually have better prices but less attentive service.

- Hardware: Independent high street hardware stores fight to stay alive in competition with the big DIY chains, but they are often still the handiest source for small home needs. Robert Dyas is a reliable chain with two dozen or so London locations.

- Household Goods: The chain department stores all have good selections, but also check out Argos, a chain of catalogue warehouse/showrooms with several London locations that has good prices on everything for the home.

- Jewellery: Regent Street, Burlington Arcade off Picadilly and New and Old Bond Streets. For run-of-the-mill stuff, there are chain jewellers in every high street.

- Kitchen Appliances: As under appliances, above. Argos also sells most major appliances through its catalogue showrooms, as do the department stores.

- Music (recorded): The three biggest shops are within walking distance of each other if you're feeling energetic: Tower Records at Picadilly Circus, and HMV and the Virgin Mega Store, both in Oxford Street.

- Second-hand Shops: Nearly every high street has a selection of these run by various charities, such as Oxfam, the British Red Cross, the Imperial Cancer Research Fund and Sue Ryder. The general rule is that the nicer the neighbourhood, the better the quality of recycled goods.

- Stationery: Ryman's is a dependable, London-wide chain. Paperchase, especially at their Tottenham Court Road shop, has a wide selection of stationery and greeting cards. Independent stationers in neighbourhoods are competitively priced.

YOU AND THE NANNY STATE

'In general, the art of government consists in
taking as much money as possible from one part
of the citizens to give to the other.'
—Voltaire

Citizens of Commonwealth countries resident in London
and Irish nationals both have the right to vote in British
elections. Other foreigners in London enjoy no rights of
participating in government at any level. If you are not of
the Commonwealth or Ireland, you cannot vote in either
local or national elections, and you can vote in European
elections (for members of the European Parliament) only if
you are already an EU national. Once you have observed the
British political process, which you can hardly avoid doing
given the saturation coverage provided by the media, you will
probably be deeply relieved that you have no responsibility
for nor obligation to the continuous drone of invective that
constitutes British politics.

The Government in a Nutshell

As a spectator in the political process, you may enjoy the
view more with a scorecard, provided herewith in the form
of a brief description. The essence of British democracy
is the House of Commons, where Members of Parliament
(MPs) sit, each representing one of the 659 constituencies
into which the United Kingdom is divided. Greater London
is divided into 84 constituencies, and thus has 84 members
of Parliament, about 13 per cent of all MPs. But London MPs
rarely, if ever, form any sort of voting bloc: the rule for MPs
is very much to follow the party line.

The government is formed by the majority party in the
House of Commons, which over the greater part of the last
two decades was the Conservative party, but since 1997
has been the Labour party. The leader of the ruling party is
the prime minister. He (or she) appoints MPs from his own
party to fill cabinet posts. These MPs are ministers, and have
responsibility for various areas of government: defence,
transport, trade, health, education and so forth.

When Parliament is in session, the ministers sit on the front bench in the House of Commons, and are sometimes collectively referred to as the front bench. The government sits on the left side of the House of Commons, as seen on television; the Opposition sits on the right side.

MPs who are not members of the governing party are members of the opposition. Members of the opposition are called upon to react to any move the government makes, and predictably, they oppose it. The opposition forms what is called a 'shadow cabinet', with various MPs serving as spokespeople for areas of government which, if they were in power, they would be responsible for. This group of MPs constitutes the opposition's front bench. The leader of the opposition would be the prime minister if the opposition had the opportunity to form a government.

Each year in November, when Parliament opens, the government announces its legislative program for the year in a speech read by the Queen. During the course of the Parliament, the government introduces its legislation in the form of bills. They are debated and voted on. In most cases, the program is successful, because the government has a majority (it would not be the government if it did not).

Chauffeurs await bigwigs at the Guildhall, where the City is governed.

A second legislative house, the House of Lords, has limited powers to review and modify legislation introduced in the House of Commons. Its members are either titled members of the aristocracy who have the right to sit in the House of Lords owing to their lofty birth, or 'life peers' who have been given a non-hereditary title by the government. Topdogs in the Church of England also sit in the House of Lords; they are called the Lords Spiritual (other Lords being called the Lords Temporal). The third element of Parliament is the monarch, currently the Queen, whose official capacity is mainly ceremonial, but who is thought to be influential in an unofficial, personal capacity.

British Law and European Law

As a member of the European Union, Britain is obliged to promulgate all laws and regulations agreed by the member states of the Union, and to defer to European law in cases where it might come into conflict with British law. This fact is the spawning ground for the most vehement political debate in Britain today, and it is a debate that will continue as long as Britain remains part of the union. A day does not pass that the media or one of the political parties does not seize upon some issue that stems from the conflict that many view as inherent in Britain's EU membership and the looming issue of monetary union—EMU as it is called—in which all member states will share in a macroeconomy and use a single currency. The foreigner in London needn't be unduly concerned with all of this, but it is worth following developments if your private or state pension might be affected by the eventual disappearance of Sterling and its replacement with ECUs (European Currency Units).

The Foreigner and the Government

While residency in Britain doesn't entitle you to any form of participation in the political process, you do not live 'outside the law' in any sense. On the contrary, residency has the effect of automatically enrolling you in a vast, mostly benign, but sometimes demanding bureaucracy. There is money for you to pay, and in some cases, benefits for you to collect. Unless you come from Scandinavia or some other wealthy and advanced socialist state, you will probably be amazed by the number and level of government handouts on offer in Britain, and you may be appalled at how much of your money goes to pay for them.

As an ordinary foreigner living in London (i.e. one not enjoying diplomatic immunity), you are subject to the same laws as the natives. If the length of time you are permitted to stay in the UK is limited, you may be subject to special laws, such as the necessity to either leave the country, or apply for an extension on your permitted stay. You have a right of appeal if a decision should be reached that you should be deported. In most such cases, you are not entitled to any free legal advice or representation.

Other aspects of your rights and benefits under the law may vary according to your type of residency, so before examining them, we will look first at the various circumstances that constitute legal, borderline and downright shady ways of being a London resident.

Living in London: The Credentials

As a foreigner having no 'right of abode' (discussed below) in Britain, there are a number of officially sanctioned ways for you to be legally resident in London. Unfortunately, simply wanting to live there will not be enough to qualify you. At the outset, it must be said that the issue of legal residency in Britain is a deep and tortuous subject that consumes the efforts and salaries of countless civil servants and lawyers. If you want to go into it in more detail than is possible here, or if you are surfing for an obscure category under which you might ride a wave into London, start with the booklet *Immigration into Britain*, published by the Foreign & Commonwealth Office and available from most British Consulates abroad.

There are several conventional categories under which foreigners can make a home in London. You will note that a few of those described below require an entry clearance. This is in effect a government-designed insurance policy against admitting anyone who is ostensibly qualified if a consular officer feels the person shouldn't be admitted. Entry clearances may be in the form of a visa, letter of consent, or entry certificate. They must be applied for and issued abroad, and must be presented on arrival in Britain. Here then are the lines that, with proper and convincing documentation to back them up, may lead you to a happy home in London.

"I've Got a Job to Do"

A UK government-issued work permit is the most straightforward, if not the easiest way to become resident in London. You may work for a UK-based concern that hires you, or for a foreign based concern that posts you to London. In either case, the Department of Employment (DOE—part of a government ministry) must first sanction your employment, and this must be done before you enter the UK. Your employer must satisfy the DOE that the job you are being hired for could not be filled by a qualified British or EU national. In practice, this means that you must have some recognised professional qualification or high level or unique expertise in your field.

When you enter the country, you must have your work permit in hand. Your passport will then be stamped in a way that permits you to work in the job you've been hired for.

Permits are usually issued for a period of a year. Thereafter, they may be extended (provided that your employer and the DOE agree) up to four years, after which time settlement can be applied for.

A small number of professions can gain provisional entry to Britain for a year without a permit, but must have an entry clearance. The main categories here are:

- Ministers and others with a full-time religious vocation
- Correspondents who work for foreign media concerns and are on assignment in Britain
- Writers and artists who can support themselves off their own work (you will have to document this convincingly)
- Servants of diplomats

All people in these categories must show that they can support themselves and their dependants without recourse to public funds.

"My Grandmother Knew Lloyd George"

If you have a grandparent who was a bona fide British subject, you may be admitted to Britain to take a job, or look for one. It is implicit for those entering under this category that you are fit to work. You will be granted provisional residency for up to four years, after which time you can apply for settlement. There is a small catch here, in that an entry clearance is required.

"They'll Kill Me If I Go Back"

Britain is a signatory of the 1951 UN Convention and Protocol relating to the Status of Refugees, and thus is required to consider the applications of those who arrive in Britain, having escaped political or religious persecution in their own country. Today, you would be hard pressed to find a hotter political potato than this: a debate rages, with vehement arguments from all points of view about the desirability of Britain absorbing ever increasing numbers of political refugees, or those who claim to be refugees, from abroad. Londoners are often at the heart of the debate since it is in London that most asylum seekers arrive, and initially settle. The trend of the government in recent years has been to confer full refugee status on fewer and fewer applicants, while the number of applications continues to grow.

Starting in 1996, applications for asylum are not entertained from those who enter Britain under any other pretext and then attempt to change their status. Another new government directive is to refuse applications from those who arrive from a 'safe' country, even if it was a stepping stone on their journey to the UK. Nevertheless, thousands of would-be refugees still arrive in Britain monthly, most of them in London, and they are given leave to remain at least until their case is decided by the Home Office.

"I Want to Set Up Shop"

If you can satisfy a deeply-probing enquiry from the DOE concerning the sincerity and viability of your intentions, you can come to London and set up your own business. In general, this requires that you will be fully occupied in the new business, that it is a needed business and that you are prepared to transfer £ 200,000 in cash at the outset to get yourself set up. You must also show that your business will support you, and will generate new, paid, full-time employment for people already in Britain. If you satisfy these conditions, you may be issued an entry clearance, which is required for those entering under this category.

"I'm Rich, and Also a Very Nice Person"

If you are aging and reasonably well-off, it may be possible for you to set up residency in London, provided that you can satisfy the Home Office of your ability to support yourself off your own wealth and that you are a person of sufficiently good character to merit a home in the UK. This category is called the retired person of independent means. You need £ 200,000 cash and evidence of a continuing income of £ 25,000 per year to pull this one off. Finally, there are stipulations that you have some connection to Britain, and that your presence would be in the general interest of the country.

"I'm Rich and Want to Get Richer"
You can enter Britain as an investor, provided that you come with disposable assets of at least £ 1,000,000 and can show that you intend to invest not less than £ 750,000 in UK companies and securities. You are forbidden from taking employment (except self-employment) and must intend to make Britain your main home. An entry clearance is required.

"I Want to Enrich My Mind"
If you are accepted for a full-time (usually at least 15 hours per week) course of study in Britain, you are entitled to residency that is coterminous with your status as a student. Your course of study must be of a single subject or of related subjects and lead to a degree or qualification. You cannot rely on public funds for any of your expenses, but you may, with permission, take work during your holidays, or part-time while studying. When your studies are finished, so is your residency. You may not switch to student status if you entered the country under some other category, nor may you switch from being a student to being some other kind of resident. There are numerous other subsidiary provisions applying to students, all designed to thwart those who would cleverly use this category of residency as a springboard for something more permanent.

"I Want to Be a Dogsbody for a Middle-Class Family While Learning English"
Unmarried, childless females aged 17–27 who come from a European country or Turkey (there are a few exceptions, most prominently Albania, Poland, Bulgaria and Rumania), can come to Britain as an au pair, to live with a British family and ostensibly learn the language, while working for the family as a domestic servant. Two years is the limit in this scheme, and no change of category is permitted.

"I Want to Live Happily Ever After"
Marrying a Briton or other person settled in London may be one of the most artless, or artful ways of getting residency.

The tabloid press thrives on the discovery of marriages of convenience (often laid bare by government investigators) that prove to have been conducted for no reason other than to confer residency on the foreign spouse or fiance; but of course there are thousands who do acquire residency in this way with complete sincerity. You should assume that your marriage to a Briton is likely to be scrutinised if you come from widely differing backgrounds (in terms of race, religion, age or income). Anyone coming to Britain with marriage on the mind, or on the books, must have an entry clearance; applications of this kind are carefully scrutinised. The same applies to those wishing to join a spouse already resident in the UK.

Registration with the Police

If you are a citizen of a Middle Eastern, or of a country with known political instability, drug trafficking problems or large-scale illegal emigration, it may be necessary for you to register with the police. Go to the Metropolitan Police Overseas Visitors Records Office, Brandon House, 180 Borough High Street, London SE 1 1LH. You must produce your passport, the documentation that gave you entry to Britain, two photos and £ 34. Here, you will be issued an alien registration card that must be endorsed by your local police station, and by other local stations should you change your address. Look under 'Law & Policy: Immigration Rules' in the Home Office website at http://www.ind.home office. gov.uk for more information.

The Easy Way: Right of Abode

You can bypass all the foregoing requirements if you have the golden key to a life in Britain called right of abode. In a nutshell, it is the right to enter and settle in Britain without formality. Right of abode is automatic for all British citizens, including those born abroad, and those who became citizens by virtue of their connection with a Commonwealth country or British colony. The various permutations of this category are too complex to detail here. If you are a citizen of the Commonwealth or a former British colony, you should apply to the British Consul or High Commission in your country for information concerning your status.

The other sort of person who may take up residence in Britain more or less at will are EU nationals, which of course includes nationals of the Irish Republic. In the case of all those other than the Irish, some restrictions may apply to permanent settlement, and they are mostly designed to prevent the admission of EU nationals who would come to Britain merely to take advantage of better welfare and social service benefits than are available in their own country. Irish nationals can live and work in Britain at will.

The Hard Way: Perpetual Tourism

If you fall into no category of person to whom the British authorities are happy to offer abode of any kind, your only business in Britain can be as a visitor. In general, visitors (tourists, in other words) are admitted to Britain for an initial period of six months. As a tourist, however, you have no right to employment, no access to welfare and no free use of the National Health Service. So in fact, this is no kind of residency at all, and is not meant to be. While the authorities are not averse to visitors being in Britain, they are very sensitive to any who may wish to take advantage of the many fine benefits available to UK residents.

Citizens of most countries of the world can enter Britain as visitors without formality, but many require visas. These include nearly every African country, most Asian countries and a handful of former Soviet or Soviet bloc countries. In all cases, visas must be applied for abroad and presented on arrival in the UK.

Permanent Residency and Citizenship

The British government doesn't confer anything it calls permanent residency, perhaps because they know that nothing is permanent in this world, or perhaps just because they don't want to create a niche for you that they can't at some point eject you from. After you have been resident in some capacity in Britain for four years, you can generally apply for settlement, which is in effect permanent residency, provided that you continue to make your home in Britain.

This sort of unrestricted residency has several advantages. The main ones are that you are no longer restricted in your activities, particularly in your means of livelihood, as you may have been under some other category; and you no longer have to apply for renewals and extensions of your stay. You also no longer have to maintain your registration with the police, and when you enter and leave the country for holidays or business, you no longer need to fill out an embarkation card (which is mandatory for those with provisional residency). So if you've been around long enough and you wish to stay, it is worth your while to get the stamp in your passport that says 'There is at present no time limit on the holder's stay in the United Kingdom.' You should apply through the Home Office, via post (slow but usually effective) or in person at Lunar House in Croydon (faster but usually maddening).

When you have been continuously settled in Britain for five years, you can apply for citizenship if you wish. You must be 'of good character', have sufficient knowledge of a UK language (in London, that means English) and intend to make your home in Britain. The British government has no restrictions on people with dual nationality, but you will be required to take an oath of allegiance if the British monarch is not already your Head of State. The chief advantages of citizenship over permanent residency are threefold:

- You acquire the right to vote in British elections, which is not available to non-citizens.
- You gain freedom of movement and residency throughout the European Union, since you are now in effect a European national.
- You can get a UK passport and use the 'British and EU Passports' queue when entering Britain, which always seems to move faster than the ones for foreign nationals.

Application for citizenship is made through the Home Office. More information about immigration generally can be found on their website (http://ind.homeoffice.gov.uk).

You Can't Bring it With You

As we have already seen in the earlier section on shopping, there is very little in the world that can't be had (for a price) in London. The start of this chapter discusses the practical aspects of bringing or leaving your various possessions behind. You should be aware of a handful of items that you can't import into the UK, or can do so only with difficulty; this will be true whether you come as a tourist, or with the intention of setting down roots. In addition to fairly standard and sensible limitations on alcoholic beverages and tobacco (you can read about these on your inbound flight), you should be aware that you cannot bring the following goods into Britain:

- Controlled drugs, firearms, weapons and pornography.
- Potatoes, chestnuts and several kinds of trees. (Importation of any other plants, seeds, fruits or vegetables can be done only after obtaining a plant health certificate from the country of origin.)
- Animals. You can import your pet (dog or cat) into Britain but only by obtaining a licence in advance from Defra, the Department for Environment, Food and

Rural Affairs. You can visit its website at http://defra. gov.uk/animalh/quarantine/index.htm—you can also download the necessary forms in PDF format).

- Meat and poultry.

THE BENEFITS BANDWAGON

The government offers a wide range of benefits under the rubric of social welfare. A contemporary and popular political debate concerns whether this generous outpouring does in fact create a healthier society, or actually develops a culture of dependency wherein welfare recipients expect something for nothing at every turn and come to the point where they are unable and unwilling to help themselves. Whether or not you wish to enter this debate, as a foreigner in London you are entitled—under certain circumstances—to most of the benefits that are available to Britons once you are granted settlement. Bona fide asylum seekers and refugees are more or less entitled to the full range of benefits, but people who enter Britain under some other guise and then attempt to switch their status to asylum seeker are entitled to no benefits whatever, under rules introduced in 1996.

A government department called the Department of Work and Pensions (DWP) is responsible for administering benefits.

They have offices all over London. The one you apply to depends on your address, and you can learn where it is by consulting neighbours or looking in the London business and services telephone directory under Benefits Agency. But before you try to book a seat on this gravy train, a few words of explanation are in order about benefits.

- Benefit can be either means tested or non-means tested. In essence, qualification for means-tested benefits involves looking at your income and other assets; non-means tested ones do not.

- Some benefits are contributory, others are non-contributory. Contributory benefits are paid for by National Insurance (NI) payments, which if you work are deducted from your salary (your employer also makes a contribution not figured in your pay), or if you are self-employed, you pay yourself on a regular basis. If you are not making such NI contributions, through salary deductions or personally, you are not entitled to contributory benefits, even though you may meet the other qualifications for them. In the case of noncontributory benefits, the benefit is payable regardless of any contribution on your part.

- It is necessary for you to pass the DWP's Habitual Residence Test in order to qualify for any benefits. This ascertains whether you are in fact habitually resident in the UK, or merely trying to take the government for a ride while soaking up sun on a beach somewhere.

- Benefits paid as replacement for earnings have a requirement that the recipient must be available to work. The only exception to this rule are certain newly arrived asylum seekers. This may be especially important if a work permit justifies your presence in Britain, because that usually means you are tied to the job that you entered Britain to take up. If you have to leave that job, it may mean that not only are you not qualified to collect unemployment benefits, but also that your gig in Britain is simply up.

With that by way of introduction and proviso, here is a brief summary of the benefits on offer, and who gets them.

As a settled foreigner in London, you are in principle entitled to the benefits that appear in the list below. You will probably not be entitled to any of these benefits before you've been in Britain for at least four years, since it is unlikely that you will have settlement until then, and it is very likely that a provision of your entry to Britain entailed your not being dependent on welfare. As in other cases, the major exceptions to this rule are asylum seekers and refugees.

- Child Benefit: Non-means tested, noncontributory. Payable to mothers, a certain amount for every child.
- Disability Working Allowance: Means tested, noncontributory. For disabled people in full-time work.
- Family Credit: Means tested, noncontributory. For full-time workers who have children and don't come close to making ends meet.
- Incapacity Benefit: Non-means tested, contributory. For those who become incapable of working owing to physical or mental incapacity.
- One Parent Benefit: Non-means tested, noncontributory. For lone parents.
- Retirement Pensions: Non-means tested, contributory. For those aged 65 and over who have contributed to the NI fund during their working life.
- Statutory Maternity Pay: Paid if you become pregnant while working full time for a UK concern.
- Statutory Sick Pay: Paid when you miss days from work, usually through your pay packet, provided that your employer is a UK concern.

The following rather important benefits are payable to foreign Londoners, but only after they are settled in the UK. However, asylum seekers and refugees, even prior to settlement, may collect Income Support, Housing Benefit and Council Tax Benefit. The government recently moved to withdraw these benefits from asylum seekers and this rule now applies to those who request asylum after they have entered Britain under some other pretext.

- Jobseeker's Allowance: Non-means tested; categories for both contributory and non-contributory. What you get when you lose your job. Recipients have to complete a 'jobseeker's agreement', detailing the steps they will take to secure full-time employment. It is time-limited. If by the end of it you haven't found work, then you may apply for

- Income Support: Means tested, non-contributory. This is basic welfare; income for those who don't have an income and is incapable of generating one. It is paid depending on the ages and number in the family as well as a range of other circumstances such as disability. It is payable in some circumstances to those who are part-time employed.
- Housing Benefit: Means tested, non-contributory. Pays part or all of your rent, depending on your circumstances. Usually goes hand-in-hand with Income Support.
- Council Tax Benefit: Means tested, non-contributory. Helps to defray the cost of the council tax for those who can't afford it. Usually goes hand-in-hand with the two foregoing benefits.

In addition to these are a number of minor categories of benefits that apply mostly to widows, disabled persons and lone parents.

All of these benefits require you to be physically present in Britain, and you must collect your benefit in person in most cases, every week from a post office. This fact notwithstanding, the media constantly uncovers various schemes by which people defraud the DWP of millions of pounds through false claims.

More about Benefits

A more detailed overview of the benefits system is given in a free booklet, *Which benefit?*, available from main post offices. For the most up-to-date information, visit the DWP website at:

http://www.dwp.gov.uk.

GETTING A NATIONAL INSURANCE CARD AND NUMBER

If you are regularly employed by a UK concern, your employer's payroll department will see to it early on that you get a National Insurance (NI) number, and will in fact probably supply you with an application form, or tell you where to get one. If you are self-employed, or a dependent of an employed person, you should apply for a NI number yourself at a DWP office; look in your telephone directory under Benefits Agency for the one nearest you. You need a NI number to ensure that your NI contributions are credited into your account, to register with a National Health Service (NHS) doctor, and to claim any contributory benefits. You must start making NI contributions as soon as you start working in Britain in order to qualify for any contributory benefits.

THE NATIONAL HEALTH SYSTEM

Britain's free health care system is probably unrivalled in the world for its quality and dependability. The quality of care in London, nearly everyone agrees, has suffered in recent years as a result of many cutbacks and closures, but it is still very good indeed, and in any case you certainly can't complain about the price.

The National Health Service is funded through ordinary government revenues (including income tax) and is not contributory as some benefits are; you qualify for care under it if you are ordinarily resident in Britain. There is no connection between the NHS and National Insurance, despite the similarity of names.

You should make it a priority to register with an NHS doctor very early on when you settle in London. This is true even if you are habitually well, if you abhor modern medicine, and if you never plan on using the health service at all. Being registered ensures that you will encounter a lot less red tape if the day should come when you have to use the health service, as in an emergency or for a catastrophic illness.

You will probably come across a doctor's surgery (office) in your

Your local GP (general practitioner) serves mainly as your front line health care provider. Anything that is beyond the realm of the GP is referred immediately to a local specialist or special clinic for treatment. You may very well have to wait weeks for an appointment for a condition that is not deemed critical or an emergency; the NHS in London is currently equipped to respond to crises fairly well, but to muddle through much of everything else that it is charged with.

neighbourhood, and there may well be more than one. If at all possible, consult with neighbours first before registering with a local doctor; some are better than others. But the important thing is to get registered and into the system. Once you are registered, you will receive your NHS Medical Card and NHS number; you may have to produce these to receive health care under the NHS.

NHS Dentists

While there are a number of dentists who work under the NHS, changes in rules over the past few years have made it increasingly unattractive for them to do so, and many have gone private. This is particularly true in London, so you may well not find an NHS dentist willing to take on new patients. In this case, your only recourse is to use a private dentist. In either case, consult your neighbours or colleagues to find a good dentist in your area, or consult the telephone directory.

Private Health Care

Despite the very good National Health Service, private medicine also thrives in Britain. If you can't tolerate the bureaucracy, slowness and the general rundown and neglected feel that many NHS surgeries, clinics and hospitals display, you will find that private health care will answer all of your needs—for a price. Private health insurance is also available and a few jobs even offer it as a perk. BUPA is the leading provider. For information about alternative health care and therapies, see the Resource Guide under 'Alternative Medicine'.

YOU AND THE COUNCIL

There are a few other points of mostly local London law and custom that are useful for you to know, and ignorance of which will probably not result in bliss. They mostly concern what your local council can do for you, and what you have to do for your local council.

The Council Tax

The Council Tax, noted briefly earlier, is assessed locally by your borough council and goes towards supporting the services that they provide: not necessarily to you personally, but to all residents of the borough. The tax is adjusted yearly, and is based on the council's budget. In principle, every council updates its council tax register yearly to learn who is living at what address, and this is the basis for sending out the yearly bills. Since people move about so often, it is impossible for the register to be completely current. Thus you may receive at your residence a council tax bill, or even a litigation threatening last chance notice, for former tenants or residents.

You should notify your local council as soon as you establish your residency. They will eventually catch up with you if you don't, but you save time, trouble and money by making your presence known to the council immediately. They will then update the register and send you an appropriate bill, pro-rated according to the time you moved in. You will be responsible for paying Council Tax arrears and possibly penalties if a borough council finds you have been resident without informing them.

Council Services

Councils are charged with providing a huge array of services to their residents, many of which you may never have the opportunity, or the qualifications, to use. In Chapter Seven, we will look at one of the main services provided at the local level that everyone can take advantage of, namely leisure services. Here is a brief look at a few of the other important services that are useful and available to nearly any London resident.

Education

Education is administered at the level of the borough council throughout London. If you have school age children (education is compulsory for children aged five to 16) and you have not arranged to educate them privately, you must register them at the school in whose catchment area you live. Your neighbours should be able to tell you about this, or you can call your council's education department for more information.

The quality of education varies widely from borough to borough, and even from school to school within boroughs. If you intend to have your children educated in state-supported schools, it is well worth your while to research the subject thoroughly with other parents to ensure that you are giving your children the best free education they can receive. It may be possible to register them in a better state-supported school outside the catchment area where you reside, but this will require forethought and planning.

Libraries

London's public library system is also administered at the level of the borough council. The quality of collections to some degree reflects each borough's population, its political slant and the state of health of its budget. All borough libraries make an attempt to accommodate the needs of ethnic groups within their borders. Left-leaning boroughs go rather further in this effort than do some others, some going so far as to neglect the range of their general collection. The quality and breadth of collections varies widely among the various boroughs, particularly in reference works, depending largely on how much they are able to spend.

Most boroughs have their entire collection catalogued on computer. If a volume is not available in a local branch but is found elsewhere in the borough, it can be fetched. An interlibrary loan system called LASER operates throughout the capital and south-east England, so it is generally not difficult (though it may be time consuming) to get your hands on a volume that can't be found in your borough.

Many of London's institutional (university and professional) libraries are quite liberal in extending visiting, if not borrowing privileges to members of the public, and they can usually be approached with specific requests to do research. This is also true of the British Library, whose holdings are generally available through the proper channels to borough libraries as well.

You can become a member of the library in the borough of your residence free, and through it you gain access, however inefficiently, to the whole of the London library system. Some boroughs, and most notably the City, extend borrowing privileges to those who work or study within their boundaries, as well as those who live there. For research purposes, two library systems stand out above the others: that of the City of London, with excellent facilities particularly at the Barbican Centre and at the Guildhall; and Westminster, whose main reference library is in the West End, just behind the new building of the National Gallery in Saint Martin's Street.

Rubbish and Recycling

We save for last perhaps the most important and appreciated function of the local council, which is rubbish collection. Once a week, on a day (usually morning) that you can find out about from your neighbours, you should place bags or bins of refuse in front of your house, or in some easily accessible place not far off the street for collection. At present, there is no curbside recycling anywhere in London, but most boroughs have facilities in various locations where you can drop off paper, glass, aluminium and sometimes other materials for recycling.

To get an idea of the range of other services provided by your council, look under the name of your council in the London business and services telephone directory, or in the front of your neighbourhood Thomson directory.

The Television Licence

Britain enjoys two commercial-free television stations, as well as five national and no end of local radio stations that carry no advertising (other than for themselves). We all know there's no such thing as a free lunch, and the same applies to broadcast media: the BBC's broadcast output is largely paid for through the television licensing scheme. Everyone who owns (or exclusively uses) a colour television pays a yearly fee of over £ 100; the fee for a black-and-white television is considerably less.

As with the council tax, a bill for a television licence may come to you for a former tenant. Whether or not it does, you should apply for a television licence as soon as you have a television. Forms are available from all post offices. Failure to do so can also result in your having to pay arrears and penalties. Special television detecting vehicles are said to prowl the streets of London regularly, and if a set is detected at a residence for which no licence is registered, heads will roll.

STUDYING IN LONDON

Studying is a full-time occupation for a sizable chunk of Londoners who do not work full-time. To make sense of the studying population we need to first acquaint ourselves with the education system.

Education is an emotive issue in British politics for several reasons. Partly because it is a *cause célèbre* and showcase for the ideologies of both main political parties; partly because the media is fond of fanning the flames under perceived controversies about education policy; and partly because parents are genuinely concerned about the quality of education that their tax money pays for. At present, education in Britain is 'free through the first degree', meaning that you shouldn't have to pay for any of it until you have a bachelor's degree, or equivalent qualification, in hand. In practice, the cost of higher education is increasingly borne by students and their families, and there is constant talk in the media of government policies that are slowly but surely changing the face of all education in Britain towards a more private enterprise with fewer governmental connections.

Primary and Secondary Education

Up to university level, parents may choose to educate their children in state schools (these may also be called government schools), in private, independent schools (which may, confusingly, be called public schools), or in any of the international schools in London. In choosing (if indeed your financial situation enables you to choose, for private education can be expensive), you probably want to consider what it is you want your children's education to prepare them for. Both the state and private sector provide good general education and preparation for higher education in Britain and elsewhere.

International schools are geared towards higher education in the country affiliated with the school, but several also offer courses leading to an International Baccalaureate, which is increasingly recognised by universities throughout the world. These schools are probably the best choice if your stay in Britain is going to be a short one and you wish to keep your children in an education system that they are already used to or will return to. International schools in London include those affiliated with France, Greece, Germany, Japan, Norway, Sweden and the United States, along with several Islamic schools connected with various Muslim countries. (See 'Schools' in the Resource Guide for more information.)

Education policy in the state sector is the responsibility of the Department for Education and Skills (DfES), which has a cabinet level minister. It is implemented by Local Education Authorities, or LEAs. Formerly, there was an omnibus education authority that looked after primary and secondary education throughout Inner London, but like many things associated with Greater London, recent Conservative governments found it far too liberal and freethinking, and so abolished it. Now each London borough has its own education authority. State schools are either LEA schools, whose budget and admissions policy is decided by the LEA, or grant-maintained schools. The latter are those that have opted out of LEA control and whose budget is grant-aided by central government.

In state-supported schools, there is a standardised system of education throughout England and Wales. Education is compulsory for children aged five to 16. The curriculum, called the National Curriculum, is an object of ongoing fascination in the media and it will not be long before you hear something about it. It is required to be taught in all schools, whether LEA-controlled, grant-maintained, or independent (but not in international schools). Primary education covers children aged five to 11. After age 11, students in the state sector go mostly to comprehensive schools, which accept all students regardless of ability. There are, however, a few grammar schools, which are selective secondary schools for better students, and these seem to be coming back into fashion.

Most students study for GCSEs (General Certificate in Secondary Education) in any number of individual subjects until the school-leaving age. Compulsory testing for proficiency in these is administered at age 15 or 16.

Since the early 1990s, a handful of secondary schools have been designated City Technology Colleges. They teach the National Curriculum, with an emphasis on maths, science and technology subjects, leading to a GCSE qualification.

Post-secondary Education

Post-secondary education in London is a major service industry that may appear, to the outsider, to have no handles on it whatever. The apparent confusion can be cleared up to some degree by mastering terminology, though it must be said that the entire system is in a state of flux and redefinition. At present, there is still a fairly dependable distinction between what is called higher education, geared towards academic qualifications, and further education, geared towards vocational qualifications. The distinction is beginning to blur, however, under pressure from government policy that would combine the two.

Learning More about Courses

A yearly publication called *Floodlight*, available in October, is a catalogue of all full-time courses in Greater London leading to qualifications or degrees, and is indispensable for the full-time student seeking a way through the maze.

There are so many ways into higher and further education, and so many degrees and qualifications offered in it, that a student coming to it from some other education system will not know where to begin. Following is a glossary of the most common terms relating to post-secondary education, which should help to point the aspiring scholar, craftsman, academic or professional in the right direction.

- A-level: A qualification required for entrance into most conventional universities. Courses last for one or two years and are taught in colleges, often called sixth-form colleges. Students typically study for A-levels immediately after completion of the GCSE (see above), and undertake study in one to four subjects: the more A-levels one has, and the higher the marks obtained, the greater the chances for being accepted into a top university.

- Access Course: A year-long course offered by a university or other institution that prepares a student coming from a non-traditional or non-British educational background for entry into the university system. There are hundreds of access courses available, geared towards particular academic subjects. These are widely attended by ethnic minorities, recent immigrants and others who have only recently gained proficiency in English.

- BTEC: (pronounced BEE-tek) The Business & Technology Education Council, a body that formulates standards for and awards GNVQs (see below). Someone enrolled in a BTEC course is working towards a GNVQ qualification.

- City and Guilds: A vocational awarding body that competes with BTEC to some degree, but defines standards for qualification in several (less prestigious) fields, some of them GNVQs and some for which there is at present no GNVQ qualification defined.

- ECCTIS: The Educational Counselling and Credit Transfer Information Service, which provides information on 100,000 post-secondary course opportunities at over 700 institutions in the UK. It is available for use on CD-ROM at numerous educational institutions.

- Foundation Course: Another name for an access course.

- GNVQ: General National Vocational Qualification. The vocational equivalent of an A-level. GNVQs began to be introduced in the early 1990s and are still in a rather formative stage. The idea is that they will eventually be standard qualifications for entry into a number of skilled trades and professions, and in some cases to higher education.

- Honours Course: A degree program with stricter entrance requirements, leading to an honours degree, which is thought more prestigious than an ordinary degree.

- Oxbridge: Oxford and Cambridge Universities, considered together. Each university consists of numerous colleges. Together they are considered the very best universities in the country. The British 'establishment'—the network of influential people generally thought to call the shots in Britain—are Oxbridge educated.
- The Open University: An institution that offers degrees to people who study at home via correspondence, lessons broadcast on television and radio and available on audio and video cassette. It provides an opportunity for non-traditional students to get academic qualifications. Regular universities are closely involved with Open University students, and requirements leading to degrees are as rigorous as those in conventional universities.
- Polytechnic: A type of school that is now obsolete, following the government's magic transformation of polytechnics into universities in 1992. Polytechnics were formerly institutions offering degrees in primarily technical subjects, and were traditionally regarded as inferior to 'red brick' universities (see below). By the end of the decade, it is intended that there will be little to choose between the older and the newer universities, as academic and vocational qualifications slowly meld, and the former polytechnics increase in prestige. In practice, however, the older universities are better established and have better faculties than the newly formed ones, and are generally regarded as superior.
- Red Brick Universities: Traditional British universities, so called because of their typical architecture. Entry is usually via the route of British secondary education with A-levels. Most university courses leading to a first degree are three years long; a few, such as medicine and veterinary medicine, are five years long.
- Student Grant: A government benefit available to post-secondary students working for their first degree or qualification, the level of which is based on the student's and the parents' income. It is meagre by any definition.

Student grants are administered by local education authorities (LEAs).

- Student Loan: A loan offered by a quasi-governmental agency, the interest on which is partially subsidised by the government.
- UCAS (pronounced YOU-cass): The Universities and Colleges Admissions Service, which fields all applications for university admission in the UK and performs the 'clearing', which matches students with available places throughout the UK on the basis of students' test scores and their stated intentions about study. The UCAS website at http://www.ucas.co.uk enables you to search for available courses based on criteria that you enter.

FOOD IN YOUR BELLY

CHAPTER 6

'On the Continent people have good food;
in England people have good table manners.'
—George Mikes, *How to Be an Alien*

THERE IS NOTHING FROM WHICH we derive a greater sense of security than food; and when we can eat familiar food that we like, no matter where in the world we may be, a part of us is at home for a little while—at least for the duration of the meal. Perhaps this explains why a vast industry exists to transport foods of all kinds around the world, to reach those people far away from where they grew up who long for a taste of home.

The food importation business is alive and well in London. After you've sampled the local fare, you will realise that the industry exists not so much to serve the tastes of foreigners as for a more important reason: to protect them from having to eat English food! It is hard to turn aside from joking when talking about English food, since the English themselves make jokes about it. Fortunately, Londoners are much more cosmopolitan in their tastes than the country generally, so it's quite easy for foreigners, if they wish, to never sample the local fare at all. You will be able to find fresh ingredients from every corner of the globe to make what you will, and you can probably find a restaurant or two that specialises in every cuisine you've ever heard of. In this chapter, we will look at all sorts of food procurement in London, whether you're buying food to cook or eating out.

THE ENGLISH HAVE A NAME FOR IT

A short glossary is in order before we begin the gastronomic tour: whatever variety of English you speak, there is a good chance that you have a different name for some fruit, vegetable or other delicacy than Londoners do. The table below sets out the most commonly used names for foodstuffs in London on the left, with equivalents from other varieties of English on the right.

Londoners say	For what you might call
Fruits	
clementine	tangerine
satsuma	tangerine
sharon fruit	persimmon
sultanas	golden raisins
Vegetables and Herbs	
aubergine	eggplant
beetroot	beet
Chinese leaves	bok choi
coriander	cilantro
courgette	zucchini
endive	chicory
ladies' fingers	okra
mangetout	snow peas
pulses	legumes (i.e. beans)
pumpkin	winter squash
spring onion	scallion, green onion
swede	rutabaga
Other Foods	
bangers	sausages
biscuits	cookies
chips	French fries
corn flour	cornstarch
crisps	potato chips
gammon	ham
mince	ground beef, hamburger

Londoners say	For what you might call
prawns	shrimp
pudding	dessert
sweets	candy

If you are shopping in any of London's street markets (discussed in Chapter Five), you may well find that fruits and vegetables are identified in the language of the predominant ethnic group in the area of the market. Thus, what is labelled as kerala in Hackney is called bitter melon in Chinatown.

THE MEAL PLAN

In London, as in any international city, the diversity of people prevents there being any general plan for when and what meals are taken, but by the same token, the sheer volume of people on the workaday schedule in London causes a pattern of sorts to prevail. Following then is an outline of the quotidian food scenario in the capital.

Breakfast

The meal advertised as 'English breakfast'—that is, some combination of eggs, toast, bacon, sausages and perhaps beans, chips or even fried mushrooms or tomatoes—is certainly not standard in London. It is in effect a working man's breakfast, for surely no one who wasn't spending the morning burning up calories could tolerate anything so rich on a daily basis. But enough people do eat this sort of breakfast to keep a whole division of restaurants in business—the ones called *cafes*, or *cafs* for short. Stop in one of these any time between 7:00 and 9:00 in the morning and you are likely to find it bustling with people stoking up before the work day begins.

Londoners who take breakfast at home, standing in the station, or at their desk at work, usually go for lighter fare: croissants or sweet rolls of some sort, perhaps a container of yogurt and coffee or tea. Ethnic London enjoys a wider variety of breakfast treats too varied to catalogue here; you'll have to visit the various neighbourhoods to ferret these out.

Elevenses

The length of time between breakfast and lunch is too long for many stomachs to tolerate, and so a break in the morning with a light snack is common everywhere. This is sometimes called *elevenses*, in honour of the time of morning when the hunger pangs attack. Tea or coffee and a bread snack of some kind is standard. Cafes normally have display cases full of treats to answer this need; scones, rock cakes (a heavy scone with raisins baked in it), bread pudding, filled croissants, Danish pastry and the like are all on offer.

Lunch

The hour of preference for lunch in London is 1:00 pm. Working or studying Londoners typically have a lightish lunch, and the hands-down favourite is a sandwich of some sort. The same cafes which hours before were serving up bacon and eggs now have their display cases filled with every conceivable sandwich filling. You can also buy your sandwiches already made up and sealed in plastic containers from just about anywhere, including supermarkets and chemists', or you can order a sandwich freshly cut from a cafe or sandwich bar. A variety of bread is available: white, wheat, granary (wheat with chunks of softened whole grains), and rolls of various kinds, including a large one called a *bap*. By default, butter (or more usually margarine) is spread on one side of the bread; if you want something on the other, such as mustard or mayonnaise, or if you don't want butter, you have to say so.

A sandwich with salad comes with pieces of lettuce, tomato and perhaps cucumber added to whatever fills the sandwich. Thus a cheese salad sandwich is a slab of cheese and pieces of the aforementioned vegetables between two pieces of bread, one of them spread with margarine. Another common sandwich addition is pickle, a sweet brown chutney more properly called Branston pickle; typically it is eaten on a cheese sandwich.

For business lunches in the City, this notion of lightness is

> Those wanting a little warmth with lunch may order a sausage roll, a baked sausage in a pastry wrapping. There is also the Cornish pasty (pronounced PASS-tee), a pastry case with a filling of mincemeat and vegetables.

tossed aside. Here the intention is to impress as well as to satiate, and there is a large tier of expensive and good restaurants that cater to the business lunch trade.

Afternoon and Evening Meals

After lunch, London splits somewhat along class and livelihood lines for the rest of the eating day. The meals served include:

High Tea

The upper classes are imagined to uphold the tradition of high tea, though whether they do in fact is open to question. It is an early evening meal at which tea, along with delicate sandwiches and sweet pastries (perhaps also scones, jam and clotted cream) are served. The expensive London hotels, knowing a cash cow when they see one, nearly all put on lavish high teas for tourists and others daily, where for a mere £ 15–20, you can ingest the foregoing in opulent splendour, often to the accompaniment of discreet live music. But high tea is not a daily affair for hardly anyone, except in the few reputed households where it is served for children who eat separately from their parents.

Tea

The working class version of high tea is merely called tea, and it is the main meal of the day for many working people and families who are all home and assembled by early evening. Thus it is indistinguishable from what you may think of as dinner or supper. There is no set fare, but 'meat and two veg' is regarded as typical. One of the veg is probably potatoes, both of the veg are probably boiled, and neither of them is seasoned with anything but salt and pepper if cooked the true English way.

Dinner or Supper

Those who don't call the evening meal tea call it dinner or supper, and if it's eaten out at a restaurant or someone else's home, it's dinner. The possibilities are limitless, and are detailed below under restaurants.

DRINKS

As with food, things to drink from all over the world find their way to London, and unless your standard beverage depends on rare tropical or alpine ingredients, chances are good that you will find it either ready-made or makable in London. The following list begins with water, where all beverages begin, and gets more complicated from there.

Water

As city water goes, London's isn't terrible, only pretty bad. You can in time get used to the taste of it, but you can also vastly improve it by investing in a water filter, available from chemists and department stores. These have disposable filters that provide about a month's worth of household drinking water. They remove the hardness and some of the taste from the water. Brita is the leading brand name; Boots and some of the supermarkets have house brands that do the same job for less money.

Mineral Waters

Many Londoners, both native and foreign, eschew what comes out of the tap for water that comes out of a bottle. A wide selection of British and European waters, both still and sparkling (or fizzy, as many prefer to call it), is available everywhere. Supermarket brands are cheaper than any others, and not noticeably inferior.

Milk

Uniquely in the European community at present, milk is still delivered door to door in London and Britain for those who want it, though the numbers are ever decreasing and it won't surprise anyone if the service disappears within the next few years.

Milk is also available from convenience stores and supermarkets. The standard is full cream, homogenised and pasteurised milk, but you can also get half-fat (also called semi-skimmed) and skim milk, as well as unhomogenised milk that has the cream floating on top. Some special varieties available at a premium include raw milk and milk from the

Channel Islands, which is creamier. Milk from supermarkets is cheaper than anywhere else.

Tea

You may get the impression that tea is to Londoners what water is to the rest of humanity. It is drunk at any time of day, and real fans of the beverage seem to have an unlimited capacity for it with no reaction to the caffeine; they may even have a 'cuppa' right before going to bed. Though loose tea makes an infinitely superior cup, tea bags are fairly standard in both homes and restaurants. The varieties are legion; even small convenience stores carry several brands, so popular is the beverage. Even if tea is not your bag, it is suggested that you develop a tolerance for it, since it will be offered wherever you go. Native Londoners always drink their tea with milk, never black. Most teas sold are in fact quite strong and need a small dose of milk to cut the bitterness. If you take sugar in your tea, it is specified in numbers of teaspoons, for example, "How much sugar?" "Two, please."

Herb Tea

A wide variety of domestic and imported, single and multiple ingredient herb teas is available from supermarkets and health food stores.

Coffee

Coffee comes in two basic varieties in London, drinkable and vile. The presence of so many Continentals has had a wonderful effect on improving the quality of coffee available and it is now possible to get good espresso almost anywhere, except in cafes in poorer neighbourhoods. Coffee that comes out of any machine other than an espresso machine should be approached with caution. Coffee is most popular as the first beverage of the day, even with those who switch to tea later on, and is also fairly standard after full meals, being the last course either after or along with dessert. Decaf is widely available.

Soft Drinks

You will find in London the products of all the international soft drink manufacturers, as well as a few purely British ones.

A few other soft drinks are British institutions and merit mention here. Ribena is blackcurrant juice, sold ready to drink or in concentrate that is mixed with water. Lucozade is a 'sports drink' that comes in various flavours and allegedly replaces nutrients lost in exercise more quickly than water or ordinary beverages will. Horlicks is a powder that dissolves in milk to create a sweet, soothing drink that is taken by some before retiring for the night.

Beer and Ale
Brewing is a major industry in Britain and drinking a major pastime. The number of people who have a 'pint' in a pub at lunch time may strike you as quite startling if you come from a more sober nation. Both beer and ale are served at or near room temperature in pubs. If you want the fizzy beverage that most of the world calls beer, ask for lager in the pub.

Wine
Though little is produced in Britain, Londoners are avid consumers of European, and to a lesser extent, American and Australian wines. Wine from all EU countries is available at reasonable prices, and wine from aspiring EU countries, such as Turkey and Bulgaria, is even cheaper. Cheap wine is derisively called *plonk*, but that doesn't stop many from drinking it. Vintage wine is available from nearly any off-licence (retail spirit outlet), from supermarkets or from specialty wine shops.

Hard Stuff
Everything you would expect to find is here, both imported and domestic. Spirits are heavily taxed, and thus there are no bargains to be found. Those with a penchant for them stock up at the airport and cross-Channel duty free outlets when entering and leaving the country.

FOOD SAFETY
Britain has roughly the same standards of food hygiene found throughout the EU, and there is no general problem about food safety. A few items merit mention owing to food

scares that have appeared at different times in the late 1980s and the 1990s. First, it is recommended that you don't eat raw eggs or make your own mayonnaise, since eggs have sometimes been found to be infected with salmonella. Secondly, some types of soft cheese have been found to be infected with listeria. This was a one-time problem in the late 1980s and has not recurred; the best advice is to eat cheeses by their sell-by date and to store them properly.

Mad about Cows?

There is an ongoing worry about British beef, following an epidemic of bovine spongiform encephalopathy (BSE), also called 'mad cow disease', in Britain in the 1980s. Since that time, speculation has been rife that some form of the disease might infect humans, and in 1996, fears were augmented by the announcement of several cases of a new form of Creutzfeldt-Jakob disease, a human form of the serious and incurable degenerative BSE. While government ministers and beef industry spokespeople rushed to assure the public that there was no danger, doubts loomed large in the mind of the public. Beef consumption in western Europe fell an average 30 per cent after this incident and tens of thousands of British cattle have been destroyed in an attempt to restore the public's confidence in British Beef. At present, there are no export restrictions on British beef but many in Britain and across Europe have simply stopped eating it.

Meat of all kinds in the UK (lamb and mutton being the possible exceptions) is produced by intensive, high technology methods that take animals rather far away from anything that might be thought of as a natural life for them. Manufactured feeds and medicines are widely used. Many complain that this leaves meat rather tasteless, and people coming from developing countries may notice a slight chemical taste in meat, though if you are from a developed country you are likely to notice little difference.

Most of the fresh produce sold in London comes either from Britain, other EU countries, or countries around the Mediterranean. Within the EU, agribusiness is highly developed and food is raised with the free and sometimes indiscriminate use of pesticides, herbicides and artificial fertilizers. If this is a concern to you, you can usually find an abundant supply of organically grown produce in ordinary supermarkets and health food stores. There is also an organic produce market on Sundays at Spitalfields E1, site of the former wholesale produce market.

WHERE TO BUY FOOD

The tradition of daily shopping for food that dates from the time before electric refrigeration is still alive and kicking in London. Supermarkets compete avidly today and have more or less won over the working shopper, but London's street markets still do a thriving business and can't be beaten for the freshness and selection of their fish and produce. Older shoppers in particular are fiercely loyal to street markets and may travel miles to shop at the market of their choice. So we'll look first at the street shopping scene before examining London's various supermarket chains and what they have to offer.

A Grammar of Street Markets

A significant part of London's retail trade is conducted in open-air street markets, and a large part of street market commerce is in food. Markets operate anywhere from one to six days a week. There are very few that sell food exclusively, but many whose main commodity is food. Street markets are much less homogenous than supermarkets or convenience stores; they cater very much to the ethnic mix and income level of their neighbourhood, so the sorts of produce, fish or processed foods that you find at Shepherd's Market in Mayfair, for example, will be quite different from those you will find in Whitechapel in East London. Prices vary considerably too between markets, with cheaper prices generally to be found in more down-at-the-heels neighbourhoods.

Haggling over food prices is not common even in street markets, but there are bargains to be had, particularly on Saturday afternoons, when nearly all markets close until Monday and inventory has to be cleared. Then you will hear the knockdown prices shouted out to you and you probably won't feel the inclination to get them any lower. At such times—in fact, at all times in street markets—the principle of *caveat emptor* applies. Market traders are not as a rule

unscrupulous, but they are experts at unloading goods of all kinds, and if anything is going cheaper than you would think possible, there is probably a reason for it.

A complete catalogue of London's street markets that deal in food would run for several pages and would in fact be of little use, since you will probably not wander far beyond your own neighbourhood—or neighbourhoods you pass on the way home from work—to shop in a market. What follows is a brief list of London food markets that are distinguished for their prices, variety and especially for their specialising in particular kinds of foods.

- Berwick Street Market W1 (Monday to Saturday), located in the heart of Soho, is noteworthy in that it is the only place in central London where you can get fresh fruit and vegetables at a reasonable price. Selection is good and runs to the exotic, perhaps catering to the cosmopolitan clientele.

- Brixton Market SW9 (Monday to Saturday) is probably the best food market south of the river. It has an astonishing variety of African and Caribbean vegetables and the best selection of fish outside of

Billingsgate, in addition to all the usual produce and staples for your kitchen.

- Church Street NW8 and W2 (Tuesday to Saturday) is the biggest general market in central London, with prices nearly as good as you will find a little further from the centre. There is a slight Middle Eastern flavour, among the shoppers if not the goods, owing to the proximity of Edgware Road.

- Leadenhall Market EC3 (Monday to Friday) in the City is one of the oldest and most interesting markets in London. It's not the place to come if you're pinching pennies, but if your taste runs towards offbeat game birds, expensive cuts of meat and unblemished produce, shop here.

- Ridley Road E8 (Monday to Saturday) in Dalston (Hackney) is a free-for-all with a good mix of Asian, Afro-Caribbean and Mediterranean merchants and shoppers. People come from miles around to inspect the wares and experience the ambiance, especially on Saturday.

- Whitechapel E1 (Monday to Saturday) combines the flavours of the old East End and the new East End, which is largely Bengali.

Fruitful trade in Liverpool Street Station.

Supermarkets

All supermarket chains in London are found throughout the UK as well. Most shoppers would agree there is little to choose among them, and chances are that the one nearest you will prove satisfactory for most of what you or your family needs in the way of processed foods and household supplies. Street markets usually have better and cheaper fish and produce than supermarkets, but in most other foods and supplies, you will find the supermarket price hard to beat—which goes a long way towards explaining why supermarkets get 75 pence in the pound of money spent on food in the UK. Recently, all the supermarkets have engaged in a price war on essential items (i.e. milk, sugar, coffee and tea and other staples) in order to attract the wavering shopper.

Food Halls and Specialty Foods

Some of the main department stores have food halls where delicacies of all kinds are sold. If you can't find what you're looking for in a supermarket, you may want to try Selfridges in Oxford Street or Harrods in Knightsbridge, surely the mother of all opulent food outlets. Both offer British and international delicacies at prices that will astound you, and not for their cheapness. Diehard foodies will also not want to miss Fortnum & Mason in Picadilly whose entire ground floor is dedicated to the art of eating well.

If you're looking for ingredients for a particular cuisine, your best bet is to go to a neighbourhood where nationals of the country in question congregate. There you may find a street market, and you will certainly find smaller grocery stores that offer what you're looking for. In nearly every London neighbourhood, you can find a Chinese grocery with Asian foods of all kinds. In most neighbourhoods, you don't have to travel too far to find a grocery store that offers a wide range of Indian foods. Other cuisines that are especially catered to in London are:

- Chinese and Far Eastern: A dense concentration of shops and supermarkets is in Chinatown. Two supermarkets in Gerrard Street (Loon Moon and Loon Fung) and one in Lisle Street (See Woo) offer the widest

London Supermarket Chains

Following are the main supermarket chains to be found in London, with brief distinguishing notes:

- Iceland: A specialty supermarket with a small and not very impressive selection of staple foods, many in economy sizes, and a wide range of frozen foods, which is their core product.

- Marks and Spencer: Though mainly a chain clothing store, M&S (affectionately nicknamed Marks and Sparks) also operates a number of supermarkets, many of them connected with their clothing stores. They stock a good and interesting variety of ready-made meals, which is perhaps their main claim to fame.

- Safeway: Shares a logo with the North American chain of the same name, but doesn't have anything else in common. A good, general purpose supermarket that is sensitive to the needs of ethnic communities in the neighbourhood of its stores. Quality of house brands (own label, as the British call them) is occasionally spotty.

- Sainsbury's: A national favourite in terms of customer loyalty, and probably deservedly so. Wider range of house brands than other chains, and generally good quality all around. If it can be faulted for anything, it would be for not carrying the national brands of many items, thereby forcing you to buy their own label or none at all.

- Tesco: Britain's largest chain. Having increased in respectability in recent years, it now has the reputation of being the cheapest chain with acceptable quality.

- Waitrose: If you need to feel that you're a cut above the *hoi polloi* of supermarket shoppers, come here. Pricier and more elegant than other chains, and offering a wider range of gourmet and exotic foods.

Other, more or less indistinguishable chains in the capital are Asda, Budgens, Gateway, Kwik-Save, Somerfield and Leo's and Pioneer, which are both part of Cooperative Retail Services.

selection. Varieties of fish not sold elsewhere in London are carried by fishmongers here, and everything that the Chinese ever did to a duck is also on offer. Oriental City (formerly Yaohan Plaza) in Colindale NW9 has an Asian supermarket. Hoo Hing on the North Circular Road NW10 is mainly a wholesaler for Chinese shops but is open to the public; good prices on Chinese foods and houseware.

- French: French cuisine being widely appreciated (if not actually eaten) in Britain, most of the supermarkets carry a range of French cheeses and wines. If you want to spend a bit more, try Randall & Aubin in Brewer Street W1.

- Greek: The Athenian Grocery in Moscow Road W2 has a good selection. Greece being in the EU, many of its more common products (cheese, olives, yogurt and wine) are widely available in supermarkets. There are also a number of Greek Cypriot food shops in the Grand Parade section of Green Lanes N4.

- Indian: For what you can't find in local Indian food stores, go to Brick Lane E1 or Southall in west London, which is the next best thing to going to India.

- Italian: The supermarket chains all stock a wide range of imported Italian pasta products, sauces and wines, all of which are fashionable with London cooks. There are a number of good, small specialty shops in Clerkenwell EC1 especially, and also in many London neighbourhoods. A good centrally located food shop is Fratelli Camisa in Berwick Street W1.

- Japanese: Marimo in Regents Park Road Finchley N3 has a selection of mostly prepared foods (and videos). Oriental City in Edgware Road Colindale NW9 has the most extensive range of imported Japanese foods.

- Jewish (Kosher): A small selection can be found in most supermarkets, with a better selection in Jewish neighbourhoods such as Golder's Green and Stamford Hill, where there are Kosher butchers, bakers and food shops. You can also try Grodzinskis in Goodge Street W1.

- Middle Eastern: There are several shops on and off Edgware Road between Marble Arch and the A40 flyover. One of the best is Green Valley, 36 Upper Berkeley Street W1, specialising in Lebanese cuisine.

- North American: Panzer Delicatessen has three locations, Circus Road NW8, Knightsbridge SW1 and Notting Hill Gate W11, where many American and Canadian imports are available—but in fact all supermarkets carry a wide range of prepared foods that have the same brand names and taste the same on both sides of the Atlantic.

- Turkish: The best supermarket is Türk Gida, also called the Turkish Food Centre, at the bottom of Ridley Road market, E8. There are also many shops along Green Lanes from Newington Green N16 northwards.

- Vegetarian and Whole Foods: Small, independent health food shops can be found in nearly every London neighbourhood, and most supermarkets carry a good supply of organically raised vegetables along with more popular items such as herb teas, soy protein concoctions and the like. Two of the better health food shops—virtual supermarkets—are Freshlands Health Store in Old Street EC1 near Old Street station and Neal's Yard Wholefoods Warehouse in Neal's Yard WC2.

The High Street

Shopping in the high street was touched on in the previous chapter. Food is not its forte, though older branches of supermarkets are often found in high streets. More typically you will find butchers and bakeries, both of them holdouts from an earlier era of shopping and these days just squeaking by. Most people buy their meat in supermarkets where prices are competitive and where there is not the abominable stench that wafts through most London butcher shops. But if you eat only halal meat (i.e. butchered according to Islamic precepts), you will probably be able to find a halal butcher not too far away, and ordinary, old-fashioned English butchers are everywhere. Kosher butchers are found in Golders Green and Stamford Hill.

A good catch with the fishmonger at Nag's Head Market.

Surviving bakeries in London are of two kinds: independents, which often specialise in particular kinds of bread (French, Turkish or Caribbean to name a few), and chain outlets, of which the leader is Percy Ingle. It sells traditional English loaves and pastries, none of which is anything to write home about.

Any high street worth its salt has a fishmonger, usually open at least five days a week, Tuesday through Saturday, sometimes on Monday. Many outdoor food markets also have one or more fishmongers, generally cheaper than their high street counterparts.

EATING OUT

Restaurant guides to London abound and are supplemented by restaurant reviews appearing in London dailies, weeklies and monthlies. If you're looking for a particular recommendation, go there. Here we discuss the London restaurant scene generally, with a few notes about where to find concentrations of particular kinds of restaurants. (See the Resource Guide under 'Restaurants' for more details.)

Londoners are as fond of eating out as people in any Western capital. They don't do it in as grand a style as the French, and they have to spend a lot more than the Canadians or Americans, but they have a limitless supply of restaurants to choose from. It is probably more ordinary than not to book or reserve a table at a restaurant, if for no other reason than to avoid the withering glares of the supercilious maître d' when you say you haven't. But it is by no means a rule to book a table, and whether it is necessary depends largely on the day and the restaurant. On Friday and Saturday evenings, it's certainly a good idea to book; likewise at any expensive, fashionable, or centrally located restaurant.

London restaurants (fast food and ethnic ones aside) are not particularly hospitable to young children or babies. Perhaps the assumption is that you should have left them home with the nanny. There is rarely a child's menu, a high chair, or a place for changing diapers. So be warned if you're going out *en groupe* to somewhere nice that they may not be so nice to you. Ethnic restaurants generally have a higher tolerance for children than non-ethnic (English and European) ones. Many, perhaps most, London restaurants do not offer a no smoking area; fast food restaurants are better at this than others.

Restaurants are about evenly divided between those with an obligatory service charge, which is in effect the tip, and those without. Scrutinise the menu and the bill for this information, and if you don't see it, don't hesitate to ask. If service is not included, a 10 per cent tip is usually acceptable, but it doesn't hurt to give more for good service. Credit cards are widely accepted. As elsewhere, when your waiter delivers the voucher without the total amount filled in, he is leaving you an opportunity to add a tip and total the voucher yourself.

The bottom of the heap of London restaurants are the fast food outlets, represented by all the American-inspired, international chains and a few strictly British ones. None deserves mention, unless it would be in the form of a warning. All are more expensive than their North American counterparts, though prices are about on a par with the rest of western Europe. From here on up, the food gets better.

Indian

The next most common sort of restaurant in London (barring the takeaways, discussed below) is probably the Indian restaurant. They are a stereotype and the vast majority do in fact conform, right down to the dishes found on the menu. Gastronomic pundits are fond of pointing out that the style of food served in London's Indian restaurants is only a tiny and not very representative sample of India's large and varied cuisine, and that most Indian restaurants are in fact owned and operated by Bangladeshis. So what? The food served up is generally quite tasty, provided that your palate appreciates a lot of spices. You may not live next door to a good Indian restaurant, but chances are there will be one within walking distance. The food is probably the most reasonably priced of all restaurant offerings in London.

Probably the best known concentrations of Indian restaurants are in Southall in far west London; or, if you don't want to travel so far, in and around Brick Lane in East London, just a stone's throw from the City. But every London neighbourhood has its share of Indian eateries, and you won't have to go very far to find a good one.

Delectations at an Indian sweet shop in Southall, Ealing.

Other Ethnic Fare

Two other cuisines are represented in the sit-down restaurants of nearly every London neighbourhood: Chinese and Italian. The average neighbourhood version of either kind of restaurant serves food that has been blanded down to please the English palate; it may or may not suit your taste. Better Italian restaurants are generally more expensive; better Chinese restaurants are generally in Chinatown. The cheap ones are in Lisle Street, the pricier ones are in Gerrard Street; the food is about the same in both.

As for the rest, there are several Japanese restaurants in the City around Liverpool Street and Moorgate, owing to the large numbers of Japanese businessmen working there. They do a roaring trade at lunch; some are not open for dinner. Golder's Green has a wide variety of restaurants featuring kosher food. There is a smattering of Greek restaurants in Charlotte Street W1 and in Camden. A few other types of restaurants are well represented in London but not confined to a particular area: these are Malaysian, French, Spanish, Turkish and vegetarian.

Pub Food

The term pub food conjures up something quite specific for most Londoners, but in fact the style and quality of food served in pubs vary widely. The general division is between pubs that serve food because it is expected that they should, and those that make an attempt to actually please their customers. Most pubs serve two menus a day (or the same menu twice), at lunch and dinner, though many of them have food available during all open hours.

An industry exists to supply meals to pubs that wish to appear to have a varied and interesting menu without putting in the work that it requires. This is what gives pub food a bad name: main dishes that are all prepackaged and frozen, and merely defrosted and cooked (often microwaved) when ordered. Favourites in this vein are breaded scampi, chicken Kiev and lasagne. Be wary of any menu that has all three. Pubs that attempt to actually attract customers on the basis of their food are likely to post their menus outdoors.

London Food

There is not much food peculiar to London that is not found elsewhere in England, and probably no food that Britons (or anyone else, for that matter) would come to London for. However, it is probably worth mentioning a type of working class London food before it disappears from the scene. This is the fare served up at old-fashioned pie and mash restaurants, of which there are a few left in the East End. The standard fare is steak-and-kidney pie served with mashed potatoes,

> Traditional English cooking is on offer at the more expensive hotels and in traditional restaurants, such as Rules in Maiden Lane WC2 (London's oldest) or Simpson's in the Strand. Everyday English food is really no different than pub food.

topped with a green parsley gravy called *likker*. Some of these shops also feature live and jellied eels. The latter cannot be described and have to be experienced. Once is enough.

EATING IN

Takeaway (or carry-out, as you may call it) food has long been popular in London. In recent years, home delivery of meals has become a growth industry, and now nearly every place that sells takeaway has been forced to offer a delivery service to keep up with the competition. It started with pizzas, and now extends to nearly every available type of food. A new menu will come through your letterbox at least weekly, advising you of the delicacies that can be delivered to your door.

As a rule, all Indian and Chinese restaurants operate a takeaway, and many offer a delivery service. A few other kinds of restaurant in London are more associated with takeaway food than for dining on the premises, and they are described below, beginning with the archetype.

The Fish and Chip Shop

If any food vendor is more ubiquitous in London than the Indian restaurant, it is the fish and chip shop, or the 'chippy,' as those fond of the places are likely to call them. Most of them are small, independently owned and operated; a surprising number of the best ones are in fact run by Asians. Typically, they have a display case for their wares which will consist of several kinds of batter coated, deep-fat-fried fish, as well as other treats such as a saveloy, which is a sausage of indeterminate ingredients, batter coated and deep-fried as if it were a fish fillet. The chips are usually made with fresh potatoes and are thus a cut above the ones you get in

Vintage London eateries: a cafe and a chippy.

a fast food chain or a pub. Whatever you order is wrapped in a paper cone and probably dowsed with salt and vinegar; indeed, the repugnant, acrid smell of a wodge of grease-soaked chips is a commonplace of the streets of London. A meal in a place like this will more than fill you up, and should never cost more than £ 4. A few provide places to eat inside but most are strictly takeaway, and few deliver.

Kebabs and Their Kin

The large Turkish and Cypriot population of London operate restaurants specialising in grilled meats served up in various ways. Doner Kebab is pressed mutton roasted on a spit and shaved off in strips, served in flat bread along with garnishes like onion, lettuce, tomato and the like. (In other parts of the world, identical food is sold by Greeks and called gyros). Restaurants serving these may also have other grilled meats available for takeaway.

Pizza and Chicken

If you just want calories and you want them now, there are a number of takeaway-and-delivery-only shops with limited menus, specialising in either pizza or fried chicken. Most are chains, many are American based, and none is exceptionally good. Pizza in London has been anaesthetised for the English palette; you may have to look around to find one to suit your taste. Chicken is served up by Kentucky Fried Chicken and its many imitators.

Street Food

Food sold on the street in London for immediate consumption has little to recommend it but convenience. The fare dished up for tourists is nondescript and predictable—the same junk food that is flogged in every Western tourist trap. Street fare that is peculiarly English is even more dire: markets often have a burger wagon that reeks of cheap meat and fried onions, the smell of which will probably send you in the other direction. Another London institution that may be serving its last enthusiastic generation is the small seafood stand, typically located outside a pub and selling highly processed seafoods such as cockles in brine, jellied eels and cooked prawns.

LONDON AT PLAY

CHAPTER 7

'It is a damned place—to be sure—but the only one
in the world (at least in the English world) for fun...
upon the whole it is the completest either to help one
in feeling oneself alive, or forgetting that one is so.'
—Lord Byron

THOSE WHO WOULD SEEK PLEASANT DIVERSION from the trials of life will find endless success in London. Unless your livelihood or financial resources force you to a strict discipline, the challenge is more in avoiding compelling distractions than in finding them. One of London's biggest industries, namely tourism, exists only to keep you amused. This chapter is a starting place for acquainting you with the various ways to enjoy your leisure time in London.

THE MEDIA

The broadcast and print media together present a formidable obstacle to anyone who wishes to avoid frittering away time at home (or elsewhere), for even though we know they exist to inform as well as to entertain, the media in Britain are second to none in keeping one amused. Here is a rundown of the major providers.

Newspapers

All the major British dailies are printed and have their editorial offices in London. They are divided into two groups, variously termed broadsheets and tabloids, quality press and popular press, or 'haughties' and 'naughties'. We start more or less at the top and work our way downwards:

- *The Daily Telegraph*: Britain's largest selling quality daily, which is also published on the World Wide Web (http://www.telegraph.co.uk) in a searchable, electronic edition. Probably the best international coverage; good financial analysis; strong Conservative slant editorially.

- *The Independent*: Britain's youngest quality daily, just over 10 years old. Purports to be free of the party political cant that characterises most other dailies, and succeeds at this most of the time. The only quality paper not to carry the daily Court Circular, telling you what all the royals are up to (in their official capacities).

- *The Guardian*: Quality daily with a long-standing love affair with the Labour Party. Slightly preachy in tone, suggesting that the world would be a better place if only capitalism and Conservatism did not flourish so. Good coverage of social issues, arts, media and education. Selections are available at http://www.guardian.co.uk.

- *The Times*: Flashiest and cheapest of the quality dailies. Popular columnists, with lots of colour pictures. Conservative slant. Also on the Internet at http://www.the-times.co.uk.

- *The Financial Times*: Strictly for the City man (or woman), with emphasis on financial news and how other world events impact economically.

Also available in London from central newsagents, usually on the day of publication, are all the major European,

Scottish and Irish dailies, as well as the *International Herald Tribune*, the *Wall Street Journal* and the international edition of *USA Today*.

London's tabloids have the effect of counteracting any positive impression that you might get of British culture from reading the quality papers. Sensationalism is the rule, and obsessive interest in the royal family generally takes precedence over any truly newsworthy matters. The tabloid approach to actual news is often uncritical and emotional, with a preference for pre-cast opinions based on simplistic ideology. Small wonder then that they outsell the broadsheets by a factor of almost 4:1.

One tabloid, the *Daily Mail*, is generally held to be slightly above the others in intellectual content. It tends to favour the Conservative party. The no-holds-barred tabloids are the *Sun* (Conservative), whose daily circulation surpasses all other papers, and the *Mirror* (Labour). Both of these feature girlie pictures every day and idolise sports figures. At a level even lower than these is the *Daily Star*, whose headlines strain credulity and which makes little pretence towards objectivity or factuality. Cheesecake is often positioned squarely on the front page.

The *Evening Standard* (Conservative) is the only evening daily in London and is only for London; it is not sold outside of south-east England. Though packed each day with endless pages of drivel and chatter specifically targeted at the exhausted commuter who is brain-dead after a day of working in the capital, it has good entertainment listings and classified ads, and is the only way to get late-breaking news in print after midday. The *Metro* (owned by the publishers of the *Daily Mail*) is a free daily tabloid aimed at the morning commuter; copies of it litter all buses and Tubes every day. The *Voice*, also published in London, is a daily tabloid targeted at Britain's black community.

The Sunday Papers

Big, multisection papers are published on Sunday, all of which have more or less separate editorial staff from the dailies but in fact are closely allied to and resemble them in content.

Free weekly television programming guides come with all the Sunday papers. They are, along with their sister dailies:

- *Mail on Sunday* (*Daily Mail*)
- *News of the World* (*Sun*)
- *Observer* (*Guardian*)
- *People* (owned by the Mirror Group)
- *Sunday Independent* (*Independent*, but owned by the Mirror Group)
- *Sunday Mirror* (*Mirror*)
- *Sunday Telegraph* (*Daily Telegraph*)
- *Sunday Times* (*Times*)

Magazines

You will be completely spoiled for choice in the matter of magazine reading in London. As many as 300 weekly or monthly titles are available at the most complete newsagents on every conceivable specialist subject and hobby, with several titles each representing motoring, gardening, horses, sports and computers. Here are a few of the better known and London-specific periodicals:

- *The Big Issue*: A weekly magazine sold by and for the benefit of homeless people. Eclectic and interesting subject matter, with some arts coverage and the underdog angle on national and international politics.

- *Country Life*: Sumptuous real estate ads, news of society and the arts. Mostly fun for imagining what house you would buy if you had a spare several million sitting around.
- *The Economist*: The thinking person's weekly news magazine. In-depth coverage of world news, with special sections devoted to Britain, Europe, the US, Asia and the rest of the world.
- *The Illustrated London News*: A 'good living' consumer magazine with a focus on London and south-east England. Published twice yearly, before Christmas and in early summer.
- *The London Review of Books*: A fortnightly highbrow literature and arts review in tabloid form.
- *London Cyclist*: The organ of the London Cycling Campaign, free to members but also available at newsagents. Essential for two-wheelers, and it also keeps a steady eye on transport issues in London.
- *New Scientist*: Weekly scholarly magazine full of the latest in science; internationally respected and essential for those who would stay in tune with the times.
- *The New Statesman and Society*: Weekly news review and analysis with some coverage of the arts. Labour-leaning; a complement to the Spectator.
- *Private Eye*: Weekly satirical magazine that walks a very delicate line between fact and rumour, and is often the subject of lawsuits on that account. Indispensable for those who wish to keep a hand on the dark underbelly of the Establishment.
- *The Spectator*: Weekly news review and analysis with some coverage of the arts. Conservative-leaning; a complement to the New Statesman and Society.
- *Time Out*: A weekly listings guide to everything happening in the capital from high culture to low, along with restaurant recommendations and television listings. Very useful when you have visitors, but also worth looking into from time to time even for residents to see what's new and different.
- *Which*: The main organ of the Consumer Association, available only by subscription, that carries out extensive

testing on consumer products and makes recommendations. Worth subscribing to, or consulting in your local library, if you will be making a lot of purchases of appliances and other household equipment.

A handful of magazines marketed elsewhere in the English-speaking world are issued in UK-specific editions: these include *Cosmopolitan*, *Esquire*, *Good Housekeeping*, *GQ*, *Men's Health*, *Readers' Digest* and *Vogue*.

Television

Anyone who doesn't concede that British TV is the best in the English-speaking world has some axe to grind. The quality and breadth of programming is unsurpassed, despite there being only five channels available without the use of cable or satellite transmission. The five channels that you can receive without special equipment are:

- BBC1: The BBC's main channel, with the main news reports, current affairs, general programming and sports. Its most popular program is *EastEnders*, a dreary soap opera whose characters spend most of their time making each other miserable in the mythical Albert Square of East London.

- BBC2: Ostensibly a more arts-and-culture oriented channel, but in practice becoming more of an auxiliary channel to BBC1. Runs several general interest programmes on topics such as gardening, cooking and motoring. It broadcasts educational programmes in the morning. Both BBC channels are commercial free (except for the BBC's tireless promotion of itself). Your TV licence fee pays for BBC television and radio programming.

- ITV: A network under the control of various regional television companies. In London, this channel is controlled by Carlton Television during the week, and by London Weekend Television on weekends. Programming is commercial and fairly popular with a mix of drama, sitcoms, documentaries and films. The *News at Ten* is widely watched. Other popular programmes include *Coronation Street*, a long-running soap about the residents of a fictional street in Manchester, and *The Bill*, a twice-a-week cop drama about the mythical but archetypal Sun Hill Metropolitan (i.e. London) Police Station.

- Channel 4: Also a commercial channel, Channel 4 provides alternative programming that is often aimed at Britain's various minority communities, but there is also a fair amount of general programming, American imports and a widely watched hour-long newscast at 7:00 pm.
- Channel 5: The third and newest of the commercial channels. Programming is similar to ITV, but of lesser quality. No programmes as yet have captured the national imagination like some of those on the older channels.

You can receive several channels, including MTV, CNN, TV Asia, the NBC Superchannel and various premium channels, via satellite by purchasing a satellite dish (available at many high street electronics shops) and subscribing to satellite service. Many parts of London are wired for cable television, also available by subscription. To find out whether cable is available in your area, you can call the Cable Television Association at tel: 0800-300-750.

The Teletext

Many televisions are equipped with a service called Teletext, which looks and acts like a rather poor relation of the World Wide Web, but has the advantage of appearing on your TV screen. Its signal is broadcast along with television signals. Each of the four main channels has a teletext service that can be accessed by a button on your remote control. Pages offering all sorts of information are indexed and can be called up by number.

Radio

The medium wave and FM dials in London are crowded with stations. Five are operated by the BBC and are commercial free. These are:

- Radio 1: Popular music aimed at a young audience, some live concerts and comedy.
- Radio 2: Popular music for an older generation that increasingly includes baby-boomers; some non-musical entertainment programming.

- Radio 3: Mostly classical music and jazz, and some cultural programmes.
- Radio 4: General, non-musical programming including news, plays, documentary reports, comedy and the like. Good weather reports and a regular shipping forecast which has a kind of cult following for its soothing recitation of the weather at various water spots around Britain. The favourite of educated Londoners.
- Radio 5 Live: Sports and news.

Commercial stations come in every flavour and are too numerous to mention: pop, rock, jazz, ethnic, classical, all-news, all-chat, oldies and the like. Long-wave radio has many programmes in French, and on short-wave, you can easily pick up European and international stations for broadcasts in other language—so it is worthwhile having a good, multiband radio. If you bring one with you from home, it is better not to bring one that has digital tuning because the interval between broadcasting frequencies in the UK may not match those of your radio, causing it to miss all the stations.

THE ARTS

Entire books are devoted to individual aspects of the London arts scene and justice cannot be done to it in a few paragraphs. Listings in the daily newspapers and the weekly entertainment guides such as *Time Out* or those distributed free with the dailies are the best place to find out what's going on—the *Guide* that comes with the Saturday *Guardian* is particularly good.

If you attend performance arts events or visit museums regularly, you will benefit by becoming a member of any of various museums, or getting a subscription to a concert or other performance series. Many performance venues, such as the Barbican Centre and Wigmore Hall, offer subscription to their mailing lists for a very nominal amount, which in turn gives you the opportunity for special ticket prices. Nearly all museums have a membership scheme that allows concessions at special exhibitions. The National Film Theatre mails its monthly program guide and offers reduced ticket prices to members—a must for the serious film buff.

ENTERTAINING

London's cosmopolitanism means that you probably don't have to be sensitive to too many cultural norms when you entertain at home, or when you are entertained in someone else's home. A London dinner party that has guests of only one nationality is either a small, private affair, or one that takes place within a relatively closed community (which could certainly include the community of native Londoners!). The following rough guidelines should suffice if you are invited to dine in the home of a Londoner not particularly well known to you.

- You can take something as a gift or contribution to the meal, e.g. a bottle of wine or other drink, a sweet for dessert, a food delicacy, a bunch of flowers or a box of chocolates.

- You should try to arrive within a quarter hour of the time you are invited for. If the named time is vague—'sevenish' or 'eightish,' for example, arrival between 7:15 and 7:30 or 8:15 and 8:30 would be quite suitable. Don't arrive early, this will startle your host. Arriving exactly at the stated time is considered early.

- Don't bring children unless they are specifically invited. It is said that English children are to be seen and not heard, but you could very easily get the impression in London that they are to be neither seen nor heard—the natives seem to prefer to leave them out of adult gatherings altogether.

- A typical evening's agenda consists of cocktails, dinner, dessert and coffee, drawn out over a period of several hours. It is suitable to leave any time after coffee. Typically, one party announces imminent departure, and then everyone decides to go in quick succession, in the midst of merely obligatory protests from the hosts.

CONTINUING EDUCATION

London provides myriad opportunities for you to put your free time to good use by expanding your horizons. All borough councils operate adult education institutes and centres that offer courses, usually at several venues, all over the borough. Fees for courses in your borough of residence

You will probably get a catalogue of courses from your borough's adult education service through your letterbox at some point during the year, but if you don't, contact them via your local education authority. Also look at your local newsagent for *Floodlight*, a three-volume publication that attempts to catalogue all education courses in Greater London. The volume for part-time courses is available in July; for summer courses in April.

will be cheaper for you than courses in another borough, but the charges are never exorbitant and the range of courses offered is quite astounding: you can learn any of 60 languages from around the world, learn to play any number of exotic musical instruments as well as the more common ones like guitar or piano, pick up various computer skills, improve your English or develop skills in some other leisure pursuit such as ceramics, gardening, archery or weaving.

One London institution merits mention, being more or less the mother of all continuing education institutes and conveniently located for those working centrally. The City Lit has its main building in Stukeley Street WC2 (off Drury Lane) and also offers courses in Keeley Street WC2 and Bolt Court, off Fleet Street EC4. A very wide range of courses is offered, many of them conveniently scheduled in the evening for those attending classes after work. Fees are reasonable, but note that you will be classified as an overseas student, and therefore subject to higher fees in some courses, until you have been resident in London for three years (asylum seekers and refugees on benefit excepted). Many courses fill up fast—pick up a prospectus and register early.

SPORTS

You can be a spectator or participant. There are amateur and professional clubs and facilities in the capital for nearly every sport you've ever heard of. Those listed below are only highlights, with a few notes of explanation about sports peculiarly English. Contact the Sports Council (Website: http://www.sportengland.org) for more particular information about any given sport in the capital. You may also want to visit the Sports Council's London headquarters at the Crystal Palace National Sports Centre SE19, where you can pick up a very useful directory of sports facilities, clubs and governing bodies in all of Greater London.

For sports activities close to home, check with the leisure services department of your borough council. Sports and leisure centres in every borough have a variety of sports facilities including swimming pools, playing fields and courts and classes. Concessions are usually available forborough residents.

Cricket

It is surely disrespectful to pretend to do justice to what is essentially a religion in a couple of paragraphs. For the uninitiated, here is an overview:

Cricket is played between two teams of 11 players, each who alternate batting (when they can score runs) and fielding (when they try to stop the other team from doing so). Batsmen work in pairs, each standing in front of an object called a wicket that consists of three vertical stakes (stumps) joined by crossbars (bails) at the top. Their job, besides trying to hit the balls bowled to them, is to defend the wicket (keep it from being toppled by the ball). The bowler bowls the ball at the wicket, attempting to disassemble it, which puts the batsman out (this being only one of a dozen ways the batsman can be 'dismissed'). Bowlers alternate and bowl six balls in each 'over'. If the batsman manages to hit the ball some distance, he runs towards the opposite wicket, while his partner runs toward the one from where he hit the ball. Each pass from one end to the other constitutes a 'run' for the batsman who hit the ball. The accumulated number of such runs from all the batsmen on each team is effectively the score of the match.

County cricket is played in summer, leading to the culminating event, the County Championship. Playing grounds in London are the Oval in Kennington SE11, connected with Surrey County Cricket Club, or Lord's in Saint John's Wood NW8, connected with the Marylebone Cricket Club. The TCCB (Test and County Cricket Board) is also located at Lord's and is the governing body of cricket.

Test cricket, which is played between teams of different countries (mostly in or formerly in the Commonwealth), in

England is played only in the summer, with two important test matches at Lord's and the Oval. The match of greatest importance is played between England and Australia for the 'Ashes', which is in effect the sacred relic of the international game, possession of which follows the victors from year to year.

Test matches last five days, and consist of two complete 'innings,' in which the 11 players on a side have the chance to bat and are dismissed, after scoring whatever number of runs possible.

A shortened version, called 'one day' or 'limited overs' cricket, is also played and for the uninitiated is undoubtedly the best introduction to the game. Each team has a set number of deliveries bowled at them and must score as many runs as possible. These games cannot end in a draw like the regular game often does and can be quite exciting, particularly in the final stages, when a team may be required to score 30 or 40 runs with only a dozen or so balls left to bowl.

Football

By football, the British mean association football, or soccer. It is probably the most rabidly followed sport in the capital. There are 13 teams in Greater London in the Football Association (FA), each having its own tribe of fiercely loyal fans. Divisions are very much a matter of prestige, as they are a hierarchy based on the number of wins a team gets against other teams in its own division in a single season. Each year, a small number of teams finishing at the top of their division are promoted to the next higher division, and teams finishing last are relegated (fall) to a lower division.

During the season, each team plays another in its division twice, once at home and once away; these games are called fixtures, and it is on them that the pools (see below under 'The Sporting Life') are based. The following table gives the 13 FA teams in Greater London. In recent years, the top divisions teams in London have included Arsenal, Tottenham, Chelsea, Charlton Athletic and West Ham.

Team	Playing Field
Arsenal	Highbury Stadium N5
Barnet	Upton Park, Barnet
Brentford	Griffin Park, Brentford
Charlton Athletic	The Valley SE7
Chelsea	Stamford Bridge SW6
Crystal Palace	Sellhurst Park SE25
Fulham	Craven Cottage SW6
Leyton Orient	Leyton Stadium E10
Millwall	The Den SE14
Queens Park Rangers	Loftus Road W12
Tottenham Hotspur	White Hart Lane N17
West Ham	Upton Park E6
Wimbledon	Selhurst Park SE25

The leading team in the premiere division gets a chance to compete for the annual European Cup against top teams from other European countries. Finally, a national representative team, drawn from premiere division clubs, also competes for the World Cup, held every four years, under the organisation of FIFA, the Fédération Internationale de Football Associations.

Golf
Big-time golf in the UK happens mostly in Scotland where they invented the game, but there are a dozen courses and clubs in Outer London, and most of them welcome visitors. The Sports Council should be able to put you on to the course nearest you, or try your borough sports authority.

Rugby
Like association football and cricket, rugby also has its origins in England. It is followed more avidly in parts of the UK outside London, but televised matches attract wide attention, especially those involving international play. Rugby has some elements of soccer and American football: players

can kick, throw, catch, or run with the ball, but not pass it forward. The essential element of the game is the 'scrum' or 'scrummage', a formation of players from both teams that face each other, with each team trying to get possession of the ball placed between them. Injuries are rife, giving rugby the reputation of being a rough game, and rugby players of being gluttons for punishment.

Rugby has two divisions, Rugby Union and Rugby League. Rules and details of the game vary slightly between the two divisions. Rugby Union games in London are played at Twickenham in south-west London. An annual competition is Five Nations Rugby, a tournament played among teams representing England, Scotland, Wales, Ireland and France.

Rugby League formed a superleague in mid-1996 that is intended to raise the public profile of the game. The London Broncos are the hometown team in this new league; their home games are played at Barnet Copthall Stadium in Mill Hill NW4. Rugby league games are also played with Australasian teams.

Snooker

This is not the sport to take up if your doctor says you need some exercise, but it is avidly followed and played everywhere in Britain, and is gaining popularity in other countries. The game is derived from billiards but is played with 22 balls: the cue ball plus 15 red, and one each of yellow, green, brown, blue, pink and black. Players must sink a red ball (worth one point) in order to earn a try at one of the coloured balls, which have ascending values from two points for the yellow to seven points for the black.

For amateurs, there are snooker clubs everywhere in London, typically in high streets. It is mostly a working class pastime, but the clubs reflect the social makeup of the neighbourhoods they are in, and it is not unheard of for those with solid middle class credentials to play, though they may consider it slumming.

Snooker Madness

Some tournaments are televised, including the World Championship (played in Sheffield) in late April, and the Masters (formerly known as the Benson & Hedges Masters), played at Wembley in February.

Tennis

The Wimbledon tennis tournament is broadcast almost continuously on BBC1 and 2 during late June and early July. Coveted tickets for the event go by lottery and must be applied for between 1 September and 31 December of the previous year. Visit http://www.wimbledon.org for more information.

For those who like to play, there are more than 2000 public courts in London that can be booked free or for a nominal fee. Check with your borough sports authority for those near you.

THE SPORTING LIFE

There is hardly a Londoner who doesn't enjoy a 'flutter' of some kind. Possibilities range from the rather unadventurous National Lottery ticket right up through a day at the races. Here are the main ways that London punters attempt to beat the odds:

- Betting Shops: The preferred euphemism for these dens of addiction is 'turf accountants', reflecting the fact that their main business is in taking wagers on horse races. You can in fact bet on just about any future event in a betting shop: the outcomes of various sports events, the likelihood of various meteorological events, the probability of various behaviours on the part of royal family members, to name only a few. Betting shops can be found in every high street. There are some big national chains such as Ladbrokes, William Hill and Coral, as well as smaller chains and independents. Despite their seemingly broad appeal, they are all frequented mostly by men that you wouldn't want your sister to marry.

- Bingo: Many of London's grand old cinemas now enjoy (if that is the right word) a second life as bingo parlours. These are also a feature of the high street, and business can be brisk on a weekend night. One visit will probably tell you whether or not you belong here.

- Casino Gambling: Games of chance are played behind closed doors in London, but you can get behind the door easily enough by joining a 'sporting club', many of which are in fact casinos. Consult the *Yellow Pages* under 'Clubs' or 'Sports Clubs'. You have to pay a membership fee and then wait 48 hours before you can play, so plan your attack in advance.

- Horse Racing: There are no tracks within greater London, but several within an hour's drive or ride. These are Ascot, Epsom, Kempton Park (Sunbury-on-Thames), Sandown Park (Esher) and Windsor. Most races are run in the summer.

- The National Lottery: Nine out of ten Londoners play the National Lottery, most of them buying at least a ticket a week. The prospect of winning millions of pounds on the wager of a single pound is irresistible to most, and the fact that the odds approach the vanishing point doesn't seem to deter anyone. The weekly drawing for the jackpot is televised on Saturday night on BBC1 at 8:00 pm amid much hoopla. Prizes are awarded for matching three or more of the six main numbers. For those who can't delay their gratification (disappointment in most cases) until the weekend, there are instant scratch cards available.

- The Pools: A complicated system of wagering on the outcome of league football games, the pools are a sacred tradition among some Londoners—mostly working class men—who play them every week, hoping to win the big pile amounting to millions of pounds. Forms and explanations can be obtained from many newsagents and shops that act as collectors for the pools. You may also receive offers in the post inviting you to participate. While an in-depth knowledge and passion about football is probably helpful in knowing how to choose bets in the pools, large amounts have also been won by people who chose randomly.

THE GREAT OUTDOORS

London's mild weather throughout the year permits outdoor activities even in the dead of winter—so long as it isn't raining. Air quality along busy roads is nearly always poor and anything but refreshing, but there is always a green space not very far away where you can escape from the noise and concrete.

Parks and Gardens

William Pitt the Elder called London's parks the 'lungs of the city' and they still function as such today, when the need for them is greater than ever as more and more motor vehicles foul up the air. London is probably unparalleled among modern cities in the amount of green spaces it affords, whether in the form of private gardens, semiprivate squares, or public parks, gardens and forests.

Here is a short list of the more popular parks in the capital, with some of their amenities. Remember that the list represents only a fraction of the total; these have been chosen mostly on the basis of their unusually large size and lack of roads and railways cutting them up, making it possible to escape the hum of motor traffic and forget for a time that you are in the city.

Parks and gardens are maintained by various authorities, usually local ones, or in the case of Hamstead Heath and Epping Forest, by the Corporation of London. The Royal Parks, marked below by an asterisk, belong to the Crown and are taken care of by the Department of the Environment. They get the most careful attention of the parks in London.

- Alexandra Park N22: Set in nearly 81 hectares (200 acres) of land which includes a boating lake, plentiful bird life and beautiful views of London to the south.
- Battersea Park SW8: Along the south bank of the Thames in Battersea. Many very old specimens of unusual trees. Also featured is a pagoda on the river's edge with four gilded statues depicting scenes from the life of the Buddha; a gift of a Japanese benefactor.
- *Bushy Park, Kingston: 445 hectares (1100 acres) of woodlands, flowering shrubs, wildlife and old-growth forest.
- Epping Forest: More than 2428 hectares (6000 acres) located mostly in Essex but extending into north-east London. Significant areas of old-growth forest remain, and large areas are undeveloped and a haven for wildlife. Trails for walking and riding crisscross in all directions.
- *Green Park and *Saint James's Park SW1: Though not very large, these two adjacent central London parks

are popular with natives and tourists alike. A resident population of exotic ducks on the lake in Saint James's Park keep visitors constantly fascinated, as do tame sparrows and pigeons who will eat from your hand.

- *Greenwich Park SE10: Some trees 300 and more years old are in this 81-hectare (200-acre) park that surrounds buildings associated with London's maritime past: the Royal Observatory, the Maritime Museum and the Royal Naval College.

- Hackney Marsh E5: More than 121.4 hectares (300 acres) of land reclaimed from marshes, this green space is now home to more than 100 football and rugby pitches. It is also the southernmost limit of Lee Valley Park which extends along the banks of the River Lee northwards out of London, covering more than 4047 hectares (10,000 acres). Trails for walking and cycling line the river. Evidence of an old towpath is found in some parts.

- Hampstead Heath NW3: Nearly 324 hectares (800 acres) of lawns, meadows, woods, playing fields and ponds (some used for swimming) in north central London. The southern part is mostly developed for organised recreation; the northern parts are old forest. There are nice views of London from Parliament Hill and other northern parts of the Heath.

- *Hyde Park and *Kensington Gardens W2: These two centrally located parks cover more than 283.4 hectares (700 acres) and contain beautiful open green spaces in between London landmarks such as Speaker's Corner, the Serpentine and the Albert Memorial.

- *Kew Gardens, Richmond: These are officially the Royal Botanical Gardens, with more than 121.4 hectares (300 acres) devoted to scientific research and species preservation. It is the most spectacular collection of plants in all of London if not in the world. As well as those growing outdoors, there are several conservatories and glass houses that mimic different climates around the world. There is an admission charge, but it's well worth the money.

- Mitcham Common, Mitcham: Just under 202 hectares (500 acres) containing green spaces, lots of wild flowers, wetlands and a public golf course.

A warm spring day at Hampstead Heath.

- *Regent's Park NW1: For the flower lover, the best of the Royal parks. Unparalleled displays of blooming things along the Broad Walk and in Queen Mary's Garden. No expense is spared to make the borders look stunning all summer long. In the northern part of the park is the London Zoo, and on its northern border, Primrose Hill, the top of which affords pleasant views of London.
- *Richmond Park, Richmond: The largest of London's Royal parks with more than 809 hectares (2000 acres) that are home to more than 200,000 trees. There is a native population of red deer in the forest. The Isabella Plantation is glorious in late spring with Azaleas and Rhododendrons in bloom.
- Syon Park, Brentford: A private park owned by the Duke of Northumberland but open to the public with an admission charge. Besides nice specimens of native trees, there is the Butterfly House (live specimens from all over the world), a beautiful 19th century conservatory and a motor car museum.
- Wimbledon Common SW15 and SW19: London's largest common with over 405 hectares (1000 acres). Grassland and woods with trails in all directions, and next to a golf course.

Gardeners greet spring at their allotments in Camden.

Gardening

Making green things grow is a national passion in Britain, and nearly any Londoner can have access to a plot. If your accommodation doesn't come with a garden, contact the environmental department of your local borough about getting an 'allotment', which is a small piece of public land for use as a flower or vegetable garden. Allotments are usually found in big groups, demarcated in squares like a checkerboard, and they tend to be fairly friendly places where you can meet others who share your gardening interests. To help you along the way to green success, there are garden centres in all neighbourhoods, and gardening magazines and broadcasts.

THE LONDON PUB SCENE

A fairly deep cross section of social classes, starting at the bottom and extending unashamedly almost up to the middle, find it acceptable to drink from an open container of beer or ale on the street. No laws prohibit this and it is fairly common in most parts of London away from the centre. Most drinkers, however, prefer more social settings.

The pub is the oldest and most revered institution for drinking and socialising. Many people frequent one close to home, referred to as their 'local'. A pub that is called a free house sells the beer or ale of more than one brewery. Other pubs are licensed to a particular brewery and sell only their beers and ales. The fizzy beverage that you may think of as beer is called lager in pubs. All pubs sell brewed beverages on tap; this is their primary function.

You can hardly walk a hundred yards anywhere in London without coming across a pub of some description and the majority of people who drink probably do so in a pub from time to time. An unwritten law says they all have to be in more or less the same style of Victorian decor; if nothing else, it makes them instantly recognisable. Typically a pub has two parts: the 'public bar', which may have only stools, is dominated by men—usually local ones—and is plainly furnished. There will likely be a dart board and a snooker table somewhere around. The 'saloon bar', on the other hand, has more comfortable places to sit and is used by those out for a social evening, rather than a quick drink.

A pub's clientele normally reflects the social makeup of its neighbourhood, but social distance and reserve is relaxed to some degree in pubs, which probably goes some way towards explaining their popularity. It is as if the natives want to be friendly and open, they are merely conditioned not to be so and need a special context to let their hair down.

A more recent addition to the drinker's world is the Wine Bar. These probably saw their heyday in the 1980s, but continue with reduced popularity today. Freed from the constraints of traditional pub architecture, they are generally more modern and less consistent in style. Most serve a smaller and less predictable selection of food than is available in pubs. There are also many private clubs in London that offer drinking as well as dining facilities to members. Membership in these usually requires nomination by one or more existing members, and they are very much an English, middle-to-upper class affair. So unless you aspire to hobnob with toffs, you will

Many pubs offer live music, especially on weekends, provided by what you could call local talent. Some pubs have a licence to be open 24 hours a day; others stay open only 11 or 12, and usually close for three or four hours in the afternoon.

Watching the passing parade from a pub in Covent Garden.

probably find drinking companions more to your liking in public houses.

THE WORLD BEYOND LONDON

Samuel Johnson's famous aphorism notwithstanding (the man who is tired of London is tired of life), there will be times when the only thing to answer your restlessness is to get away from it all for a while. Take heart! A whole industry exists to cater for those who wish to leave London for a short break. You can be in the heart of Brussels or Paris in three hours via the Eurostar service through the channel tunnel. For the less adventurous, try a day outside of London via one of the National Rail lines: you can get a cheap day return ticket to destinations served by all London mainline stations, and most stations have brochures suggesting typical destinations for a day out. Visit the British Travel Centre in Lower Regent Street SW1 to whet your appetite for the places within easy reach of London.

NIGHTMARE LONDON

As a shot at fun, we present a very subjective list of traps in London: places and events that are touted as being fun, but that are in fact irksome and exhausting at the best of times. If there is a common theme here, it is that all are victims of their own success: too many people clamouring to experience the thing that, because of its very popularity, is no longer enjoyable. Here then are the attractions to be avoided by those who would rather go placidly, bypassing the noise and waste altogether:

- The Hard Rock Cafe: It's getting to the point where there's one of these in every city. If you must experience one, why not find one that doesn't force you to stand outside in the rain and then wedge you into a table where the patrons and the music are too loud.

- Harrods January Sale: The ads say, 'There is only one Harrods. There is only one Sale.' But there are multiple kinds of headaches, and you will get to experience them all if you go to this consumerist orgy.

- Madame Tussaud's Wax Museum: The queue snaking along the Marylebone Road should tell you all you need to know about this place. If it doesn't, you'll find yourself inside a hot, airless, one way track, passing by unconvincing mock-ups of famous people, most of whom you wouldn't go out of your way to see even in the flesh.

- The National Gallery during school holidays: Pity the poor children. They thought they were coming to

London for some fun, and now they're getting culture stuffed down their throats. The Canalletos are a lot more enjoyable without 10-year-olds whingeing all around you.

- Oxford Street Shopping on Saturday: The shops are open at least six days a week. You'll like it better if you can negotiate the pavements without having multiple collisions.

- Planet Hollywood: See 'Hard Rock Cafe' on the previous page for reasons why.

- Camden Market: It is said to be one of the biggest tourist draws in London. If you're between 15 and 30, you'll probably know why; otherwise you'll wonder how anybody could have dragged you here!

- Trafalgar Square on New Year's Eve: There is the possibility of kissing a London policeman with complete impunity, but this hardly compensates for the terror of being surrounded by thousands of inebriated louts. The view from the telly is much better.

- The Rock Circus: The queue of dazed young people waiting to get in and the bitty snippets of music blasting out the front door are vital clues to what goes on inside. Even if you grew up loving rock and roll, you'll be happier just to leave your memories intact.

- Speaker's Corner on Sunday Morning: The day may have been when people came here to have their ideas and imaginations challenged. About the only thing that gets challenged nowadays is your patience. The speakers are mostly rabid religious and political fanatics, and if they could get an audience anywhere else, they wouldn't have to come here!

A YEAR IN LONDON

'In London I had been by turns poor and rich, hopeful and despondent, successful and down-and-out, utterly miserable and ecstatically, dizzily happy. I belonged to London as each of us can belong to only one place on earth. And, in the same way, London belonged to me.'
—Gertrude Lawrence, *A Star Danced*

This section is a month by month guide to London life that records the events whose recurrence is dependable. Both those not to be missed, and those to be avoided at all costs, are noted here.

January
Holidays
New Year's Day is a holiday for all. Since the late 1980s, there has been a New Year's Day parade sponsored by the Lord Mayor of Westminster that features floats, marching bands and the occasional celebrity. It all starts at Westminster Abbey around midday.

Sports
The Five Nations Rugby Tournament begins, a showdown among teams from England, Ireland, Scotland, Wales and France. Some games are played in Twickenham, south-west London; many games are televised.

Events
If you have any money left after Christmas, various stores have their annual sales. The mother of them all is Harrods Sale, which cannot fail to come to your attention in light of all the hype that surrounds it. Whether anything offered is an actual bargain depends very much on your sense of proportion. Other distractions to get you out of the house include the Boat Show at Earl's Court, where more than 600 exhibitors display their wave-plying wares, and the Contemporary Art Fair at the Business Design Centre (Islington N1), where artists great and small display their work—mostly paintings—all of it for sale.

February
Holidays
There are none on the official calendar, but if you must celebrate, consider Chinese New Year, which usually falls near the beginning of February. There are colourful events in Chinatown for several days running, particularly on the Sunday nearest the full moon.

Sports

The Masters Snooker Tournament (previously known as the Benson & Hedges Masters) is held at the Wembley Conference Centre. You can see lots of it on TV.

Events

If Shrove Tuesday comes this early (the beginning of Christian Lent), pancakes are traditionally eaten and pancake races are held at Lincoln's Inn Fields and Spitalfields.

March
Holidays

There are none that will get you off work, but Mothers' Day (or Mothering Sunday, as it is quaintly styled) is celebrated on a Sunday in the middle of the month. Saint Patrick's Day is celebrated by London's Irish community (especially in Kilburn) on the 17th, but largely ignored by the English. The Kurdish community celebrates Newroz (New Year) around the time of the spring equinox.

Events

There are two major exhibitions: the Ideal Home Show at Earl's Court, and the International Book Fair at Olympia. Also held in March at the latest is Cruft's, the biggest dog show in the UK, in Birmingham. Parts of this are televised, and you will probably find that the view is much better from the couch unless you long for the press of the fur.

March also sees London's fashion week in which UK designers preview their fall collections. British Summer Time starts on the Sunday morning after the third Saturday in the month: move your clocks ahead one hour. This is usually coordinated with the time change on the Continent so that Britain remains, as usual, one hour behind, but North Americans often don't change their clocks until a week later. Also in March, the Chancellor of the Exchequer (treasury minister) announces the budget for the coming year on Budget Day, and the media have a feeding frenzy.

April
Holidays

April Fool's Day is observed on the first by no end of practical jokes. The print media and radio often participate, and you have to have an astute eye or ear for the entirely bogus stories that appear, truth being increasingly harder to distinguish from fiction. Easter, if it hasn't already passed, will be coming along and it carries two bank holidays with it: Good Friday and Easter Monday. There is a tradition of eating hot-cross buns on Good Friday; you'll see them being sold in more than usually large numbers. On Easter Day, there is a parade in Battersea Park which can be a lovely affair, weather permitting. On Easter Monday, there is a Horse Harness Parade in the Inner Circle of Regent's Park.

Sports

Cricket season opens. The Rugby League Cup Final is played. The London Marathon, largest in the world, is run in late April and televised. The course starts and ends in South London.

The Oxford-Cambridge Boat Race on the Thames takes place starting around Putney Bridge and racing upstream to Mortlake. It is a tradition nearly 170 years old and a symbol of the good-natured rivalry between the two universities. Finally, the Grand National, the world's greatest steeplechase, is run. Though the race is at Aintree outside of Liverpool, it is a national obsession; the horses and jockeys are featured in all the newspapers, and many informal pools form to take bets.

Events

The old tax year ends on 5 April, and the new one begins on 6 April. The London 'season' begins, a 19th century throwback in which young ladies of social distinction, dressed in expensive frocks, are presented at various London charity balls. The Royal Horticultural Society holds its Spring Flower Show at their halls in Vincent Square SW1.

May

Holidays

The first and last Mondays of the month are Bank Holidays. With the improving weather, many Londoners like to head for the countryside. If you plan to join them, book your accommodation early.

Sports

There is usually a one-day cricket match at Lords.

Events

The Chelsea Flower Show takes place the last week in May on the grounds of the Chelsea Royal Hospital SW3. Staged by the Royal Horticultural Society, it is open to members only on the first two days, and to the public on the last two. Several television programmes show highlights of the more than 700 exhibitors' blooms. The Regent's Park Open Air Theatre opens at the end of the month; performances run throughout the summer. Local elections (for local government) are held every four years; the next ones in London will be in 2006.

June
Holidays
A Sunday in the middle of the month is designated as Father's Day.

Sports
Wimbledon, the most famous of all tennis championships, is played out over a two-week period towards the end of the month. The BBC provides excellent television coverage. The Derby, a classic horse race, is run at Epsom Downs racetrack in far South London on the first or second Saturday of the month. Another important horse race meeting (in terms of the media hype that surrounds it) is at Ascot in Berkshire. Outlandish hats and royals generally get as much attention as the hoofed quadrupeds. The London to Brighton Bicycle Race is held. Finally, there is a Test Match at Lord's Cricket Ground in Saint John's Wood NW8.

Events
The Royal Academy Summer Exhibition opens at the Royal Academy in Picadilly. It is a chance to see work by contemporary British artists who have received the nod of approval from the academy. Lakeside Concerts begin at Kenwood (in Hampstead Heath) and continue on Saturdays until the end of August. The Tourist Season begins in earnest: hordes descend. The Queen's official birthday is celebrated with a spectacle at Horse Guards Parade, off Whitehall. Tickets are required and must be applied for in advance from the Brigade Major, Household Division, Horse Guards, Whitehall SW1.

July
Holidays
There are no official ones, but it is prime time for people to take their summer holidays, and the rush hour traffic is marginally reduced on account of this. Ditto for August.

Sports
The Henley Royal Regatta, a rowing festival featuring several races on the Thames at Henley-on-Thames, west of London,

The Trooping of the Colour: one of the events performed during the Queen's birthday parade.

is an opportunity for high society and those who aspire to it to show their faces and new clothes.

Events

The Royal Tournament at Earl's Court is a rather creepy spectacle that combines Britain's fascination with pageantry and military might, flavoured with nostalgia for the glories of Empire. The Proms, short form for the Henry Wood Promenade Concerts, begin and play through the summer at Royal Albert Hall. They are popular events, providing an opportunity for the masses to enjoy classical music with many tickets offered at very reasonable prices. The Hampton Court Palace Flower Show takes place, not as grand an affair as Chelsea, but worth the trip out just to enjoy the sumptuous setting.

August
Holidays

The first Monday of the month is a Bank Holiday. Fairs are held on Hampstead Heath, Blackheath and at Wormwood Scrubs.

Sports
There is a Test Match (cricket) at the Oval, Kennington Road SE1. The regular football season begins.

Events
Coinciding with the Bank Holiday Weekend is the Notting Hill Carnival, the largest street carnival in Europe and the third largest in the world. It is the chief popular cultural event of the Afro-Caribbean community. Owing to so many movers and shakers taking their holidays, and Parliament being in recess, the press indulges in what is usually called the Silly Season, wherein trivial matters normally not meriting public attention suddenly become newsworthy.

September
Holidays
No official ones. The new school year begins, which may be viewed as a holiday by some parents.

Events
The Last Night of the Proms, at which there is much flag-waving and moments of nostalgia for the passing of summer, takes place at Albert Hall. The political season begins in earnest with the conference of the Liberal Democrats. The news media will tell you more about it than you want to know. Watch for the City of London Flower Show in the Guildhall, a small but charming affair for the green-fingered. The waves of tourists begin to subside. Fighter planes fly past Westminster Palace to commemorate the Battle of Britain on the Sunday nearest 15 September. There is a Jazz Festival in Soho.

October
Events
London's other fashion week, in which designers preview their spring collections, takes place mid-month. The Conservative and Labour parties have their conferences, and the media steps into high gear, fanning the flames of political controversy. Remember that mute button on your remote control! Finally, British Summer Time ends on the Sunday

after the fourth Saturday of the month and clocks are set back one hour. The London Motor Show parks at Earl's Court. A service is held for judges in Westminster Abbey, marking the opening of the law courts. After the service, the judges proceed, in gowns and wigs, to the House of Lords—not something you see every day.

November
Holidays

Guy Fawkes Day (not an official holiday) is on 5 November. It is also called bonfire night, when many private and public bonfires are lit and effigies of Guy Fawkes are burnt, commemorating the time in 1605 when the eponymous rogue tried to blow up Parliament. Starting a week or so before the day, children may go through the streets with their home-made effigy soliciting money with the phrase "Penny for the Guy!"

Though not a day off from work, Remembrance Sunday is a day of solemn observation on the Sunday nearest 11 November, when Britain remembers its war dead. On this day, the Queen lays a wreath at the Cenotaph to commemorate Britain's war dead in a solemn, televised ceremony. In the week or so leading up to the day, plastic or paper poppies are sold for charity, and no public figure is seen without one.

Sports

The London to Brighton Vintage Car Run takes place on the first Sunday.

Events

The London International Film Festival runs for about two weeks, when new and unusual films from around the world are shown at nearly all major cinemas in the West End and at the National Film Theatre. The Queen presides over the State Opening of Parliament, a tradition steeped in ritual in which she processes to the House of Lords to read the speech prepared by the government in power, outlining their legislative program for the coming year. Best viewing spot: in front of your television. The Lord Mayor's Procession and Show takes place in the City, in which the newly elected

Lord Mayor parades from the Guildhall to the Royal Courts of Justice amid much pomp and finery. Towards the end of the month, Christmas decorations go up in Covent Garden, and along Bond Street, Regent Street and Oxford Street.

December
Holidays
Christmas Day and the day following, Boxing Day, are holidays. Many businesses and offices close or run on reduced hours for the entire week between Christmas Eve and the end of the year. There are several carol and midnight mass services on or near Christmas Eve.

Events
Numerous neighbourhood theatres stage pantomimes, a traditional form of British comedy featuring stock characters and plays—fun for children and adults alike. Early in the month, there is a Christmas tree lighting ceremony in Trafalgar Square. The tree each year is the gift of the people of Norway, thanking Britain for assistance rendered during World War II. New Year's Eve, for the stout-hearted, is celebrated en masse in the same locale, where Big Ben's chimes can be heard ringing in the New Year at midnight.

CALENDAR OF FESTIVALS AND HOLIDAYS
Holidays and festivals in London, both official and unofficial, are always greatly appreciated and wholeheartedly celebrated. London's multicultural and multinational residents have also left their colourful mark on a number of festivities. This is a succinct guide to holidays and festivals you can look out for.

- 1 January—New Year's Day
  A holiday for all and a good time to take in the spectacle of the New Year's Day Parade.
- January/February—Chinese New Year
  Though not a holiday, colourful events run for several days in Chinatown.
- February/March—Shrove Tuesday
  Join in the pancake races at Lincoln's Inn Fields and Spitalfields.

- 17 March—Saint Patrick's Day
  The Irish community, especially in Kilburn, will get together for a day of joviality.
- March—Newroz
  The Kurdish New Year falls around the time of the Spring Equinox.
- March/April—Easter
  Two bank holidays—Good Friday and Easter Monday, hot-cross buns, a parade in Battersea Park and a Horse Harness Parade to look forward to.
- May—May Day and Spring Bank Holiday
  Both are bank holidays and they fall on the first and last Mondays of the month respectively.
- Mid-June—Trooping the Colour
  The Queen's official birthday is celebrated in grand style at Horse Guards Parade.
- July–August
  Summer holidays begin.
- August—Summer Bank Holiday
  First Monday of the month is a bank holiday and over the weekend, the Notting Hill Carnival is held.
- 5 November—Guy Fawkes Day
  Also known as Bonfire Night, private and public bonfires will be lit and effigies burnt. For about a week or so prior to this day, children may go around with their home-made effigies soliciting for money.
- 11 November—Remembrance Day
  Britons remember their war dead on the Sunday nearest 11 November and the Queen will lay a wreath on the Cenotaph.
- 25 & 26 December—Christmas Day and Boxing Day
  Two holidays always eagerly anticipated by all. Events to look out for include the Christmas tree lighting ceremony in Trafalgar Square and pantomines.
- 31 December—New Year's Eve
  Listen out for Big Ben's chimes as it rings in the New Year.

LEARNING THE LANGUAGE

CHAPTER 8

'I don't hold with abroad and think foreigners
speak English when our backs are turned.'
—Quentin Crisp

SPEAK ENGLISH?

London can rightly be called the English-language capital of the world. Thousands flock here yearly to learn, study and practise the language, and many also come to get credentials for teaching English abroad. There is no shortage of either teachers or students of English in London, so whatever state your English is in, you will have every opportunity to improve it.

WHICH ENGLISH?

It doesn't take very long in London to observe that English is not one monolithic language, but instead many dialects that blend into one another other to form what we call English. Living in London will give you the opportunity to listen to all the dialects of the UK and if you have a good ear, you will soon be able to distinguish the major distinctions —that is, the different pronunciations and intonations that are peculiar to Irish, Scottish, Welsh, Northern and West Country English. If you take an interest, you will eventually be able to take it to the next step, and recognise a Yorkshire accent from a Lancashire one, or perhaps to recognise the difference when you're listening to a *brummie* (a native of Birmingham) as opposed to a *geordie* (a native of Tyneside, in north-east England). But let's start at a more basic level: what sort of English are you most likely to hear in London, and what kind is the best one for you to speak?

RP

If you've never been to the UK and your main acquaintance with British English is from listening to or watching the BBC, the accent that you are most familiar with is probably RP: that stands for Received Pronunciation. Received from whom, you may ask? The answer seems to be, from people who know better than you. RP is the most standardised, the least regional, and in some ways, the most respectable British dialect. It is the one most often used by newsreaders, by actors when they are not portraying some regional or historical character, and by most university-educated English people of the middle and upper middle class. If you have the ability to imitate accents well, this is the one to shoot for. It is the accent that is taught to people who take elocution lessons—that is, lessons for British people and others who want to get rid of their less respectable accent.

Cockney and Estuary English

Despite its claims to respectability, it is probably safe to say that RP is not the accent that comes naturally to most Londoners, or the one you will hear most often on the street. Instead, native speakers in London fall broadly into two classes: speakers of Cockney and speakers of Estuary English. Cockney is the accent of working-class Londoners. You will hear good examples of it on the long-running television program *East Enders*, but you don't need to watch television to know what Cockney sounds like. Working people all over London, and particularly on buses, on the Underground and in street markets, are speakers of Cockney; you will learn to recognise the accent very soon.

Many of the poorer and working immigrant communities in London, while retaining the accent of their native language, end up speaking English that sounds a bit like Cockney.

Estuary English, though its speakers might not agree with this characterisation, is a dialect that is somewhere between RP and Cockney. You might call it the regional dialect of South-east England. The Estuary part refers to the Thames estuary, because this is roughly the area where the dialect is spoken: in Greater London, Essex and Kent. It is the English of many middle-class Londoners and commuters to London. Young Londoners probably make up the largest group of estuary speakers and they come at it from two directions: working-class youth who want to sound less Cockney than their parents did, and middle-class youth who want to be more earthy than their parents were.

Talking Posh

Transcending all regional variations in UK English is an accent that is associated with the aristocracy. The Queen's flawless pronunciation is the best representative of this form of English. You are not likely to come in regular contact with a large number of people to whom this 'posh' accent comes naturally, but you will find that many Londoners imitate it in a humorous way when making a joke intended to send up an aristocratic attitude or response to a situation. In addition to older members of the royal family, this sort of English can also be captured in its native habitat among some members of the House of Lords and in the titled aristocracy. Actors portraying such people in contemporary or historical dramas also reproduce it very well.

LEARNERS' TOOLKIT

If you manage to walk from one end of Oxford Street to the other without collecting a handful of flyers about where you can take English lessons, it is only because you kept your hands to yourself. London is littered with English courses of every description. You will encounter no difficulty in locating a course to enrol in; the only difficulty is in deciding which one. Here are a few pointers.

Look close to home first. The English courses offered by the Adult Education Institutes in the various London boroughs offer good value for money, especially in the borough that you live in: you will pay reduced fees based on your residency.

Shop around and do not settle on a course—certainly, do not part with any money—till you have at least met the teacher. Ask if you can sit in on one class before you commit yourself. The quality of instruction and curriculum organisation varies dramatically from one course and institution to the next, and it is no secret that there are a few 'junk' English courses on offer in London.

If you are coming to London specifically to study English and have to make arrangements before you get there, the best place to start is probably International House in Piccadilly (Website: http://www.ihlondon.com). It qualifies hundreds of teachers every year to teach English abroad and offers a variety of classes for learners, all of them monitored by top professionals in the field.

Supplement your classroom learning with written materials. This will help consolidate your learning experience, and insure that your written and reading skills keep pace with your progress in speech. Besides being the English-language capital of the world, London is also the English-language publishing capital; most bookstores have large selection of books aimed at learners of English. Fogle's in Tottenham Court Road and Dillon's in Gower Street are both particularly good.

> If it is within your budget, get a private tutor in addition to, or in place of, your classroom experience. A good private teacher can individualise your learning and help you to progress much faster.

BEYOND WORDS

Because London is such a cosmopolitan city where people of every culture and language have to make themselves mutually understood, there is a tendency to be explicit where communication is concerned, and to leave as little as possible to chance. In practical terms, this is to your advantage: there is no detailed secret code of nonlinguistic and metalinguistic communication that you must master in order to figure out what's really going on. The gestures, body language and euphemisms in the repertory of the average Londoner are relatively small and easily mastered.

SENTENCE SUBSTITUTES

Things that people do in London with their hands, heads and bodies as speech substitutes are similar to what is found elsewhere in the English-speaking world: nodding the head one or more times means yes; the more nods and the faster they come, the more enthusiasm you may infer. Shaking the head from side to side means no. Shrugging the shoulders indicates uncertainty, doubt, or lack of concern.

Other body language that you may observe in London is pretty much universal, or at least common to all Western culture, and not peculiar to Londoners or British people. Men, and less frequently women, may cross their arms over their chest as a sort of closing-up gesture—a sudden indication of less openness than before. It is generally considered rude to point with the finger at anyone; a discreet nod of the head in the direction of a person you are trying to indicate is usually acceptable. A 'thumbs-up' gesture (fist closed, thumb pointing upwards with a slight thrust) is generally a sign of approval, or a request for you to signal your approval or assent. A 'thumbs-down' gesture is the opposite: a signal of disapproval, or a request for you to confirm that your answer is no.

DEATH BY SUBMODIFICATION

Because Britons tend to avoid awkwardness at all costs, there is a habit of making sharp communication less direct by using words that take the edge off of pronounced judgments. The words to watch out for are what grammarians these days call submodifiers—that is, adverbs that modify other modifiers. The two chief culprits in British English are 'rather' and 'quite'. 'Rather' is used to lessen the force of a negative statement. 'Quite' often suggests that something could have been much better than it was, but the speaker doesn't wish to say so directly. In other words, Britons often use these words to blunt the force of a statement that might otherwise seem too pointed. Example: 'The conference was rather disorganised' might well mean just what it says, but in many cases it is a veiled way of saying 'Complete chaos reigned at the shambles that was called 'a conference''. Similarly, a remark such as 'The hors d'oeuvres were quite good' may be a way of saying just that, but more probably means 'I was shocked that they couldn't come up with hors d'oeuvres that were more imaginative/tasty/fresh', etc.

LONDON AT WORK

CHAPTER 9

'Those who can and do work are emphatically London. ...
London wears a dismal exterior to the eye of
the foreigner, because all London is hard at work.'
—Blanchard Jerrold, *London: a Pilgrimage*

THE CULTURE OF THE WORKPLACE

Two perils loom for anyone who would attempt to generalise about working life in London. First, the working population is itself so diverse that any observation about its characteristics can only apply in a limited way. Second, what will be considered remarkable or noteworthy about working life in London will differ a great deal according to what you have experienced before and what you expect. With these as our guidelines, we make a limited foray into the London workplace to see what features of it may apply to or affect nearly everyone.

They've Got Class

It is probably safe to say that in any London workplace where there are even a handful of natives (we mean here the English), class distinctions will affect nearly all forms of communication. The great comfort for you as a foreigner is that you will not necessarily be included in this system of classifying humanity, and in the beginning you may not even notice that it is operating. Class in London is a bit like cricket and the weather: it's always going on in the background, and you can pay as little or as much attention to it as you like. It is different, however, in that you stand a fair chance of understanding it, and working with it to your advantage (this may never be true of cricket or the weather). The ramifications of class in the workplace can be seen from several points of view, and it is arguable that those presented here derive largely from matters other than class, and that class only plays a small part in them. You will have the opportunity to observe and decide for yourself.

Levels of operation within companies tend to be clearly stratified, reflecting the hierarchical division of British society. People called 'staff' are likely to be paid hourly, get paid a premium for working overtime and are likely to be, well, working class. Management, on the other hand, is usually salaried and do not punch a time clock. It would not be fair, however, to say that people in management are middle class, since a large group that would identify themselves as working class are also managers.

There is often a tendency for groups within a company to perceive themselves in an adversarial relationship with those at lower or higher levels; in other words, an 'us versus them' mentality is common in London workplaces. This is especially true in companies or institutions where there is a real division in the qualifications and background of, for example, production workers and management. This sort of mentality also prevails strongly in companies that employ unionised labour.

> It is typical for people doing the same job in a company to be at roughly the same level in the social hierarchy and, barring any foreign or regional influences, to speak with roughly the same accent.

While unions are considerably reduced in size, power and influence from the pre-Conservative era, they are still very much alive in clerical trades, manual labour and manufacturing industries. Union membership is typically working class, and so labour-management disputes tend to be aggravated by class conflict.

Manners are Important

As in British culture generally, the culture of the London workplace puts a high value on decorum, politeness and courtesy. The dictum that 'awkwardness shall be avoided' prevails at work, as everywhere. This doesn't mean, however, that everyone is stiff and inexpressive. Humour is very much a part of everyone's workday, and in fact it very often eases the way in the absence of other open avenues for expressing emotions. In short, silliness is almost always in order, and humour can often be sarcastic and mocking, but is rarely cruel or derisive, at least not when the butt of the joke is present. There is a very healthy give-and-take attitude regarding humour between different groups in the workplace, and again, this sort of repartee often eases relationships that might otherwise be strained. Humour may often be based on stereotypes, but the tendency is towards making fun of the stereotypes themselves rather than taking them seriously.

Women at Work

The tendency to ease tensions by the use of humour in the workplace is quite evident in the relationships between men and women. Women in the workplace can be routinely subjected to teasing and sexual innuendo that American women would initiate litigation for. But in London, the working woman is probably as adept at dishing it out as at taking it, and is more likely to play along with the game than to react against it. There is a limit, however, and cases of sexual harassment can and do reach the courts.

Such is the variety of the status of working women in the world today that you may find their situation in London either refreshing or appalling, depending on where you come from. In comparison with its peers—the other developed European capitals—London probably offers women as many opportunities, and affords them about the same status, which is by no means equal to that of men. In the world of business and management, women are far under-represented. In other professions, however, they are found in numbers significantly higher than in other modern capitals, particularly in medicine, dentistry and the law (working as solicitors, though not so much as barristers or judges). Women MPs are only a tiny fraction of the British Parliament.

Childcare is now almost entirely private, though there are government initiatives afoot, funded centrally and administered locally, to provide more nursery places. Childcare in a competent, licensed day nursery starts at around £ 20 per day. There is, however, a government scheme that ensures three- and four-year-olds a place in a full-time nursery school, playgroup or school reception class, among other benefits. This programme is administered by the Sure Start division of DfES (Department for Education and Skills). For more information, look up http://www.sure start.gov.uk.

For Mothers

Provisions for maternity leave are mandated by law but are generally below average by Western European standards. Statutory maternity pay (SMP) is available to women who have worked in the same job for six months and should be arranged by the employer on presentation of proof of pregnancy. The benefit continues for up to 18 weeks.

Understanding Your Boss

If you are supervised by a British person or otherwise report to one, don't expect to be dictated to. The values of fairness and civility usually prevail at work as everywhere else, and communication between superiors and inferiors, whatever may be going on under the surface, has a gloss of ease and fair play. A polite request from your boss may be the strongest form of his or her telling you what to do. You will be assumed to be honest and fair in your approach to work, and you should assume that your boss will be too.

If there is not a great (real or perceived) social distance between you and your boss, you may be invited, after some time, to a social occasion outside of work, typically a meal at a restaurant or at home. You can expect this to be more informal than work, but not all that informal. See the section on 'Entertaining' in the Chapter Seven for some tips.

Corporate London

Professional life in the City or elsewhere in London gets its flavour partly from British culture and partly from the increasingly global culture of business. If this is the environment that you're used to, the adjustment required of you in London may be very small indeed. If you're used to wearing a suit and tie or tortuous high heels, you'll keep them here. Professional attire is formal, perhaps reflecting the Londoner's lifelong habit of dressing up that begins with school uniforms.

Meetings are a common part of business culture, and tend to be well organised, with a set agenda and adequate briefing for all who attend in the form of memos or reports available in advance. There is a strong tendency to document everything in writing. Minutes of meetings are quite detailed, and points that require action are typically noted with someone's initials next to them, showing who is expected to do what as a result of decisions made at the meeting.

There is an emphasis on teamwork, cooperation and harmony. Individual initiative taken without getting consensus or opinions from others is not well regarded. The overall approach to taking decisions and formulating policy is conservative and cautious. Change is not undertaken for its own sake, but rather only when circumstances point to no profitable way of preserving the status quo.

The Work Routine

Except in retail trade and catering, the world of business is pretty much a Monday to Friday, nine to five affair in London. As in other modern capitals, there is a trend towards implementing flexitime and telecommuting, but the day when these have a significant impact on the rat race of the rush hour seems very far off. The concourses of all London train and Underground stations are the proverbial wave of humanity from 8:00 am to just after 9:00 am and again from 4:30 pm to about 6:00 pm. If you don't have a good reason to be moving about at these times, stay off the roads and steer clear of public transportation! The driving force of a commuter running for a train that's about to depart is something you don't want to get in the way of. Lunchtime usually starts within half an hour of 1:00 pm and usually lasts an hour. A whole industry exists to provide cheap lunches, usually sandwiches. A dismaying proportion of working

A summer afternoon break in the city.

people, from tradesmen to professionals, spend part of the lunch hour in a pub or wine bar over a drink.

When Things Go Terribly Wrong

Under UK employment law, there is a special body called an industrial tribunal that exists to resolve disputes between employers and employees or employers and labour unions, when the normal channels for reconciliation have failed. A tribunal consists of an appointed professional and two independent laypeople. Claims in such matters as unfair dismissal, sexual or racial discrimination or harassment and equal pay are heard. The tribunal has fairly wide powers to order compensation or the reinstatement of a dismissed employee.

If you should find yourself in a position where you think you are entitled to better than you have got under the terms of your work, you should seek advice at a Citizen's Advice Bureau (see the Resource Guide under 'Advice') to pursue your claim further.

STARTING A BUSINESS IN LONDON

Companies formed under British law are either limited liability companies (indicated by the letters 'Ltd' following the company name) or Public Limited Companies (indicated by the letters 'Plc'). Plcs are publicly owned and their shares trade on the London Stock Exchange, or a smaller exchange. Limited companies are privately held by individuals, partners, families or groups. Shares are issued, but are privately controlled and do not trade openly.

Ltd or Plc?

A limited company operates in very much the same way as a small business in most parts of the world, with decisions about policy and management in the hands of the owners. Plcs are governed by a board of directors (minimum membership two people, a managing director and a secretary). The main executive of a Plc is usually called a managing director (MD), though there is a modern trend to use the more American term chief executive, or CEO (chief executive officer).

Provided that you have the necessary credentials and documentation for living in London, there is nothing to stop you either buying or starting up a company; there are only some formalities to observe. (If you wish to come to London for the sole purpose of starting a company, see Chapter Five: Settling In on page 155 for the requirements.) The assumption here is that you intend to start up a small, limited liability company. Those with grander designs will no doubt have a bevy of lawyers, accountants and other advisers at hand to guide them through the red tape.

The concept of a company with limited liability was born in London, and still thrives there. While you are not required to form a company in order to do business (it is possible to trade as a sole proprietor, or in a partnership, with full liability), forming a company is the standard procedure, especially if you mean to have business premises or take on employees. Being a company necessarily involves more paperwork and legal complications than trading as an individual, but in most cases brings advantages.

A company is regarded as an entity separate from the individuals who form it, and like individuals, its birth, death and activities in between are of some interest to record-keeping authorities. In London, an institution called Companies House (in City Road EC1) is the repository of statistics on all trading companies, and those who would form a company must register it there. Once a company is formed, there is also a requirement to submit its audited accounts yearly to Companies House.

Off-the-Shelf Companies

The legal process of forming a company from scratch is rather tortuous and time consuming. Because of this, the more common procedure is to buy an 'off-the-shelf' company and then tailor it to your needs. Several agencies specialise in forming and offering such companies, and many of them, conveniently, are located a stone's throw away from Companies House. They are called Company Registration Agents and their business essentially is to form companies that meet all legal requirements but that exist only on paper. Individuals who wish to start up a company then buy one of these businesses and register the necessary changes, which will certainly include the names of the company directors, the address of the company and probably the name of the company. Off-the-shelf companies come with all sorts of not very meaningful names such as Fieldview Ltd, Hopecrest Ltd, etc. The cost of buying such a company starts at around £ 200; the more complicated your requirements, the more you'll have to pay the agents.

In choosing the name of your company, you must be sure that you have not chosen a name identical or suspiciously similar to one that already exists. Certain words suggesting connection with the government, such as Council, Board and Authority are forbidden, and you must get permission to use words in the name of your company that would suggest something to the customer about your business ('dentist', for example) or the range of your interests ('international', for example).

You should not undertake the process of forming a company without the help of a solicitor and an accountant to steer you past the pitfalls. You will also want to win the confidence of a bank manager early on in your venture. (See the Resource Guide under 'Business Information'.)

Acquiring Premises

If your company requires premises, you can enlist the help of a commercial estate agent. There is a high turnover of commercial properties in London and there is always a very wide range of premises available. Tenure in business premises is more often leasehold than freehold, and leases are as a rule shorter than in residential property, usually running from three to 21 years.

The most important consideration in acquiring business premises is planning permission: you should make sure that the sort of business you wish to operate is a permitted activity on the premises you have chosen. The planning department of the borough council is the authority that oversees this matter. The agent who shows you premises should be able to put you in touch with the authorities who can advise about permission. Obtaining a change of use, in the case where your envisioned activity is not permitted, is a long, fraught and not always successful process. You are far better off choosing premises on which you can be assured your business will be legal and permitted from the outset.

LONDON
AT A GLANCE

CHAPTER 10

'Nothing is certain in London but expense.'
—William Shenstone

Official Name
London

Flag
Blue field with the red cross of Saint George (patron saint of England) edged in white superimposed on the diagonal red cross of Saint Patrick (patron saint of Ireland), which is superimposed on the diagonal white cross of Saint Andrew (patron saint of Scotland); commonly called the Union Jack

National Anthem
Although England does not have an official national anthem, 'God save the Queen' is often sung at national events

Time
Greenwich Mean Time (GMT). However , London is 1 hour ahead of GMT during summer time (GMT + 1)

Telephone Country Code
Country Code for Britain: 44
Area Code for London: 020

Climate
Temperate, with mild and damp winters and moderate summers. Cloudy weather and rain can be expected even

in the height of summer. In July and August, temperatures average around 18°C (64.4°F) but can occasionally soar to 30°C (86°F) or more. In spring and autumn, temperatures drop to between 11°C (51.8°F) and 15°C (59°F). In winter, they hover just below 6°C (42.8°F); snow is uncommon

Land Area
1,600 sq km (617.8 sq miles)

Population
7,421,328 (January 2005 est.)

Ethnic Groups
Although predominantly white and Anglo-Saxon, more than a quarter of its population is from an alternative ethnic background, making up half of the UK's total ethnic minorities. This gives London the largest non-white population of any European city and is an important part of its cosmopolitan feel. Over 250 languages are spoken in the city

Religion
Religion is very diverse, with all major world religions represented in the city. 3 million residents encompass Sikh, Buddhist, Hindu, Jewish, and Muslim minorities and other religious denominations

Official Language
English

Government Structure
Elected mayor and assembly

Administrative Divisions
There are 32 London boroughs. These include Barking & Dagenham, Barnet, Bexley, Brent, Bromley, Camden, Corporation of London, Croydon, Ealing, Enfield, Greenwich, Hackney, Hammersmith & Fulham, Haringey, Harrow, Havering, Hillingdon, Hounslow, Islington, Kensington and Chelsea, Kingston upon Thames, Lambeth, Lewisham,

Merton, Newham, Redbridge, Richmond upon Thames, Southwark, Sutton, Tower Hamlets, Waltham Forest, Wandsworth, Westminster

Currency
Pound sterling (GBP or £)

Gross Domestic Product (GDP)
£ 147 billion

Industries
The financial and business services are at the centre of London's economy. London is also a major centre for European e-commerce and related sectors. Attracted by solid reliable infrastructure and an impressive track record in research, development, innovation and manufacturing, many of the worlds leading companies in the field have invested in London. London is also home to several other thriving industries including arts and fashion, film, media, design, law and computing. Tourism is another important industry for London with typical yearly expenditure by tourists being in the region of £ 7–10 billion

Exports
Manufactured goods, fuels, chemicals; food, beverages and tobacco

Imports
Manufactured goods, machinery, fuels and foodstuffs

Airports
London has five airports: Heathrow, Gatwick, Luton, Stansted and London City airport

FAMOUS LONDONERS
Geoffrey Chaucer (c1342–1400)
Best known for his work, *The Cantebury Tales*, Chaucer is one of England's renowned poets who also served as a diplomat for the English court.

Sir Christopher Wren (1632–1733)

Known as the greatest architect of his time, Sir Christopher Wren is the brains behind many London buildings, including 53 churches, among them Saint Paul's Cathedral.

Dr Samuel Johnson (1709–1784)

One of the most famous literary figures from the 18th century, Dr Johnson was originally born in Lichfield, Straffordshire, but later made his home in London. His works include essays, biographies, parliamentary reports, poetry, pamphlets and his well-known dictionary. He is one of the most quoted Londoner and he is reknowned for claiming that, 'when a man is tired of London, he is tired of life.' He is buried in Westminster Abbey.

Joseph Mallord William Turner (1775–1851)

Born in London, Joseph Turner is one of England's finest landscape artists whose works were exhibited when he was a teenager. Some of his famous works include 'Dido Building Carthage', 'Burial at Sea' and 'Calais Pier'.

John Keats (1795–1821)

A famous Romantic poet, John Keats is probably best known for his poems, 'Ode to a Grecian Urn' and 'Ode to Autumn'. His prolific career was tragically cut short when he succumbed to tuberculosis and died at the young age of 26.

Florence Nightingale (1820–1910)

Born in Florence, Italy, Nightingale grew up in London and trained as a nurse there. Her achievements, against many adversities, during the Crimean War earned her the name, 'Lady of the Lamp'. She would later establish the Nightingale School for Nurses in 1860, ths first of its kind in the world.

Dame Millicent Garrett Fawcett (1847–1929)

A leading proponent in the women's suffrage movement for 50 years. She founded one of the first English university colleges for women, Newnham College located in Cambridge.

Virginia Woolfe (1882–1941)

The author of such books as *To the Lighthouse* and *Mrs Dalloway*, Virginia Woolfe is renowned for using a stylistic writing technique known as 'stream of consciousness'.

Charlie Chaplin (1889–1997)

A native Londoner, Charlie Chaplin is best known the world over as the 'Little Tramp'. But Chaplin was much more than a comic artist in black-and-white silent films, and his credits include writer, producer, director and composer.

Alfred Hitchcock (1899–1980)

Perhaps one of the most famous movie directors in the world, Hitchcock was born in London and only moved to Hollywood, California in the USA in 1939. The year after, in 1940, he won his first academy award for the film *Rebecca*. His ability to maintain suspense onscreen was legendary in such films as *Vertigo*, *Rear Window*, *North by Northwest* and of course, *Psycho*.

Barbara Windsor (1937–)

Born Barbara-Ann Deeks in Shoreditch, London, this British actress made a name for herself on the *Carry On* films from the 1960s to 1970s. More recently, she has been seen in the BBC drama *EastEnders*.

Sir Trevor McDonald (1939–)

Born in Trinidad and Tobago, West Indies, he is a well-known newscaster and television presenter on Britain's ITN. He was knighted in 1999 and is also the Chancellor of London South Bank University.

John Major (1943–)

British politician who was prime minister from 1990–1997.

Naomi Campbell (1970–)

Originally from South London, Naomi Campbell is a top fashion model who has graced the covers of many top international fashion and lifestyle magazines, as well as many runways of the world's fashion capitals.

Talvin Singh (1970–)

London-born DJ who has fused classical Hindustani music with Western drums and bass.

Kate Moss (1974–)

A leading fashion model from Addiscombe, in Croydon, who was the 'Face of Calvin Kein' in the 1990s.

Zadie Smith (1975–)

A promising young writer from London, Zadie Smith's first novel *White Teeth* won critical acclaim when it was released in 2000. It won the Whitbread First Novel Award in the same year.

Martine McCutcheon (1976–)

British actress who became a household name through her role as 'Tiffany' in the BBC drama *EastEnders*. Her stage work won her the Laurence Olivier Award for best actress in a musical in 2002. Her more recent work include a role in the British comedy *Love Actually,* as well as a video in London's bid for the 2012 Olympics.

Rio Ferdinand (1978–)

Born in South London, Ferdinand is a footballer for the Manchester United team and represented the UK at the World Cup in 2002.

Ms Dynamite (1980–)

Moniker of Niomi McLean-Daley, Ms Dynamite is talented performer of urban music.

ACRONYMS AND ABBREVIATIONS

The following acronyms and abbreviations are among the commonest in British English and often appear without expansion in newspapers, on signs and in other places where it is assumed the reader will be familiar with the meaning.

If the pronunciation is other than what is obvious, it is given in parenthesis.

AA	Automobile Association (commercial organisation that aids motorists)
ABTA	Association of British Travel Agents
ACAS	Advisory Conciliation & Arbitration Service (sorts out employer-employee disputes)
BMA	British Medical Association
BR	British Rail (the former national rail service)
BUPA	British United Provident Association (private health insurance company)
C of E	Church of England
CAB	Citizens' Advice Bureau
CBI	Confederation of British Industry (industry trade group)
CID	Criminal Investigation Department (where serious crimes are investigated)
CPS	Crown Prosecution Service (government department that prosecutes crime)
DoE	Department of the Environment
DEFRA	Department for Environment, Food and Rural Affairs
DfES	Department for Education and Skills
DoT	Department of Transportation
DPP	Director of Public Prosecutions (head of the CPS)
DTI	Department of Trade and Industry
DVLA	Driver and Vehicle Licensing Agency
DWP	Department for Work and Pensions
FRCS	Fellow of the Royal College of Surgeons
HGV	Heavy goods vehicle (a truck or lorry)
HMSO	Her Majesty's Stationery Office (publisher of government documents)
IATA	International Association of Travel Agents
IMRO	Investment Management Regulatory Organisation (watchdog organisation for stock markets and securities trading)

LB	London Borough (usually followed by the name of one of them)
MENCAP	National Society for Mentally Handicapped Children and Adults
MoD	Ministry of Defence
RUC	Royal Ulster Constabulary (Northern Ireland police)
TA	Territorial Army (an auxiliary force of government troops)
TUC	Trades Union Congress
OFGEM	watchdog organisation for the gas and electricity industries
OFSTED	watchdog organisation for educational institutions
OFT	Office of Fair Trading (government consumer protection agency)
OFTEL	watchdog organisation for the telecommunications industry
OFWAT	Office of Water Services (watchdog organisation for water supply companies)
QC	Queen's Counsel (title for big-time barristers)
RAC	Royal Auto Club (commercial organisation that aids motorists)

PLACES OF INTEREST

There are numerous places to visit in London but here are some of those you shouldn't miss:

Albert Memorial

Built by Queen Victoria in memory of her late husband, Prince Albert, the memorial is located in Kensington Gardens and was opened in 1872.

Buckingham Palace

The official residence of the British monarch is probably one of the most famous landmarks in London. Not to be missed is the Changing of the Guard ceremony which takes place every day.

Covent Garden

Originally a flower, fruit and vegetable market, the Covent Garden of today is a sophisticated entertainment and shopping complex in Westminster, central London.

Downing Street

For two centuries, Downing Street has been home to the official residences of the Prime Minister of the United Kingdom (Number 10) and the First Lord of the Treasury (Number 11).

London Eye

Also known as the Millennium Wheel, this is the world's largest observation wheel. It stands 135 m (443 ft) high on the south bank of the River Thames. Although officially opened on 31 December 1999, the London Eye was only open to the public in March the following year.

Saint Paul's Cathedral

Designed by Sir Christopher Wren, Saint Paul's Cathedral is now the seat of the Bishop of London.

Shakespeare's Globe Theatre

Located in Bankside, Southwark, this is a reconstruction of the famous Globe Theatre where Shakespeare worked for many years and where many of his plays were performed.

Tower Bridge

Often misidentified as the infamous 'London Bridge', the Tower Bridge is a bascule bridge (a drawbridge that makes use of counterbalances) that was originally built to ease the traffic crossing the River Thames of the actual London Bridge that lies further upstream. The Tower Bridge was finally completed 1894 after eight years of construction.

Tower of London

Located along the River Thames, this complex of buildings has served as a palace, treasury, armoury, fortress, observatory, mint, office of public records and place of execution. At one time, it was also a prison for the gentry, especially those suspected of treason. One such famous prisoner was Elizabeth I.

Trafalgar Square

Located in central London, this square commemorates the 1805 Battle of Trafalgar but is more well-known for its vast numbers of pigeons.

Westminster Abbey

The resting place of many great names, this is an architectural masterpiece and historical testament to the different historical periods of the city.

Iconic of London, the Tower Bridge is a sight that one should not miss.

CULTURE QUIZ

You might occasionally trip up as you clamber over the obstacles of London culture; the situations below are typical of the ones that might confound your instincts. Remember that a sense of humour is your most reliable companion in any case of awkwardness; anyhow, it's what the natives use!

SITUATION 1

You are riding on a Tube train and pull into a station. You hear a disembodied voice repeating the phrase "Mind the gap" at regular intervals. Therefore you should:

A Brace yourself for a shock.
B Sound an alarm.
C Mind the gap.
D Leave the train immediately.

Comments

The correct response is **C**, though you will do quite well to simply ignore the message if you're not getting off at this station. 'Mind the gap' is the peculiarly English way of telling you that there is a small space between the train and the platform that you could put your foot into, if you're not paying attention.

SITUATION 2

A work colleague invites you to dinner at his home. You ask what time, and he says, "Oh, sevenish." Therefore you show up at:

A 6:45 pm
B 7:00 pm
C 7:15 pm
D 7:30 pm

Comments

Either **C** or **D** is acceptable. 'Fashionably late' is the rule. Don't show up early, this would never be expected.

SITUATION 3

You are standing at a zebra crossing, waiting for a safe moment to cross the street. A driver approaching the crossing flashes her headlights. This means:

A She has seen you and is telling you to cross.
B She has seen you and is warning you that she is faster than you.
C She wants to give you a lift.
D She is merely obeying a law requiring motorists to flash their lights at pedestrian crossings.

Comments

The answer is probably **A**; this is a common courtesy but it has no sanction in law, so exercise caution as you normally would.

SITUATION 4

You are riding in a lift at work with several colleagues. Someone in the lift makes a sour face and announces, "Ooh! Someone's been eating garlic." You realise that this person is you. You should therefore:

A Keep your mouth shut and get off at the next floor.
B Vow never to eat garlic again.
C Accuse someone else.
D Make a full confession in a good-natured way.

Comments

Any of these responses will work, but only **D** is recommended. The blandness of English food seems to make many Londoners unusually sensitive to smells that would pass unnoticed in other parts of the world. This is their problem, not yours.

SITUATION 5

You are sitting on the grass in a park in the city on a warm summer day. A businessman in a suit sits down nearby and proceeds to strip to the waist. You should:

Ⓐ Remove your clothing as well.

Ⓑ Move away.

Ⓒ Establish eye contact to see if he appears sane.

Ⓓ Ignore him.

Comments

Ⓓ is the correct answer. English sunshine is appreciated as a rare thing and the natives take full advantage. You can rest assured that he will put his shirt back on before leaving the park.

SITUATION 6

You invite the five English people you know—none of whom have ever met the others—to a dinner party. Despite your best efforts, the conversation never really gets going and everyone wants to leave right after dinner. What happened?

Ⓐ The food was terrible.

Ⓑ They don't like you.

Ⓒ You failed to note that there was something unmissable on the telly tonight.

Ⓓ You attempted to mix people of different social classes on equal terms.

Comments

Any of the answers is possible, but don't torment yourself with Ⓐ, Ⓑ or Ⓒ until you're sure that Ⓓ is not the answer: English people are reserved by nature and generally socialise mainly with people from their own social class. If you're new to London, these distinctions might be completely invisible to you.

SITUATION 7

During a meeting at work, you find that you have completely lost patience with a colleague whom you find incompetent, untrustworthy and the source of all trouble. You feel confident that everyone else shares your views. You lose your temper and angrily denounce him, but everyone ignores you. This is because:

Ⓐ Everyone else is more tolerant and sympathetic than you.

Ⓑ No one likes a scene.

Ⓒ You spoke out of turn.

Ⓓ You didn't approach the problem through proper channels.

Comments

All of these reasons probably apply. Civility is the rule in all areas of public life and showing strong emotions, particularly negative ones, marks you as someone who has no control, and therefore not much credibility. As an additional factor, there is a very wide tolerance for all shades of imperfection in the workplace, as well as other areas of life. Most Britons would be more comfortable with 'muddling through' a situation with a difficult person, if the alternative is an emotional confrontation with him or her.

SITUATION 8

You are getting along fantastically with one of your work colleagues and you think there is a strong possibility of developing a friendship outside of work. You realise that you will be in the neighbourhood where your colleague lives on the weekend, so you repeatedly drop hints about this, hoping to elicit an invitation to visit. But alas, no invitation is forthcoming. What should you do?

Ⓐ You should invite yourself to visit your colleague at home.

Ⓑ You have done everything you can; now just shut up.

Ⓒ You should propose a meeting with your colleague at a neutral place, such as a café.

Ⓓ You should just drop in on your colleague when you're in the neighbourhood.

Comments

Avoid **Ⓐ** and **Ⓓ** at all costs; both of these would be an awkward imposition. You can try **Ⓒ** if you're really determined but the best answer is **Ⓑ**. British people are expert at the kindness, thoughtfulness and civility that make working relationships easy, but they are private about their life at home. They will let you know if they want to share it with you.

SITUATION 9

You are at a street market that you have never visited before, admiring a delightful mound of fresh mushrooms that are offered at a good price. You say, "I'll have a kilogramme of these, please." The trader fills a bag with other, inferior mushrooms that you had not noticed from a box behind him and holds them out to you. Now is the time for you to:

A Hand over the money.
B Protest that you were not given the mushrooms you indicated.
C Try to haggle in order to bring the price down further.
D Alert the authorities to this unscrupulous practice.

Comments

B is the best answer, and the time to give it is actually the moment you detect something going awry. Many market traders will try to see what they can get away with, particularly with someone who is not a regular customer. Always be alert!

SITUATION 10

After three months in your new job, you think that you have accurately diagnosed a major problem in your department's working methods, and you have worked out a sensible solution. You outline your plan at a meeting and everyone agrees that it's a great idea, but then no one shows any enthusiasm for taking the next step. What's going on?

A No one really agrees with you, they are just being polite.
B No one wants to take responsibility for a plan that might fail.
C Everyone fears you are trying to take over the department.
D You have failed to perceive the underlying reasons for maintaining inefficient working methods.

Comments

Any of these reasons is possible and bear your looking into; but it's more likely that you place more importance on the value of change and innovation than everyone else does.

There is a British tendency to mistrust change and progress, or at the very least, a tendency to resist change merely for the sake of change. If you want your proposals to succeed, you would be better advised to quietly win over several key people first and let them in turn win over others, until everyone agrees that a change is in order.

DO'S AND DON'TS

DO'S

- Do offer to shake hands when you are meeting someone for the first time, or after a long interval; however, it is not necessary to shake the hands of people you see regularly.
- Do join a queue if one has formed: at the post office, in a bank, at a bus stop or anywhere.
- Do say "Sorry" and then continue on your way when you have a walking collision with someone, even if you think it was their fault. This is what both parties always do.
- Do let people off on buses and trains before you try to get on.
- Do show up a little bit past the stated time when you are invited to a party or other gathering in someone's home.
- Do always be polite and friendly to tradespeople, bus drivers, waitstaff and any other working people you encounter every day.
- Do keep your shoes on when you visit someone's home, unless you observe lots of shoes by the door and you see that others have taken their shoes off.
- British people don't often kiss each other on the cheeks, but if you do this, twice is enough: once on each cheek.

DON'TS

- Don't stand too close in talking to a person you don't know very well. British people like to have their personal space.
- Don't be rude or argumentative with beggars or homeless people. If you do not have any spare change to give them, it is better to avoid engaging with them at all.
- Don't smack your lips or make other noises when you eat; this is considered rude and uncultivated.
- Don't eat food with your fingers unless you see that others are doing this.
- Don't sound your horn because you are frustrated that traffic isn't moving. Horns should be used only to warn of danger.

- Don't sound your horn outside the house of someone to let them know you have arrived to pick them up; go to the door and announce yourself.
- Don't try to haggle with market traders for items that have a posted price.
- Don't ask how much money someone earns, and don't ask how much someone paid for an item that they own.

GLOSSARY

Here are some British colloquialism and their explanations:

All over the gaff/shop	To describe something that has no direction or that is in a mess
A bun in the oven	Pregnant
A load of codswallop	Speaking a lot of nonsense
A lot of malarkey	A load of nonsense
A toff	An upper class gentleman
Ballistic	To be mad with rage
Bangers	Sausages
Barf	To vomit
Bell	A telephone call ("Give us a bell later")
Blimey	An exclamation of surprise or annoyance
Bloke	An informal term for a man
Booze/Boozer	An alcoholic drink / someone who drinks a lot
Bottle	Courage, boldness
Brekkie	Breakfast.
Brew	A cup of tea or a pint of beer
Bugger	A mild term of abuse or an exclamation ("You crafty bugger", "Bugger off")
Chippy/chippie	A fish and chips shop
Chuffed	Very happy, delighted
Damage	Cost ("What's the damage?")
Do a runner	Leave an area unexpectedly
Dodgy	Dubious person or thing

Doing porridge	To be in jail
Don't get sarkie with me	Don't play around with me / you better watch your behaviour
Don't give a toss	To be indifferent
Dosh	Money
Footie	Football
Geezer	Another common term for a man
Git	Popular mildly offensive word for someone you don't like
Gobsmacked	To be very surprised
Grass	To expose someone to the police, an informer
Gutted	To be very upset about something
Have a swig	Have a drink
Having a knee up	To enjoy oneself
Iffy	Dubious, doubtful
Keep your hair on	To stay calm
Knackered	Exhausted
Laddish	To be one of the boys
Mate/Matey	A common address for a friend
Mucking	To mess around
Nipper	A young child
Not on your Nelly	No way
Off your trolley/rocker	To be crazy
Prezzie	A present
Plonker	An idiot, a fool
Punter	A paying customer
Skint	To have no money
Snog	Kiss

Suss	To perceive hidden facts or information
The Bill	The police force.
Treading the boards	The acting profession
Winding one up	Doing something to annoy someone.

RESOURCE GUIDE

This is an alphabetical listing of resources for Londoners. Consult the index as well for information that may be elsewhere in this book; the items in this list are intended to take you further along roads that we have only had time to point out in the other chapters.

ADVICE

Borough councils throughout London operate a service called the Citizen's Advice Bureau. Such bureaus are typically found in high streets and are open at erratic and unpredictable hours. They have a lot of general information in pamphlet form and can advise on many other personal, legal, or financial matters. For one near you, look in the *Yellow Pages* under 'Counselling and Advice'. It's best to make an appointment rather than drop in if you have a particular or complicated problem.

ALTERNATIVE MEDICINE

Alternative medicine of all kinds thrives in London, and many people find that this is the best choice for routine and chronic complaints. Alternative practitioners offer reasonable prices, a lot of personal attention and none of the bureaucracy of the NHS. Homeopathy is very well established with several highly respected schools and pharmacies, in addition to thousands of private practitioners. Osteopaths are also everywhere to be found.

You can consult friends and colleagues, directories or professional registration bodies to find any sort of alternative practitioner. *The Time Out Shopping & Services Guide* has a complete listing of the professional bodies of various therapies which can provide referrals. Also look in the *Yellow Pages* under any of these classifications: 'Acupuncturists', 'Alexander Technique', 'Chiropractors', 'Herbalists', 'Homeopaths' or 'Osteopaths'.

BOOKSHOPS

Bookshops of London is a handy guide to London booksellers, indexed by area, name of shop and subject. Currently the most up-to-date directory is the one published by Skoob, available in bookshops or in the Skoob bookshop itself in Sicilian Avenue WC1.

BUSINESS INFORMATION

Most of the high street banks, in cooperation with various publishers, bring out small manuals giving the essentials of law for the small business. Examples are *Law for Small Businesses* (Pitman and NatWest Bank) and *Law for the Small Business* (Blackwell and Barclays Bank). These are sold commercially but may be available through your bank as well.

You can research any existing company in England at Companies House in City Road EC1, using their public database. Also visit the City of London Business Library in Brewer's Hall Gardens EC2. The library is in a basement and the entrance is in the aforementioned tiny street that doesn't even appear on most maps; it's between London Wall and Aldermanbury Square. The library is strictly for reference but is open to the public and has an unparalleled collection of British, European and international trade and professional directories, as well as subscription to 750 business periodicals and 80 newspapers. The library also operates a fee-based research service; for details, ring Tel: (020) 7600-1461. Their general enquiry number, usually engaged, is Tel: (020) 7638-8215.

CHILDREN

When school doesn't occupy your children there is a lot in London for them to see and enjoy. *Children's London* is a handy collection of activities arranged by type with maps, an index and a shopping guide. *Family London* (London Transport) lists five walks around the capital that take in activities for children along the way. There is also a calendar of traditional events that kids can watch or participate in. *Kids Out* is a monthly magazine from the publishers of *Time Out*, loaded with kids' activities.

CONSUMER INFORMATION

The *Time Out Shopping and Services Guide* is a useful general reference for the new (or established) Londoner on every legal way to spend your money in the capital. The Consumer Association on Marylebone Road NW1, through its many publications, offers more considered advice along the same lines.

EMBASSIES

Addresses and phone numbers are listed variously in the business phone book under 'embassy' or under the name of the country. The biggest concentrations are in W1, SW1 and SW7. Listings of all the better known ones can be found in most tourist guides.

EMERGENCIES

Call 999 for either the police, an ambulance or the fire department. Be prepared to specify which service you require, and to say what telephone number you are calling from.

ETHNIC GROUPS

Guide to Ethnic London by Ian McAuley has summary chapters on several of the 'ethnic' (i.e. non-Anglo-Saxon) communities in London, including Chinese, Asians, Poles, Italians, Irish, Greek, Turkish, West Indians and Arabs.

EXPATRIATE ISSUES

A wide range of issues affecting expatriate life in Britain is explored regularly in the monthly magazine *The International in Britain*. It is available from central newsagents, or by subscription. Enquire for details on (020) 7405-6969. You may also want to consider joining Focus Information Services, which offers numerous seminars, workshops and social events for English-speaking expatriates in London. It also publishes a newsletter ten times a year, and a very useful Expatriate Calendar. It currently has members representing 23 nationalities, though the focus is strongly American. Their website is http://www.focus-info.org.

GAY AND LESBIAN CULTURE

London has the most visible and active gay life in the United Kingdom and draws young people from all corners of the country. There are numerous organisations that cater to all aspects of gay life, as well as the 'scene', which consists of cafes, clubs and pubs. You can try the Lesbian and Gay Switchboard (Tel: (020) 7837-7324) for specific enquiries but you will probably never get through. You might also buy a copy of the monthly magazine *Gay Times*, available from most newsagents, or the *Pink Paper*, distributed free in gay venues. Gay's The Word is a gay bookstore with a frequently visited notice board in Marchmont Street WC1. A direct way in is to go to Old Compton Street in Soho W1 and follow your nose.

GOVERNMENT (LOCAL)

If you have to work with anything having to do with London as a whole, rather than an individual borough council, two books will help to guide you through the fragmented minefield of London government: the *London Government Directory* has a short abstract on each borough and names and phone numbers of all the movers and shakers. *The London Government Handbook* edited by Hebbert and Travers explains what all the bodies with London-wide authority are, what they do and how they came to be.

GOVERNMENT PUBLICATIONS AND INFORMATION

Information on a wide range of subjects that the government wishes to make known is published and sold more or less at cost through an institution called HMSO, which stands for Her Majesty's Stationery Office. The main London HMSO bookshop is in High Holborn WC1. You will find that your public library stocks many HMSO publications.

The UK government maintains hundreds of pages on the Internet. The way in is through website: http://www.open.gov.uk. This is a top-level link page from where you can navigate to all other areas.

GUIDEBOOKS

If, heaven forbid, the volume in hand proves insufficient in any regard for the newly established Londoner, the author modestly refers the reader to three guides that stand out for their ease of use, superiority of design and usefulness for the London resident, as opposed to the London tourist. These are: *The London Transport Capital Guide: London for Londoners*, *Out and About in London* by Francesca Collin and the *Time Out London Guide*. All are widely available in bookshops and libraries.

HAIRCARE

In London as elsewhere, the difference between a hairdresser and a barber is mainly one of price, as far as men's haircuts are concerned. Barbers and hairdressers can be found throughout London, typically in high streets and in most mainline train stations. The further you are from the centre, the less you'll pay, though rarely less than £ 5 for a barber, £ 10 for a hairdresser.

London barbers use a number system to specify the length to which they cut your hair. The numbers most commonly used are 1 (1/8 inch), 2 (1/4 inch), 4 (1/2 inch) and 8 (1 inch). Specify the length you want left by number, e.g. "1 on the sides, 2 on the top."

There is no formal licensing scheme for people who make a living cutting hair in London, and just about anyone can set up shop. You might want to get a recommendation from someone before trusting your tresses to any particular practitioner.

HANDICAPPED ACCESS

Nicholson's Access Guide to London is the most up-to-date publication for those who have to negotiate the capital by wheelchair. Very little of London Underground or rail networks within London are easily accessible, but specially equipped 'Mobility Buses' operate on major London routes at least one day per week. Contact your borough council for information about these and other services available.

HELPLINES

All of the ones listed here will be found to be busy most of the time—it is all a part of the queuing culture.

- Alcoholics Anonymous National Helpline
  Tel: 0845-769-7555
- Al Anon (for those detrimentally affected by alcoholism in others)
  Tel: (020) 7403-0888
  Website: http://www.al-anonuk.org.uk
- Narcotics Anonymous
  Tel: (020) 7730-0009
  Website: http://www. ukna.org
- National AIDS Helpline
  Tel: 0800-567-123
- The Samaritans (for the suicidal and desperate)
  Tel: 0845-790-9090
  Website: http://www.samaritans.org.uk

IMMIGRATION, RESIDENCY AND NATIONALITY ISSUES

Everything is dealt with by the Home Office at Tel: 0870-606-7766. Getting through to someone on this number is the first rite of passage. If you're feeling really brave and have a lot of time to kill, proceed with all documentation in hand to Lunar House in Croydon. (Take a train from London Bridge to East Croydon and follow the signs). If your issue is straightforward, you may be able to deal with it there in a day, as opposed to spending months waiting for something to be resolved through the post. But do consult others for horror stories first. You may also want to look up the Home Office website at website: http://www.ind.homeoffice.gov.uk for more information.

INTERNET

Internet providers advertise widely in the daily press and in computer magazines. Quality of service varies dramatically; some of the biggest and best known providers give the worst service because they have more traffic than their equipment can handle. Consult colleagues if possible before settling on a provider, but also be prepared to shop around and switch until you find one that suits your needs. Any provider who asks a high startup fee should also give a money back guarantee, in case you find soon after establishing service that it isn't satisfactory. Providers with a North America-based server, despite their high advertising profiles, are not recommended: they are the slowest of all.

BT is in the process of upgrading its network to provide broadband access for residential use. Visit their website (http://www.bt.com) to see if this service is available for your area. Many other providers also offer broadband access to the Internet.

Information about London on the Internet is more extensive than can even be hinted at here. Searches using the conventional Web engines on the word 'London' yield hundreds or thousands of hits. If you're looking for something particular, narrow your search with suitable keywords. A good one stop shop for all sorts of London information, especially useful to those on their way but not quite there yet, is http://www.londononline.co.uk.

LANGUAGE

Even native speakers of English will find some language used in London unfamiliar. If your dialect of English comes from some part of the world other than the British Isles, you may want to get a copy of the *Longman Dictionary of English Language and Culture*, which, though a learner's dictionary, probably does a better job than any other in covering dialectal variants of a wide range of terms. It also has a lot of cultural information associated with various words that is not usually found in dictionaries, but can be very useful to someone new to the nuances of English on its native soil. Particularly useful is its feature on social class in Britain, which gives some insight into the associations of various cultural features and activities with different social classes.

MARKETS

The Markets of London by Alec Forshaw and Theo Bergström lists the best known markets in London by area, commodity and type, along with opening hours, pictures and some history.

MUSEUMS

See conventional tourist guides or listings magazines for information about special exhibitions. More in-depth information about collections can be found in any of numerous published museum guides. A concise, easy-to-use one is the *London Museum Guide*, with details of over 200 museums in the capital.

NEIGHBOURHOOD RESOURCES

Once a year, you should get through your letterbox a *Thomson Directory*, which is a privately published, freely distributed set of telephone directories for London neighbourhoods. Pages in the front of the book are a valuable condensation of council and other public services available in your area.

PARKING

The London Parking Atlas is a short and handy book of maps with a coded scheme showing parking available in all of central and most of Inner London. Available from bookshops and newsagents.

PUBLIC TRANSPORTATION

If your head is spinning after looking at Tube, bus and train maps, or you want to know when a given service runs, call the London Travel information hotline [Tel: (020) 7222-1234]. It provides travel information for London Underground, London buses and national trains within London. To get a free bus guide to your area or some other area of London, call London Transport's bus information [Tel: (020) 7371-0247]. LT Travel Information Centres, where detailed and specific advice can be given on all public transport matters (after you've done your time in the queue), are found at Heathrow, at Euston and Victoria train stations, and at King's Cross, Liverpool Street, Oxford Circus, Picadilly Circus and Saint James's Park underground stations.

To look up train routes and schedules out of London and around the UK, log onto the National Rail website at http://www.nationalrail.co.uk.

PUBS

The *Evening Standard* publishes a yearly (maybe) pub guide to London with opinionated but descriptive notes on hundreds of pubs in the capital. *Nicholson's London Pub Guide* is more concise and more tourist oriented.

RESTAURANTS

The print media give lots of attention to restaurants old and new in London, and there are several guides available from bookshops and newsagents. Both the *Evening Standard Restaurant Guide* and the *Time Out Eating and Drinking Guide* are updated regularly and are generally reliable, but there is really no definitive guide: there are too many restaurants, and they come and go too quickly for anyone to keep up.

Here are five restaurants that I frequent, and personally recommend for these reasons: the food is good; they are off the beaten tourist track; the staff is friendly and professional; and the prices are reasonable.

- The Angel
  Rotherhithe Bermondsey Wall East SE16
  Tel: (020) 7237-3608
  A neighbourhood pub downstairs and an elegant restaurant upstairs, serving traditional British and Continental cuisine. Situated on the river, it has spectacular views of Tower Bridge and the London skyline. The fact that it is almost impossible to find seems to keep it from ever being overcrowded, but you should book a table with a good view.
- Beyoglu
  756 Finchley Road NW11
  Tel: (020) 8731-7473
  A small, family-run Turkish restaurant with delicious, fresh food and friendly waiters. Booking recommended on weekends.

- Ravi Shankar
  133 Drummond Street NW1
  Tel: (020) 7388-6458
  This restaurant is one in a whole street full of restaurants featuring south Indian vegetarian fare. Good service from friendly and professional waiters, and delicious food. Go early, it gets busy later.
- Poons
  27 Lisle Street WC2
  Tel: (020) 7437-4549
  One of about seven Chinese restaurants in London called Poons. Though in the heart of Chinatown, its nondescript entrance doesn't lure the unknowing tourist. It has an extensive menu, quick service and an informal atmosphere. You don't pay for the decor because there isn't any. No need to book, they'll seat you anywhere there's a spot, often with strangers. After extensive testing, the menu has not been found to contain any duds.
- Toff's
  38 Muswell Hill Broadway N10
  Tel: (020) 8883-8656
  A fish-and-chip restaurant and takeaway. Service is fast, portions are huge and the fish is cooked to perfection. Get chips and mushy peas to go along with it for the full treatment. Several traditional sweets are available as well if you've got room for them. Often busy, but the turnover is pretty fast.

SCHOOLS

Which London School? (phone Tel; (0728) 663-666, or see if there is a copy in your local library), lists hundreds of private primary and secondary schools in the Greater London area. Many of the schools have paid listings in which they give details of their offerings. There is also a detailed and very useful question and answer section for parents considering private education for their children.

STATISTICS

Raw data about London for market research is gathered efficiently in three places:

- The 2001 census, which has separate volumes for Greater, Inner and Outer London.
- *London 95* (London Research Centre) which details various areas of social, political and economic life in London.
- *London: Facts and Figures* (HMSO) which is longer on tables and charts but shorter on interpretation than the foregoing work.

TELEPHONE DIRECTORIES

British Telecom publishes telephone numbers for all of the UK in a multi-volume work called *The Phone Book*. You may find some volumes in the accommodation you move into, or if you establish new phone service, the BT installer will leave you some books. Essential for Londoners are:

- *Volume 101*
  London postal area business and service numbers. It has the numbers of all businesses, government offices and public services. This is the directory referred to as the 'Business Phone Book' in this guide. Don't be without it.
- *Volumes 102–103*
  The London-wide residential directory, published in two volumes, A–K and L–Z
- *Yellow Pages* for Central London
  There are seven *Yellow Pages* directories for different areas of London. If you don't live in central London, you should request for the central London *Yellow Pages* in addition to your local area *Yellow Pages*. It lists many important numbers that you won't find in your local *Yellow Pages*, and also has a section entitled 'Living in London' in the centre of the book, full of important and useful numbers.
- *Thomson Directory*
  Published privately and distributed free, Thomson directories break down the capital into manageable chunks and contain many useful numbers and a lot of information about your neighbourhood. If you don't find one in your house or flat, call Thomson at Tel: (01252) 555-555.

FURTHER READING

BOOKSHOPS
Bookshops of London. Charles Frewin and Derek Lubner. London, UK: Two Heads Publishing, 1998.

FAMILY
Children's London. London, UK: Nicholson/HarperCollins,1993.

ETHNIC GROUPS
Guide to Ethnic London. Ian McAuley. London, UK: Immel Publishing Ltd, 1993.

GOVERNMENT
London Government Directory. London. UK: Association of London Government, 2006.

The London Government Handbook. Michael Hebbert and Tony Travers. London, UK: Cassell, 1988.

GUIDEBOOKS
The London Transport Capital Guide: London for Londoners. Elaine Gallagher. London, UK: Boxtree Ltd, 1995.

Out and About in London. Francesca Collin. London, UK: Cassell Illustrated, 1995.

Time Out London Guide. London, UK: Penguin Books Ltd, 2003.

HANDICAPPED
Nicholson's Access in London: A Guide for Those Who Have Problems Getting Around. Gordon Couch. London, UK: Collins, 1984.

LANGUAGE
Longman Dictionary of English Language and Culture. Martin Aitchison. New York, NY: Longman, 2005.

Mighty Fine Words and Smashing Expressions: Making Sense of Transatlantic English. Orin Hargraves. New York, NY: Oxford University Press, 2003.

MARKETS
The Markets of London. Alec Forshaw and Theo Bergström. (Penguin). London, UK: Penguin Books Ltd, 1983.

MUSEUMS
London Museums Guide. Jemima Johnstone and Fiona Talbott. London, UK: London Transport Museum, 1995.

PARKING
The London Parking Atlas. Timothy Williams and Hakon Lawal. London, UK: Pathmedia Communications Ltd, 1994.

PUBS
Evening Standard London Pub and Bar Guide. Edward Sullivan. London, UK: Simon & Schuster Ltd, 1999.

London Pub Guide. Judy Allen. Ayrshire, Scotland: Nicolson Maps, 1995.

RESTAURANTS
Evening Standard London Restaurant Guide. Nicholas Foulkes. London, UK: Simon & Schuster Ltd, 2000.

Time Out London Eating and Drinking Guide. Ed Cathy Phillips. London, UK: Time Out Publications Ltd, 2005.

SCHOOLS
Which London School? Vivienne Wright. Suffolk, UK: John Catt Educational, 2005.

SHOPPING
Time Out Shopping and Services Guide. London, UK: Time Out Publications Ltd, 1997.

ABOUT THE AUTHOR

Orin Hargraves grew up in the mountains of south-western Colorado and graduated from the University of Chicago. During seven years in London, he worked variously as a computer system manager, teacher of English and lexicographer. Today, he divides his time between rural Maryland and London. He is also the author of two other books in the *CultureShock!* series (Morocco and Chicago). His e-mail address is orinkh@carr.org and he welcomes comments from readers and any information that will help to keep this book up to date in future editions.

INDEX

Argentina
Australia
Austria
Bahrain
Barcelona
Beijing
Belgium
Bolivia
Borneo
Brazil
Britain
Cambodia
Canada
Chicago
Chile
China
Costa Rica
Cuba
Czech Republic
Denmark
Ecuador
Egypt
Finland
France
Germany
Greece

Hawaii
Hong Kong
Hungary
India
Indonesia
Iran
Ireland
Israel
Italy
Jakarta
Japan
Korea
Laos
London
Malaysia
Mauritius
Mexico
Morocco
Moscow
Munich
Myanmar
Nepal
Netherlands
New York
New Zealand
Norway

Paris
Philippines
Portugal
San Francisco
Saudi Arabia
Scotland
Sri Lanka
Shanghai
Singapore
South Africa
Spain
Sweden
Switzerland
Syria
Taiwan
Thailand
Tokyo
Turkey
Ukraine
United Arab
  Emirates
USA
Vancouver
Venezuela
Vietnam

WITHDRAWN

For more information about any of these titles, please contact any of
our Marshall Cavendish offices around the world (listed on page ii)
or visit our website at:

www.marshallcavendish.com/genref